Who Was Who
in Orkney

Who Was Who

in Orkney

Compiled by

W. S. Hewison

Bellavista Publications
1998

The Publishers gratefully acknowledge the financial assistance given by the
Orkney Islands Council.

ISBN 0 9525350 3 3

Printed by The Orcadian Limited, Hell's Half Acre, Hatston, Kirkwall, Orkney.

Published by Bellavista Publications, Bellavista, Carness Road,
Kirkwall, Orkney, KW15 1TB. Tel. 01856 872306

Foreword

by

Edwin R. Eunson, O.B.E.

Convener, Orkney Islands Council, 1978-90

"Of making many books there is no end," said the wise men in old times, and when one considers all the books which have been written about Orkney in the last century and a half, one might think that enough is enough and little new can be said. We have sagas, histories, books of legends, poetry, studies in archaeology, anthologies and works of fiction. But no-one has so far compiled an Orkney Who Was Who, and my old friend Bill Hewison is to be congratulated on rectifying this omission, and on producing such a readable and comprehensive volume, stretching from Agricola in the first century A.D. up to the present decade.

The Norse period has always been depicted as Orkney's Golden Age. As is said in this volume, to some people the sagas were regarded as almost Holy Writ, and the descriptions of the heroes and villains were taken at face value. I remember a debate on the motion that Orkney in the twelfth century was a better place in which to live than the twentieth century. The proposer was horrified when I suggested that Earl Rognvald, great figure though he was, had feet of clay, and that for example his behaviour on his crusade when he was entertained by Lady Ermingerd hardly qualified him for sainthood. The author of this book, while giving Rognvald full credit for his many accomplishments, describes him as 'a most improbable saint.' I remember another writer who suggested that his sainthood was rather as if the English had canonised Richard Lionheart or Henry V!

One of the features of this volume is that unlike the normal 'Who's Who' it features not only the great and good but others who can only be described as colourful characters, such as 'Skatehorn' who was a well-known figure on the roads of the islands around the turn of the century. Then there were the smugglers, highly popular among the Orcadians at a time of strict regulations and high taxation on wines and spirits. These include two who had my own surname. One of them, George Eunson, was obviously a versatile and gifted character, but undoubtedly a rascal.

Magnus Eunson was also a successful smuggler, who has become somewhat rehabilitated in recent years through having been given the credit of being the founder of Highland Park Distillery. I see that a new meeting room and VIP lounge in the distillery has been named the Eunson Room in his honour.

The first half of the 20th century was the time when it was said that the main exports from Orkney were 'eggs and professors.' A look through this work shows how many professors were born or brought up in the islands. I used to see many of them during the summers before the Second World War when I was with the firm of J. & W. Tait on Broad Street, Kirkwall. The proprietor, Mr Charles Tait, was a brother of Prof. John Tait of McGill University, Montreal, and brother-in-law of Prof. Ernest Shearer, Edinburgh and also a relative through marriage of Prof. R. C. Wallace, Ontario, all of whom, with their families were frequent visitors to the shop when on holiday in Kirkwall.

I remember, and frequently confused, Col. T. Smith Peace the auctioneer and his namesake the architect, who lived in King Street. John Shearer the Director of Education, who figures in the book, told me a story about the latter. His father had been one of the Secession Church elders in Shapinsay who were evicted by David Balfour for daring to criticise the 'promiscuous dancing' which had taken place at the laird's 'muckle supper' or harvest home. Many years later the laird, still pursuing the improvements to his estate for which he was noted, sent for the rising young architect who was making a name for himself in Kirkwall to design a new set of farm buildings on one of his holdings. The tenant was called on to be present and explain some features. Obviously overawed by having to speak to the laird, the farmer was standing with his cap in his hand and showing great humility, and in fact cringing as he answered his master's questions. At length Peace could stand this no longer and burst out "Good God, man, to think that if you hadn't evicted my father I would have had to speak to you in the same way as this poor fellow here."

Of the Peace family the member I knew best was David B. Peace, mentioned as having succeeded his uncle, Col. Peace as County Assessor and head of the auctioneering firm. He was a son of David B. Peace who introduced the first silent films and eventually the 'talkies' to Kirkwall. D. B. Peace snr lived to be a very old man and his son, though officially described as 'D. B. Peace jnr' was universally known even when in his seventies as 'Young Davie Peace'.

Robert Garden the 'Merchant Prince' of Orkney was before my time but I remember his wife, who lived in Ayre House, now the Ayre Hotel. As well as bringing up a large family she played an active part in the business. She was very kind to the travelling people, who were numerous in Orkney at that period. She supplied them with cheap goods for their packs and dealt with them personally. She and her husband went on a trip to Jerusalem, a most unusual journey at that time when Palestine was still part of Turkey. One day a tinker woman came in to shop and asked one of the staff for the mistress. "Oh," said the assistant, "she's in the Holy Land." "Oh, the poor lady," said the woman, "dead and buried, and I didn't even know she was ill."

I well remember Peter Shearer the tailor, who always kept up with the changes in trade. When the Kirkwall Burgh School became the Grammar School it became fashionable for the pupils to have school uniforms, and Mr Shearer became the main supplier. There were two Peter Shearers in business in Kirkwall, one a coal merchant and the other the tailor. The citizens distinguished them as 'Coaly Peter' and 'Clootie Peter.'

The subjects of the biographies in this book are now all in the past. Two elderly Orcadians were exchanging reminiscences about old-time worthies and one said to the other, "Man there's no characters like that nooadays." "Boy," said the other, "we don't ken whut the young folk are saying aboot thee and me!"

Perhaps sometime in the next millennium a writer will find enough characters now living to justify an update of Orkney's 'Who Was Who.'

Edwin R. Eunson

Inverness,
Autumn, 1998.

To the Memory of

Evan MacGillivray, M.B.E.

Introduction

Orkney history teems with colourful characters, some good, saints even, some not so good and quite a few just plain bad. But all of them vivid personalities with lives full of incident and action.

I became acutely conscious of this during my time on *The Orcadian* especially when having to write about them during the various historical conferences of the 1960s and '70s. My trouble was remembering who was who, which was which and when.

I had read my Orkney history, of course, but I don't think I was alone in finding it hard to separate one Thorfinn from another, getting the Sigurds mixed up, and as for all those Erlends, Einars and even the Rognvalds and Magnuses - well, they could and did get me all confused. Sorting them out meant the tedious search through a labyrinth of sagas, histories and reference books every time my memory failed me - as it often did.

And they were only the Norsemen. There were still the Stewarts and the Mortons, the Balfours, Baikies, countless Sinclairs, multitudinous Traills and the odd Bishop or two with some other notable clerics thrown in for good measure. Add a bunch of botanists, a few pirates, a lot of MPs and a dozen or so professors, not forgetting a generous sprinkling of writers, and the problem of finding out who they all were became not only time-consuming but mind-bending especially with a deadline to meet. And still I found them fascinating. But the crying need for an Orkney reference book where such consolidated information would be easily accessible became ever more obvious.

Such a single volume, however, did not exist and the required information was spread over dozens if not hundreds of books and papers, sometimes in rather obscure publications. The obvious answer, of course, was to compile the book myself - and I did make a start - but the demands of day-to-day journalism caught up with me and the project faded after I had written only a few thumbnail sketches of some of the more prominent Vikings. Since retiring from more active newspaper work, however, I have had time to expand that little list and there are now just on 700 names on it ranging from the Norsemen, and even a few before them, right up to the present day but, with one possible exception, Domenico Chiocchetti, excluding anyone still alive at the time of going to press, in autumn 1998. This means, of course, having to omit several prominent personalities like the distinguished composer Sir Peter Maxwell Davies, who has chosen to make his home in Orkney and is renowned not only for his music but more locally as having been the inspiration behind the annual St Magnus Festival. Long may he lack the essential qualification for an entry in this 'Who Was Who', he already has all the others.

Fortunately the Orkney story and its *dramatis personae* has been well covered by historians both local and international so that when I first started making up that early 'honours list' just after the Second World War there were already plenty of published sources to draw upon - when I could find them. Among the most valuable were A. B. Taylor's great translation of the Orkneyinga Saga, Storer Clouston's very readable 'History of Orkney', particularly strong on the Norse period, Hossack's monumental 'Kirkwall in the Orkneys', Tudor's 'Orkney and Shetland' and quite a few more such as the Old Lore Miscellany of the Viking Club and the Proceedings of the pre-war Orkney Antiquarian Society particularly those with Hugh Marwick's genealogical studies of prominent Orkney families which he continued in the 'Orkney Miscellanies' of the Orkney Antiquarian and Record Society of the 1950s.

Most of these books, of course, dated from the first half of the century and much had happened since they were written, both academically and historically, and some of the information they contained was naturally in need of re-interpretation and an up-date.

That up-date has certainly been achieved. Much valuable research both in Orkney and beyond has, in the last half-century or so, illuminated many previously dark corners of our past, letting us see what their occupants had been up to - and some of those corners were dark in every sense of the word.

And so the time-lapse between my first tentative effort to compile an Orkney 'Who Was Who' and this one has turned out to be an advantage for now I have been able to draw on many more and up-to-date sources among which pride of place must go to William P. L. Thomson's 'History of Orkney' published in 1987 on which I have leaned heavily. On the mainly Norse side Barbara Crawford's 'Scandinavian Scotland' has corrected the excessive enthusiasm of a few early Norse addicts for whom the sagas were almost Holy Writ while Peter Anderson has given us a clearer unslanted picture of the Stewart Earls in his 'Robert Stewart, Earl of Orkney' and 'Black Patie'. For the 18th century there are Ray Fereday's 'The Orkney Balfours' and 'Orkney Feuds and the '45' and his invaluable section on 'Lairds and Historians' in 'The People of Orkney' in the Aspects of Orkney series. And as I have already mentioned, there are also the papers to the Orkney Record and Antiquarian Society of the 1950s published in its 'Miscellanies'. To them all I am deeply indebted and there are many others besides.

More directly I have to thank Chief Librarian Bobby Leslie, Principal Archivist Alison Fraser, her second-in-command, Phil Astley, and the staffs at the Library and the Archive for their invariably courteous and friendly responses, to my repeated cries for assistance with unstinted professional help and advice at all times. Without their encouragement, and indeed active participation, the project would probably have suffered the fate of my first effort and faded into oblivion. Museums Officer Bryce Wilson, Tom Muir, Ann Brundle of the Tankerness House Museum staff, too, have been of great assistance and encouragement and like the Library and Archive staffs have read and given constructive comments on my original typescript.

I have already mentioned how heavily I have depended on the publications by W. P. L.Thomson, Ray Fereday, Barbara Crawford and Peter Anderson, but better still I have had their personal assistance, for not only have they read my typescript and proofs for any blemishes but they have all come up with suggestions for improvement and additions which I have incorporated and for which I can hardly thank them enough, and I am also very grateful to Mrs Sheena Wenham for reading proofs with special reference to the Graeme family and Olaf Cuthbert for his help with George Low and Bishop Reid.

There are many others to whom I am indebted not least my publishers Stewart Davidson and his wife Leslie of Bellavista Publications for their friendly practical advice and for their suggestions on possible improvements. Any errors or omissions, however, are entirely my responsibility for the final selection of material to be included was mine alone though backed by the best of advice.

And finally I am deeply grateful to my wife, Nancy, who has not only endured the constant procession of these historical characters through our house but has brought them to life in her design for the dust-cover in addition to researching material, reading the typescript and proofs.

To them all I offer my sincere thanks in the hope that our combined efforts will remind the present and future generations of Orcadians and others now living here of the people who came before them and made Orkney what it is today.

W.S.H.,
Kirkwall.
Autumn, 1998.

If you want to know more

Norsemen are listed under their first names eg Sweyn Asleifsson NOT Asleifsson, Sweyn; similarly the Norse Earls of Orkney are listed as Thorfinn II Sigurdsson The Mighty NOT Sigurdsson, Thorfinn. The later Earls of Orkney are listed under their family surname eg Sinclair, William or Stewart, Patrick.

Where possible dates of birth (b.) and death (d.) are given but when these are not available with any degree of accuracy the dates of the actual rule of earls, reigns of kings or tenure of official appointments are used. Where such hard-and-fast dates are not known, at least one date, such as a marriage (m.) or acquisition of an estate, has been used where available in order to establish the appropriate period.

There are three spellings of the family name Stuart, Stewart or Steuart but for the purpose of this book Stuart refers to the Royal family eg Prince Charles Edward Stuart; Stewart refers to the Stewart Earls and their family connections eg Stewart of Brugh which last may also be spelt Brough; and Steuart refers exclusively to the Burray family eg Sir James Steuart of Burray. The word 'Stewart' can also be used occasionally as an alternative for 'Sheriff' or 'Sheriff Substitute'.

It should be noted that there are fairly wide variations in the spellings of Norse proper names arising from different translations of the sagas, eg Pal/Paul, Haco/Hacon/Haakon/Hakon, Sweyn/Svein and, more extremely, Unn the Deep-Minded for Aud the Deep-Minded who may also be found as Aud the Pensive. These descriptive nick-names commonly added to the actual names of prominent Norsemen can also vary considerably in translation and interpretation, eg King Harald Fair Hair is also called Fairhair, Harfager, Haafagri, Hairfair, Fine-Hair and even in one instance, The Shaggy, all derived from the original Old Norse harfagri. The spellings adopted for this book are those now in most common use as eg in Thomson's 'History of Orkney'.

Numbers following entries as listed below refer to suggested sources of further and more detailed information but are by no means exhaustive. Many of the books or papers listed may well be out of print but virtually all are available in the Orkney Room of The Orkney Library including those listed as 'manuscript' or 'typescript'. Figures in brackets immediately after such numbers indicate the actual volume in a series such as the 9 volumes of the Old Lore Miscellany (OLM) or the 15 of the Proceedings of the Orkney Antiquarian Society (POAS) eg 20(11) refers to POAS Volume 11 (1932-3). Orc and OH refer to *The Orcadian* and *Orkney Herald* newspapers respectively followed by the appropriate date of issue eg 5/11/16.

Most of the individuals listed are either native Orcadians or persons who have had a long connection within Orkney itself playing an important part in its history but there are some, often of national or international stature, whose physical presence in the islands was brief or spasmodic but who nevertheless influenced the course of the islands' history. Sir Winston Churchill is a case in point. He visited Orkney only half-a-dozen times but his decisions concerning Scapa Flow as a naval base had a profound and lasting effect on Orkney. Other world-famous visitors like Sir Walter Scott or Gladstone are of local interest, perhaps only for having been even briefly in Orkney or for their comments about the islands. The full story of their lives can be obtained in such works as the Dictionary of National Biography or in Who Was Who. I have listed only their direct connection with Orkney. Then, again, there are the native-born Orcadians who have gone out to play important parts in the wider world - such as the scholars in universities of many nations, the administrators, scientists and members of many other professions or trades.

Almost all the sources quoted have been published in book or pamphlet form but in a very few instances there are references to a prime source in the Orkney Archive (OA) of The Orkney Library.

Abbreviations used - b. = born, bro. = brother, c = circa (approximately), d. = died, dau. = daughter, e. = eldest, m. = married, s. = son. OA = Orkney Archive. OS = Orkneyinga Saga.
Asterisk * denotes cross-reference.

Brief Glossary

Bailie = Officer delegated by Chief Magistrate to preside over Parish or Island Bailie Courts dealing with petty crime, weights and measures, maintaining watch against possible invasion and general administration. Also Burgh magistrate next in rank after Provost on Town Council.

Bonder = Lesser landowners, small farmers.

Factor = Manager of estate.

Farmer see Tacksman.

Feu = Land or property held on feudal tenure subject to duties payable in cash or kind to the Superior.

Fief = Land held of a superior in return for service.

Foud = Senior legal official in Shetland. Title also given to local magistrates. Equivalent to Sheriff in Orkney.

Gøding = Member of sub-aristocracy of leading Norse landowners usually kinsmen of the Earls.

Hird = Royal or Earl's retinue; bodyguard.

Laird = owner of tenanted estate.

Lendirman = Norwegian aristocrat.

Mormaer = Petty king often of the Moray area.

Skald - poet; usually member of Earl's hird.

Stewart/Steward = Sheriff or Sheriff Substitute.

Superior = Overall landowner to whom feu duties are payable eg Earls of Morton and the Dundas family.

Sysselman = Representative of Norwegian or Danish Crown in Orkney and Shetland especially during an earl's minority or during an interregnum when there was no clear succession to the Earldom; Royal administrator of kingsland in Orkney confiscated from the earl after Florvåg.

Tack = Lease of land or right to collect revenue for payment of a fixed sum.

Tacksman = holder of such a lease sometimes referred to as farmer of a tack.

Udaller/odaller = Outright owner of land without a Superior and usually without title deeds under Norse system of land tenure as applied in Orkney until feudal system was introduced after the islands were annexed by Scotland in 15th century.

Writer = lawyer.

Sources
(see numbers following individual entries)

1. History of Orkney - J. Storer Clouston, 1932.
2. History of Orkney - W. P. L. Thomson, 1987.
3. Orkneyinga Saga - A. B. Taylor translation, 1938; H. Palsson and P. Edwards translation 1978; Hjaltalin and Goudie translation, ed. by Joseph Anderson, 1873, reprint 1973.
4. Kirkwall in the Orkneys - B. H. Hossack, 1900, reprint 1986.
5. Anthology of Orkney Verse - E. W. Marwick, 1949.
6. The Church in Orkney - J. Smith, 1907.
7. Sanday Church History - Alexander Goodfellow, 1912.
8. Orkney and Shetland - J. Tudor, 1883.
9. The Little General and the Rousay Crofters - W. P. L. Thomson, 1981.
10. Orkney - Hugh Marwick, 1951.
11. Orkney Feuds and the '45 - R. P. Fereday, 1980.
12. Robert Stewart, Earl of Orkney - Peter Anderson, 1982.
13. Black Patie - Peter Anderson, 1992.
14. Orkney Miscellany (1953-57).
15. Curious Incidents from Ancient Records of Kirkwall - W. R. Mackintosh, 1892.
16. Eric Linklater - Michael Parnell, 1984.
17. The Orkney Balfours - R. P. Fereday, 1990.
18. Life & Letters of an Orkney Naturalist Rev. George Low 1747-93 - Olaf D. Cuthbert, 1995.
19. St Magnus, Earl of Orkney - J. Mooney, 1938.
20. Proceedings of the Orkney Antiquarian Society (POAS) (1923-39).
21. History of the Church in Orkney - J. B. Craven, 1901-12.
22. Orkney & Shetland - Eric Linklater, 1965.
23. No Ordinary Journey, John Rae, Arctic Explorer 1813-1893, 1993.
24. An Island Shore, Life and Work of Robert Rendall - Neil Dickson,1990.
25. Kelp-making in Orkney - W. P. L. Thomson, 1983.
26. This Great Harbour Scapa Flow - W. S. Hewison, 1985.
27. The Orcadian Centenary Supplement Nov 1954.
28. Kirkwall Charters - J. Mooney, 1948.
29. The Grand Fleet 1914-1916 - H. Jellicoe, 1919.
30. Heimskringla - Monsen/Smith 1932 Cambridge translation.
31. Orkney Anthology - E. W. Marwick - ed. J. D. M. Robertson, 1991.
32. The Balfours and Balfour Castle - M. Zawadski, 1986.
33. The Story and the Fable - Edwin Muir, 1940.
34. History of the Kirkwall UP Congregation - Rev. David Webster, 1910.
35. Old Lore Miscellany of Orkney, Shetland, Caithness and Sutherland Vols 1-10, 1907-1946.
36. Orkney Folklore and Traditions - W. T. Dennison, ed. E. W. Marwick, 1961.

37. Northern Lights - Walter Scott, 1982.
38. Njal's Saga - Magnusson/Palsson translation, 1960.
39. The Real Captain Cleveland - Alan Fea, 1912.
40. The Pirate Gow - Daniel Defoe, 1725, 1890, 1978.
41. The Moodie Book - The Marquis of Ruvigny and Raineval, 1906.
42. The St Clairs of the Isles - Roland William Saint Clair, 1893.
43. An Orkney Estate (Graemeshall) - Gilbert Schrank, 1995.
44. Dictionary of National Biography.
45. Orkney Shore - Robert Rendall, 1960.
46. The People of Orkney - R. J. Berry & H. N. Firth, 1986.
47. Natural History of Orkney - R. J. Berry, 1985.
48. The Diary of Patrick Fea of Stove - ed. W. S. Hewison, 1997.
49. Who Was Who - of appropriate date.
50. The Ultimate Viking - Eric Linklater, 1955.
51. Scottish Art - Stanley Cursiter, 1949.
52. Looking Back - Stanley Cursiter, 1974.
53. Orkney Folklore & Sea Legends - W. T. Dennison ed. Tom Muir, 1995.
54. New History of Scotland Vol 2 - George S. Pryde, 1962.
55. Scapa and a Camera - C. W. Burrows, 1921.
56. Orkney and the Last Great War - ed. P. N. Sutherland Graeme, 1915.
57. Pateas Amicas - P. N. Sutherland Graeme, 1936.
58. Memoirs - Jo Grimond, 1979.
59. The Peggy and Isabella - Ian Hustwick, 1996.
60. Air Road to the Isles - E. E. Fresson, 1967.
61. The Grand Scuttle - Dan van der Vat, 1982.
62. The Kitchener Enigma - Trevor Royle, 1985.
63. Scapa Flow: The Greatest Scuttle of All Time - L. von Reuter.
64. A Genealogical Account of the Traills of Orkney - Wm. Traill, 1883.
65. For the Islands I Sing - An Autobiography - George Mackay Brown, 1998.
66. The Alexander Graham Case - Ian MacInnes - Orkney Heritage Vol I, 1981.
67. The Breckness Estate - James Irvine, 1997.
68. William Balfour Baikie - E. W. Marwick, 1965.
69. Diary of Thomas Brown NP - ed A. Francis Steuart, 1898.
70. Agriculture of the Islands of Orkney - Robt. Pringle, 1873.
71. Laxdaela Saga - trans. Magnusson/Palsson, 1969.
72. Orkney, Illustrated Architectural Guide - L. Burgher, 1991.
73. Merchant Lairds of Long Ago - Hugh Marwick, 1936.
74. Orkney Archive - Skaill Collection D3, Watt of Breckness and Skaill.
75. The Royal House of Scotland - Eric Linklater, 1970.
76. Scandinavian Scotland - Barbara Crawford, 1987.
77. Northern and Western Islands of Scotland - F. J. Shaw, 1980.
78. The Man who bought a Navy - Gerald Bowman, 1964.

79. The Northern Isles: Orkney and Shetland - A. Fenton, 1978.
80. The History of Orkney - George Barry, 1805.
81. Connections, Orkney and Australia - Frank Foden, 1992.
82. The Northern and Western Isles in the Viking World - ed.
    Alexander Fenton and Hermann Palsson, 1984.
83. Burke's Peerage.
84. Book of Saints - A. & C. Black, London, 1966.
85. The Laird, the Factor and the Elders, Stress and Strain in
    Shapinsay 1847 - Paul Sutherland. KGS SYS 1989.
86. Orkney and the Earls of Morton - Jane Ross. KGS SYS 1977.
87. Family of Heddle of Cletts and Melsetter - Joan Heddle,
    Orkney Archive Misc 1/2.
88. History of Sierra Leone - Christopher Fyffe, 1965.
89. Around the Orkney Peat Fires - W. R. Mackintosh, 1914 ed.
90. Samuel Laing - Autobiography, Orkney Archive D 1/466.
91. Dr. Robert Paterson of Orkney - Alexander Goodfellow, 1920.
92. In the Tracks of Bishop Andrew Pictoris and Henry
    Phankouth, Archdeacon of Shetland - Brian Smith (Innes
    Review Vol XI No. 2 1989).
93. William Sinclair, Earl of Orkney and his Family - Barbara
    Crawford (Essays on the Nobility of Medieval Scotland).
94. Days of Orkney Steam - A. and A. Cormack, 1971.
95. Scapa Flow in War and Peace - W. S. Hewison, 1995.
96. Oxford Companion to British History.
97. 1492 Rental - ed. W. P. L. Thomson.
98. Agriculture of the Islands of Orkney - R. O. Pringle, 1873.
99. Mary, Queen of Scots - Eric Linklater.
100. Birsay and the early Earls and Bishops of Orkney - Barbara
    Crawford in Orkney Heritage Vol II, 1983.
101. Birsay and the Sixteenth Century - Peter Anderson in Orkney
    Heritage Vol II, 1983.
102. King Harald's Saga - trans Magnusson/Palsson,
    Penguin Classic Series, 1966.

Who Was Who

in Orkney

A

Aberdeen, Alexander - Land Surveyor of Orkney Earldom to the *14th Earl of Morton in mid 18th century. Like those of his bro. *William, his maps are decoratively illustrated. 2.

Aberdeen, William - Succeeded his brother *Alexander as Land Surveyor of the Orkney Earldom estates after they were bought by *Sir Lawrence Dundas from *14th Earl of Morton 1766. Produced maps and plans of various parts of Orkney illustrated with vignettes and sketches notably one of Kirkwall from the west. 1,2.

Adalbert - Bishop of Orkney during time of Earl *Thorfinn II. Bremen-Hamburg consecration. 2,21,100.

Afreka - dau. of Earl of Fife, first wife of Earl *Harald Maddadsson c1158 who divorced her and then married *Hvarflod, dau. of Malcolm MacHeth, Earl of Ross, Pretender to the Scottish Throne. 1,2,3.

Agricola, Gnaeus Julius - b.40 d.93 AD. Roman general. Governor of Britain 78-84 AD during which period his fleet sailed round the north of the British Isles. Tacitus later wrote that they 'discovered and subdued Orkney' although Agricola was not on the voyage himself. 2.

Aidan macGabrian - King of Dalriada; conducted campaign in Orkney c580. *Early Sources of Scottish History* - A.O. and M.O. Anderson 1922.

Aitken, Henry - d.1643 Orkney. Commissary and Sheriff Depute Orkney and Shetland under *Bishop Law 1611/12. 13.

Alexander de Ard - Sysselman in Orkney 1375-6, s. of Weland de Ard and Matilda, dau. of Earl *Malise. Had claims to Earldoms of Orkney, Caithness and Strathearn which he pursued without success for 20 years. 2.

Amundi of Sandwick, Deerness - c1015; father of *Thorkell Fostri. Most important chieftain of his time outside the Earl's immediate family. 1,3.

Amundi Hnefason of Freswick, Caithness - First husband of Ingirid, who later m. *Sweyn Asleifsson. 1,3.

Amundi Illingisson - Shetlander cured of leprosy by one of the miracles attributed to St *Magnus after his martyrdom c1117. 3.

Anakol - Hebridean-born 'viking of good family and a valiant fellow' (OS) foster-father and Councillor-in-Chief to Earl *Erlend III.   1,3.

Anderson, James Urquhart - b.1799 d.1874. Founder/editor of *The Orcadian*; s. of Magnus Anderson, Kirkwall, catechist and bookbinder. Educated Kirkwall Grammar School and served apprenticeship as bookbinder in Leith where became interested in printing. Returning to Orkney entered bookbinding firm his father Magnus Anderson had started in 1798; m. (1) Janet King, Kirkcaldy (2) Jessie Reid, Kirkwall. Acquired hand-press in 1820s and added printing to the business. In 1854, aged 55, fulfilled life-long ambition by founding county newspaper, *The Orcadian*, with son James who had been learning the newspaper and printing crafts in the south. Continued as editor until his death when James succeeded him.   27, Orc 17/2/1874.

Anderson, Dr. Joseph - b.1832 d.1916. Distinguished Scots antiquarian. Curator of Museum of Antiquities of Scotland, Edinburgh. Edited and wrote introductions to both 1873 translation of 'Orkneyinga Saga' by Jan Hjaltalin and Gilbert Goudie and *Low's 'Tour of Orkney and Schetland' 1779.   3.

Andrew, Bishop - see Paynter.

Angel, Archie - A little boy, only survivor of a Russian ship wrecked on Aikerness, Westray in 1730s. Legend has it he was found tied to his mother's body, some say to a dog. He was unable to tell his rescuers who he was, not even his name, the only clue to his identity being part of the ship's sternpost washed ashore with her port of registration on it - Archangel. So his foster-parents, who took him into their home and brought him up as one of their own family, christened him - Archie Angel, by which name he was known throughout his Orcadian life. He married Jean Drever of Aikerness and the name passed on in Westray until it died out in the 19th century.
          31, Orc 1/11/1990, *The Orkney View* Dec 1977/Jan 1978.

Angus Earls of Orkney - see Gilbert I & II, John II, Magnus II,III,IV,V.

Armadale, Lord - see Honyman.

Armod - Icelandic skald (poet). Joined hird of Earl *Rognvald II in Kirkwall c1150 along with 2 other Icelandic skalds, Oddi the Little and Thorbjorn the Black all 3 sailing with him on crusade to the Holy Land 1151.   1,3.

Armour, Rev. Matthew - b.1820 Paisley d.1903 Sanday. Educ. Glasgow and St.Andrews Universities. Free Kirk Minister in Sanday 1848-1903. Congregation split 1858 over his manner of preaching, the dissidents following *Walter Traill Dennison and his bro. Jerome, to form break-away congregation in what became known as the Mission Station.

There was a strong evangelical revival movement 1860 in his own kirk which spread throughout Orkney. He held strong Radical views and advocated land reform including the division of big farms into smaller units to provide holdings for the poorer people, a policy which did not endear him to the land-owning classes. He gave evidence to the Napier Commission on crofting 1883 encouraging the Sanday crofters to do likewise.

In autumn 1885 he was involved in a disturbance at a Tory party meeting in Sanday for which in January 1886 he was arrested, charged and sentenced to four days in prison. Hundreds of people protested against the sentence outside the Tolbooth in Kirkwall where he was confined and on instructions direct from the Court of Session in Edinburgh he was released within 7 hours of being sentenced much to the delight of the crowd shouting 'The Minister's oot'.

At various times he served on the Parish and County Councils and the School Board. 6,7.

Arnfinn Thorfinnsson - Earl of Orkney for a period between 976-991. Eldest s. of Earl *Thorfinn I Skullsplitter; m. *Ragnhild, dau. of *Erik Bloodaxe, King of Norway and Gunnhild. Murdered in Caithness at instigation of his wife. 1,2,3,76,100.

Arni Lorja or Loria - d.c1202. First Royal sysselman imposed on Orkney by *King Sverre after he defeated the Island Beardies at battle of Florvåg 1193. Killed, possibly at instigation of Earl *Harald II Maddadsson after Sverre's death 1202. 1,2.

Arni Spindleshanks - Norse chieftain killed by *Sweyn Asleifsson for non-payment of debt to one of Sweyn's North Isles tenants during the Norsemen's winter stop-over in Orkney prior to *Rognvald II's crusade in 1151. A henchman of *Eindridi. 3.

Arnkell Einarsson - Joint Earl of Orkney c.946-954; s. of *Torf-Einar. Ruled Earldom together with brother *Erlend I until both were killed with *Erik Bloodaxe, at battle of Stainmore in England 954. 1,2,3,76.

Arnljot - Steward of Earl *Sigurd II based on Stroma from where he could keep watch against possible invasion of Orkney by the Scots. 38,100.

Arnor Thordarsson Earlskald - Icelandic skald (poet) who lived in

Orkney. Close friend and kinsman by marriage of Earl *Thorfinn II and was with him at sea-battle off Deerness c1030 when Scots fleet under King *Karl Hundason was put to flight and also at the subsequent battle of Tarbatness recording both in skaldic verse. Again he was present with Thorfinn during the Pentland Firth battle off the Berry 1046 when *Rognvald I Brusisson, pressing his claim to share of Earldom, was defeated although ambivalently Arnor composed eulogistic odes to both of them.   1,3,35(1),76,82.

Arnot, Sir John - Lord Provost of Edinburgh 1592-1615. Treasurer Depute of Scotland, and tacksman of Orkney Earldom. Loaned considerable sums of money to Earl *Patrick Stewart and also to James VI of Scotland who in 1594 granted him £2,000 out of the Orkney and Shetland revenue in part payment of these loans. Assumed designation 'of Barswick' in South Ronaldsday from one of the estates he acquired from Patrick as settlement of some of his debts. Appointed Sheriff and Commissioner of Orkney and Shetland jointly with Bishop *Law 1608.   2,13.

Arthur, George Thomas (Geordie) - b.1899 Kirkwall d.1952 Kirkwall - Naturalist with emphasis on bird-life, conservationist, musician, yachtsman, baker. Educ. Kirkwall Grammar School and after army service in France during World War I when twice wounded, entered family bakery business in Kirkwall which he subsequently owned. His great interest was observation and study of birds in which he became an acknowledged expert nation-wide and was the first person in Scotland to be awarded the Silver Medal of the Royal Society for the Protection of Birds 1950. He was particularly proud of having been largely responsible for saving the Hen Harrier, in danger of becoming extinct during the 1940s, not only in Orkney but nationally.

Frequent contributor on natural history to local and national press and radio. Played cello in Kirkwall Orchestra and a keen yachtsman winning many trophies in local regattas with his *Naughty Girl*.
                                          OH 15/11/52, Orc 17/11/52.

Asleif - m. *Olaf Hrolfsson of Duncansby and Gairsay; mother of *Sweyn Asleifsson. 'A wise woman of good family and strong character' (OS).2,3.

Asolf Gunnisson - 18-year-old Norwegian member of Earl *Rognvald II's company during fatal hunting expedition in Caithness 1158 with Earl Harald II Maddadsson when Rognvald was surprised and murdered by *Thorbjorn Klerk and his men at Forss. Asolf lost a hand trying to deflect Thorbjorn's sword.   3.

Asquith, Herbert Henry, b.1852 d.1928. 1st Earl of Oxford and Asquith -

Liberal Prime Minister 1908-1916. Visited Scapa Flow and Kirkwall with First Lord of the Admiralty, *Winston Churchill October 1913. Grd. father of *Laura Bonham Carter, wife of *Jo Grimond, MP for Orkney and Shetland 1950-83.					26,44.

Auchinleck, Thomas - b.1550 Perth d.1612 possibly Orkney. Notary. Commissary of Orkney and servitor to both Earls *Robert and *Patrick Stewart.					12,13.

Aud the Deep-minded - dau. of *Ketil Flatnose, a Norse chieftain who controlled much of northern Scotland and the Western Isles c870; mother of *Thorstein the Red. After he was killed by Scots in Caithness she had a ship built secretly and when it was launched sailed to Orkney where she married off her grd dau., Groa, to a Caithness chieftain, Dungad, apparently exiled in Orkney; the dau. of this marriage, Grelod, m. Earl *Thorfinn I Skullsplitter. Aud went on to Faroe and then Iceland where she settled.			1,2,3,35(7),71,76.

Aytoun, Professor William Edmondstoune - b.1813 Edinburgh d.1865. Professor of Rhetoric and Belles Lettres, Edinburgh University 1845. Sheriff Depute of Orkney and Zetland 1852-1865. Student friend of *David Balfour 5th of Trenaby; frequent visitor to Balfour Castle. Prolific writer of heroic verse. Keen angler and *bon viveur*.				85.

B

Baikie, James, b.1712 d.1764, 6th of Tankerness - Provost of Kirkwall 1737-1764. Eldest s. of Robert Baikie, 5th of Tankerness and Margaret Sinclair of Quendale, Shetland; m. Janet Douglas, dau. and heiress of *William Douglas of Egilsay whereby he acquired that island for the Baikie estate.

The Douglases of Egilsay were connected with the Earl of Morton family and James remained pro-Morton throughout his life and therefore anti-Jacobite. As a result he did not co-operate with the dissident anti-Morton Jacobite lairds in the Pundlar Process 1733-59 and, in fact, as Provost of Kirkwall collaborated with *Andrew Ross, Sheriff Depute and Chancellor of the Earldom, in attempts to arrest them after the '45. Along with Ross he deemed it advisable to take refuge in Shetland in 1746 for several weeks when Melsetter, Kirkwall and Stromness were

invaded and temporarily occupied by a pro-Stuart raiding party of
Highlanders led by *Mackenzie of Ardloch.   4,11,14(4).

Baikie, James, b.1786 d.1869, 8th of Tankerness - Close associate of *Rev.
Dr. Robert Paterson. Bequeathed part of estate to be used for religious
and educational purposes. Instrumental in starting up first steamship
service between Orkney and Scottish Mainland.   2,14(4).

Baikie, Captain John, RN - b.1787 d.1875. Father of explorer *Dr.. William
Baikie. Joined Navy 1800 serving in HMS *Lynx* for 2 years on North
Sea station. Midshipman and master's mate in HMS *Lapwing* 1803.
Then in 98-gun *Barfleur*, and frigates *Camilla* and *Amiable* on
Newfoundland and home stations. Promoted Lieutenant in flagship
Majestic 1807. In 1810 in 64-gun *Dictator* on Baltic convoy duty and
1812 on West Indies and Canada convoys in flagship *Gloucester*.
Retired from Navy 1814 to Orkney, only being commissioned Captain
40 years later 1854. Was appointed first agent of National Bank of
Scotland in Kirkwall 1825.   4.

Baikie, Robert, d.1817, 7th of Tankerness - Only s. of *James Baikie, 6th of
Tankerness and Janet Douglas of Egilsay; m. 1785 Mary Balfour, dau.
of *Thomas Balfour of Huip.
    Elected MP for Orkney in 1780 defeating *Charles Dundas but then
unseated for alleged irregularities during the election. Involved with
notorious firebrand and smuggler *George Eunson in anti-smuggling
campaign aimed at discrediting his political opponents.   14(1&4),17.

Baikie, Dr. Robert, 9th of Tankerness - bro. of *James, 8th of Tankerness.
Joined East India Company. Interested in scientific subjects. Translated
several books from Indian languages into English.   14(4),70.

Baikie, Thomas - Kirkwall skipper and probably boat-builder. His
specification for building 'ane great boat' is dated 1662.   20(5).

Baikie, Rev. Thomas - b.1672 d.1740, of Burness; 2nd s. of James Baikie 1st
of Burness; m. (1) Elizabeth Fea, dau. of Patrick Fea of Whitehall (2)
Elizabeth Traill, dau. of Patrick Traill of Sebay. Educ. St Andrews
University. Ordained 1697.
    First Presbyterian Minister of St Magnus Cathedral (1697-1740)
following the revolution of 1689 and the thorough purging of Orkney's
Episcopalian ministers but in the early years of his ministry he had
trouble with those members of his congregation remaining loyal to
their Episcopalian faith who attempted to slander him.
    While lying in bed unwell one Sunday morning in 1703 he was
astonished to hear the Cathedral bells just across the street from his

house ringing for morning service although to his knowledge there was no relief minister to conduct it. But his popular Episcopalian predecessor, John Wilson, who had continued preaching in the cathedrad until finally deposed 1703, believing him to be too ill to officiate that morning took the opportunity to preach there once more. Baikie, however, was having none of this. Hurriedly throwing on some clothes with the help of his wife he stalked across the Kirk Green still in his nightcap and dragged Wilson from the pulpit, dismissed the congregation, locked the Kirk door behind them and later sacked the Kirk officer who had had the temerity to ring the bells. He did not, however, come through unscathed for the meeting of the Kirk Session scheduled for the following day had to be postponed due to the 'Minister's great tenderness'.

Manuscripts of many of his lengthy sermons, characteristic of 18th century 'Moderates', are preserved in the Orkney Archive.   4,6,21.

Baikie, Rev. William, d.1683, of Holland, Stronsay - 3rd s. of James Baikie 1st of Tankerness and Barbara Smith. Bequeathed his library of 160 volumes to 'the Ministers of Kirkwall for a Publick Library to be kept within the Toune.' *Rev. James Wallace added 30 more books and many pamphlets to form what became known as the 'Bibliotheck of Kirkwall' housed in St Magnus Cathedral - the oldest public library in Scotland, forerunner of present Orkney County Library.   14(4),69.

Baikie, Dr. William Balfour, b.1825 Kirkwall d.1864 Sierra Leone - Explorer, Naval Surgeon; s. of *Captain John Baikie RN. Studied medicine Edinburgh University becoming interested in natural history and zoology.

Served in Royal Navy as assistant surgeon both at sea and ashore at the Naval Hospital, Gosport. Made first expedition to explore River Niger in West Africa in 1854 during course of which he took over command when the original leader died. Penetrated some 700 miles up river from the coast and also navigated 250 miles further up the Niger's tributary, the Benue, than had previously been explored.

Led second expedition to Niger 1857 being stranded for two years when his river steamer failed to reach him with supplies. Although racked with bouts of fever and frequently on starvation rations he continued surveying and mapping new territory. He also studied local languages, translating some of the Bible, particularly the Psalms, into Arabic and Hausa. He travelled widely throughout the region, often in extremely difficult climatic and jungle conditions and setting up a trading centre at the confluence of the Niger and Benue, clearing the bush with his own people in order to establish what became the town of Lakojo. He died in Sierra Leone, 1864 at the Freetown home of a fellow Orcadian, *Charles Heddle.   44,68.

Balfour, Alison - d.1595 Kirkwall executed for witchcraft. A native of Ireland in Stenness. Accused of using supernatural powers to advise plotters in scheme to kill Earl *Patrick Stewart and confessed under torture of herself and family supervised by *Rev. Henry Colville of Orphir, a supporter of the Earl, but retracted her confession before dying at the stake.   6,13.

Balfour, David - b.1754 Westray d.1813 Edinburgh; s. of *William Balfour 2nd of Trenaby; bro. of *John Balfour 1750-1842 3rd of Trenaby and *Col. Thomas Balfour 1752-99; m. Marion Mackintosh 1782 dau. of Glasgow merchant.
A respected man of business operating from Edinburgh where he dealt with kelp sales, law suits and politics for many Orkney lairds and in particular for his 2 bros.   17.

Balfour, David, b.1811 Orkney d.1887 Edinburgh, 5th of Balfour and Trenaby - 3rd s. of *Capt. William Balfour RN, his older bros. John and Thomas pre-deceased him. Educ. privately, then studied law Edinburgh University; succeeded his father who died 1846 his older bro. Thomas having died 1838; m. Eleanor Edmeston 1844.
Orkney's most important landowner in 19th century owning all Shapinsay with extensive holdings elsewhere including Westray, from where the family derived its territorial designation 'of Trenaby', Stronsay, Sanday including West Brough, Gairsay and on the Orkney Mainland in Stenness, Orphir and Evie. One of the leading agricultural improvers of the century. Along with his factor, *Marcus Calder, abolished the old inefficient run-rig system of farming, drained and squared off Shapinsay into conveniently sized holdings for letting and played active part in improving the breeding of livestock.
Convener of Orkney Commissioners of Supply (forerunner of County Council), Deputy Lieutenant, Provost of Kirkwall, Chairman of School Boards in Kirkwall and Shapinsay, Chairman of Harbour Trust and in addition to building first Shapinsay pier inaugurated similar projects for Westray and Stronsay and as Kirkwall Town Councillor was largely responsible for organising installation of burgh's first piped water supply. Honorary Colonel 1st Orkney Artillery Volunteers raising a battery in Shapinsay. Made Freeman of Kirkwall 1861.
Between 1847 and 1850 engaged leading Scots architect of the day, *David Bryce, to design and build Balfour Castle in the then fashionable Scots baronial style, at the same time extending the village of Balfour. Had wide interests in literature, music, local history and folklore. Author of 'Odal Rights and Feudal Wrongs, Memorial for Orkney', transcriber and editor of 'Oppressions in the Islands of Orkney and Zetland' and 'Orkney Melodies'.
32,70,79, Orc Nov 1887, OH 23/11/1887.

Balfour, David Hubert Antony, b.1908 d.1961 Devon. The last Balfour laird he came into the estate through descent from 7th laird of Trenaby Col. William Ligonier Balfour.

Described as 'a charming, convivial, utterly irresponsible man-about-town'. Married and divorced 4 times without fathering a legitimate heir he left the Castle and most of Balfour village to his companion and house-keeper, Mrs Florence Matthews who in turn sold it to Capt. T. Zawadski who already owned the home farm, Balfour Mains.

Balfour, Edward (Eddie) - b.c1916 d.1974. Orkney's leading ornithologist and conservationist of his day. Recognised as world authority on the Hen Harrier which came from 43 years study in the field, i.e. the Orkney moorlands. Also produced studies on the Kestrel and Cormorant among many other birds. Appointed honorary officer for Royal Society for the Protection of Birds (RSPB) in Orkney 1937 and Society's 1st full-time Officer in Orkney 1954.   47, Orc 22/8/1974.

Balfour, Edward John Ligonier - b.1780 d.1799. Army officer; eldest s. of *Col. Thomas Balfour of Elwick and Frances Ligonier, sister of Earl Ligonier. While still at school (Harrow) aged 14, appointed nominal Ensign in Orkney and Shetland Fencibles raised by his father. Later appointed Lieutenant, also nominal, in 105th Foot (King's Own Yorkshire Light Infantry) and eventually Captain in the North Lowland Fencibles which his father had also raised and commanded. They served together in Ireland for a time before, having caused his father considerable distress by his rather wild teen-age life-style in Edinburgh, London and Orkney, he joined the Regular Army as Captain in 9th Foot (Norfolk Regiment) formerly commanded by his late uncle, Earl Ligonier, and took part in the ill-fated Netherlands campaign against the French. Killed in action at Den Helder 1799 aged 19.   17.

Balfour, Sir Gilbert, of Westray - b. early 16th century, probably in Fife d.1570 executed Sweden; m. Margaret Bothwell, half-sister of Bishop *Adam Bothwell.

Involved in murder of Cardinal Beaton 1546 and imprisoned, along with John Knox, in the French galleys. Back in Scotland became Master of Household to Mary Queen of Scots who appointed him Sheriff of Orkney, Keeper of Kirkwall Castle. Granted extensive Church lands in Orkney 1560 by his bro.-in-law, Bishop Adam Bothwell, and in 1567 received Westray, where he built Noltland Castle, Papay and Pharay from the Queen.

Implicated in killing of the Queen's husband, Lord Darnley, at Kirk o' Field 1567. After collapse of Queen's Party in Scotland following

battle of Langside 1568 escaped to Sweden where he was executed
1570 for an attempt on the Swedish King's life. Founder of the Orkney
Balfour family.   2,4,12,35(4),75,101.

Balfour, Colonel James William. b.1828 d.1907, 6th of Balfour - Army
officer, Black Watch, Dragoon Guards; s. of *Captain William Balfour,
RN; succeeded his half bro. Col. David Balfour 1887; m. Isabella
Craster.
   Retired from Army 1878 and settled at Balfour Dower house,
Berstane, St. Ola. Deputy Lieutenant, JP, Convener Orkney
Commissioners of Supply (forerunner of County Council), Chairman
of Orkney Harbours Commissioners and Orkney Steam Navigation
Company, succeeded *General Burroughs in command of Orkney
Artillery Volunteer Corps.   4.

Balfour, Sir James, b.c1525 d.1583, of Pittendreich - bro. of *Gilbert
Balfour; owned Kirk o' Field, Edinburgh where Darnley was
murdered 1567 and implicated in the killing. Eminent lawyer, advisor
to Mary Queen of Scots. Represented his brother in disputes with
*Bishop Adam Bothwell over Gilbert's acquisition of bishopric lands in
Orkney. Described as 'the most corrupt man of his age'.   2,12.

Balfour, John - Sheriff Depute of Orkney 1566. Bro. of *Sir Gilbert of
Westray and *Sir James of Pittendreich.   2.

Balfour, John, b.1750 Westray d.1842 London - 3rd of Trenaby. Eldest s. of
*William Balfour and Elizabeth Coventrie. Educ. Aberdeen University.
Writer in East India Company, Madras 1772 where he made his fortune
trading on his own account as well as for the Company. Promoted
Factor and became merchant banker marrying a wealthy widow with
even better prospects, Harriet MacLellan. Returned to Britain 1790, a
'Nabob'. MP for Orkney and Shetland 1790-1796. After return from
India lived mainly in Curzon Street, Mayfair, London and at his
country villa, Charlton Grove, Kent but retained close contacts with
Orkney and the family whose interests he furthered through influence
he was able to exert in high places. Endowed Trust to fund Balfour
Hospital 1836.   17.

Balfour, Mary - see Brunton.

Balfour, Michael, of Montquhanie - nephew of *Gilbert Balfour from
whom he inherited Westray estate including Noltland Castle 1588.
Appointed Commissioner 1589 by Earl *Robert Stewart, with whom
he had been previously associated, to set feus and tacks in Shetland.
But disillusioned and at litigious odds with the Stewart Earls to such

an extent that *Patrick, who had succeeded to the Earldom, seized Noltland Castle from him 1597 on pretext of an unpaid debt of £8,000. Balfour escaped to Scotland and laid a complaint before the Privy Council and through the Courts obtained surety against the Earl. 13.

Balfour, Thomas, b.1721 d.1782, of Huip - Kirkwall merchant. 2nd s. of *John Balfour, 1st of Trenaby; m. Mary Mackenzie of Groundwater.

Involved in Pundlar Process and also acted for his bro. *William during his bankruptcy. Traded in meal, kelp, flax and lint with a little smuggling and in early days sailed as skipper of his own ships. Was banker and guarantor for the family in Kirkwall. After being factor for Huip in Stronsay he acquired it for himself 1762 also buying the island mill. Became factor for farm of Holland in Stronsay 1768. Assisted financially in education of his three nephews, sons of *William. Politically opposed to Kerse Dundases, owners of Orkney Earldom estate, voting against *Thomas Dundas in 1780 election but pro-Henry Dundas of Arniston branch (later Viscount Melville) who wielded great political power nationally. 14(3),17.

Balfour, Dr. (later Colonel) Thomas, b.1752 Westray d.1799 Bath, of Elwick - 2nd s. of *William Balfour 2nd of Trenaby and Elizabeth Coventrie of Newark, Deerness; bro. of *John Balfour MP, 3rd of Trenaby; m. Frances Ligonier, sister of 2nd Earl Ligonier. Studied medicine Edinburgh and Aberdeen Universities.

Appointed nominal Ensign in 9th Regiment of Foot (Norfolk Regt) commanded by bro-in-law Earl Ligonier but never served with it although on payroll. Returned Orkney after marriage to manage family estates acting as their agent in Kirkwall, Deerness and elsewhere in the county. Leased Burray from *Sir Lawrence Dundas, 1778 and carried out extensive improvements to the Bu before buying Sound in Shapinsay 1784 where he built Cliffdale for his seat. Appointed Sheriff Substitute of Orkney.

As merchant laird engaged in kelp industry, agricultural improvement, shipping, fisheries with as many as 10 smacks; involved with Northern Lighthouse Commissioners in building Orkney's first lighthouse on North Ronaldsay and another on the Pentland Skerries.

Raised Orkney and Shetland Fencibles 1792 and North Lowland Fencibles 1794 seeing service in Ireland with the latter as Colonel 1795. Contracted typhus and returned to Scotland for recuperation before rejoining his unit in Ireland. Still involved in family and Orkney affairs but owing to deteriorating health went to Bath for a cure where he died 1799 only shortly before his son, *John, was killed in action. 17.

Balfour, William, b.1719 Orkney d.1786 Edinburgh, 2nd of Trenaby - s. of

*John Balfour, 1st of Trenaby and Elizabeth Traill of Westness; m. Elizabeth Coventrie 1744.

One of the North Isles Jacobite lairds who took refuge in Gentlemen's Ha' caves, Westray after the '45 to elude troops under *Benjamin Moodie of Melsetter who failed to find them.

Opposed to Earl of Morton and active in the Pundlar Process. Following bankruptcy recovered with the help of his bro. *Thos Balfour of Huip and became politically active. After early misgivings accepted *Sir Lawrence Dundas who acquired the Earldom estates in 1766 and was his factor in Shetland 1769 where he introduced kelp making. Chamberlain for Dundas also in Orkney 1775 to 1780 but lost Shetland factorship 1778.   11,17.

Balfour, Captain William RN, b.1781 Burray d.1846 Edinburgh, 2nd of Elwick, 4th of Trenaby - Younger s. of *Col. Thomas Balfour of Elwick and Frances Ligonier; m. (1) cousin Mary Balfour Manson 1806 (2) Mary Margaret Baikie 1823.

Educ. Harrow. Joined Navy as Midshipman 1795 in HMS *Irresistible* with Channel Fleet. Wounded in battle of Cape St Vincent 1797. Took part in naval blockade of Spanish fleet in Cadiz and engaged in several minor actions before joining Nelson's Mediterranean fleet in HMS *Northumberland* for the re-taking of Malta from the French 1799. In action off Bergen 1804 as Second Lieut., in HMS *Amethyst* 1804 and as First Lieut. in HMS *Cleopatra* against the French ship *Ville de Milan* 1805 when he was wounded. Promoted Commander 1806. Retired from Navy on half pay 1808 with rank of Captain and returned to Orkney living at Cliffdale, Shapinsay where after gaining some experience was factor 1812 for his uncle *John's Orkney estate which he subsequently inherited 1842. Retired to Edinburgh 1843.   17,32.

Banks, Sir Joseph - b.1743 d.1820. Naturalist, explorer, founder of Royal Botanic Gardens at Kew. Visited Orkney 1772 on way to Iceland. With *Rev. George Low excavated 2 burial mounds on Skaill Links, Sandwick. Artists accompanying him made sketches of the area, cist burials and the Ring of Brogar.   *Proceedings of Society of Antiquaries Scotland* Vol 104, 1971/2, *Biography* - Patrick O'Brian.

Barclay, Dr. Robert Steven, BSc, FRSE - b. Hurkisgarth, Sandwick, Orkney d.1973 Edinburgh. Statistician, sailor. Educ. Oxtro School, Birsay, Heriots and Edinburgh University.

Went to sea as ordinary seaman in coasters, cargo ships and ocean liners obtaining Ticket as First Mate (Deep Sea). Commissioned Lieutenant in RNR during World War II engaged in manning, equipping and trials of wooden minesweepers. Returning to academic career gained PhD with thesis on mortality and fertility 1947, established interest in population figures and appointed statistician in the General Register Office, Edinburgh. Publications include 'Population of Orkney 1755-1961' and editing of 2 'Court Books of Orkney and Shetland 1614/15 and 1615/6.   Orc 29/3/73.

Barry, Rev. Dr. George - b.1748 Berwickshire d.1805 Orkney - Tutor to lairds' families before being ordained Second Minister St Magnus Cathedral 1782 being translated to Shapinsay 1793; m. Sibella, dau. of *Rev. John Yule, Minister St Magnus Cathedral. Contributed the sections on Kirkwall and St Ola and also Shapinsay for the Old Statistical Account as well as writing the 'History of Orkney' 1805. 6.

Battenberg, Admiral of the Fleet Prince Louis of - b.1854 d.1921; s. of Prince Alexander of Hesse and Princess Alice, dau. of Queen Victoria. Served in Royal Navy becoming First Sea Lord 1912-1914 having commanded Atlantic Fleet. Surveyed possible coastal defence positions around Scapa Flow 1892. In Kirkwall Bay 1898 as Flag Captain Channel Fleet and led parade on horseback in Broad Street watched by Duke of York (later King George V) then commanding one of the cruisers in the Bay. Visited Scapa Flow as Commander-in-Chief Atlantic Fleet 1909. Return visit with 90 ships of Fleet 1910. Retired from Navy as Admiral of the Fleet 1914 following press smear campaign regarding his Teutonic ancestry. Became Marquis of Milford Haven·changing name to Mountbatten. Father of *Earl Mountbatten of Burma.   26,44.

Beatty, Admiral of the Fleet Sir (later Earl) David - b.1871 d.1936. Commanded 1st Battlecruiser Squadron at battles of Heligoland Bight, Dogger Bank and Jutland before succeeding *Jellicoe as Commander-in-Chief Grand Fleet in Scapa Flow 1916. Received surrender of German High Seas Fleet ships in the Forth November 1918 and dispatched them to Scapa Flow for internment.   26,44,95.

Bellenden, George - Sheriff Depute 1563.   2.

Bellenden, Sir John, d.1577, of Auchnoull - Succeeded his father, Thomas Bellenden as Justice Clerk of Scotland; bro. of *Patrick Bellenden of Evie and Stenness; cousin of *Bishop Adam Bothwell; m. Barbara Kennedy, dau. of Sir Hugh Kennedy of Girvanmains.
    Power behind the throne of cousin's episcopate and early part of Earl *Robert Stewart's rule. Had control of bishopric temporalities following death of *Bishop Reid 1558; maintained political contacts in Edinburgh while bro. *Patrick of Evie and Stenness managed affairs in Orkney. Feued Birsay estate which he leased back to cousin Bishop Bothwell.   12,101.

Bellenden, Katherine - wife of *Oliver Sinclair of Pitcairns; mother of *Bishop Bothwell by previous marriage to *Francis Bothwell, lawyer and Lord Provost of Edinburgh; sister of *Sir John Bellenden; mother-in-law of *Gilbert Balfour of Westray.   12.

Bellenden, Sir Lewis d.1591, of Auchnoull - s. of *Sir John Bellenden whom he succeeded as Justice Clerk of Scotland; granted Crown Charter 1587 jointly with Sir John Maitland of Thirlestane, Chancellor of Scotland, to manage Earl *Robert Stewart's forfeited Orkney Earldom and Shetland (Lordship) estates.   13,101.

Bellenden, Sir Patrick. b.1532 d.1611 of Evie and Stenness - s. of Thomas Bellenden, Justice Clerk of Scotland; bro. of *Sir John Bellenden whose interests he managed in Orkney; m. Katherine Kennedy, widow of *Henry Sinclair of Strom (later of Brough).

Granted charter of land in Stenness 1563 on which he built 'Palace' which became principal family residence in Orkney. Acquired even more extensive lands mainly in Evie from Bishopric estate 1565 and was appointed Sheriff only to be supplanted in this appointment almost immediately by *Robert Stewart who had been granted Orkney and Shetland by Queen Mary though not as yet the title of Earl - that came later. Tightening his grip on Orkney, Robert deprived Bellenden of many of his estates engendering bitter animosity between them. Bellenden left Orkney but continued feud with Robert from the south aided by powerful friends such as the Earl of Caithness and the then Regent, the Earl of Morton.

Was involved in assassination of Rizzio, secretary and favourite of *Queen Mary at Holyroodhouse 1566. Arrived at a grudging accommodation with Earl Robert 1577, but supported efforts of his nephew *Sir Lewis Bellenden and Sir John Maitland of Thirlestane, the Secretary of Scotland, against the earl with an abortive invasion of Orkney in 1587. Thereafter did not return to Orkney until after Robert's death 1593. Continued opposition to the Stewarts when *Patrick succeeded his father as Earl.   12,13.

Bellus - Mythical pre-Norse king of Orkney sometimes erroneously connected with the now broken stone from the former episcopal palace in Birsay bearing the inscription 'Mons Bellus' (Mount Pleasant).   80.

Ben, Jo - An otherwise unknown 16th century author who wrote a Latin 'Description of Orkney' supposedly in 1529 but the material contained in it shows it was actually written much later in the 16th century.

Attempts have been made to identify him with the poet John Bellenden and with John Bonar, who was briefly minister in North

Ronaldsay in the 1590s. The former has proved untenable but there is more to be said for the latter. The amount of space in the manuscript devoted to North Ronaldsay and Stronsay with which Bonar may have had family connections through Margaret Bonar, wife of *William Henderson makes this identification plausible but no more definite conclusion can be reached. 10, *Macfarlane's Geographical Collections, Scottish Historical Society*, Vol 3, 1908.

Bergfinn Skatisson - Blind Shetland farmer who regained his sight after vigil at the St Magnus shrine in Birsay c1117 and, in a later vigil at St Olaf's Church, Kirkwall after the saint's relics had been transferred there from Birsay, his son Halfdan was cured of leprosy. 3.

Berry, Harry - b.1905, Peckham, South London d.1994 Orkney. Served in Royal Navy 1920-45 rising to rank of Chief Petty Officer. He had married Orkney girl, Margaret June Guthrie, and having trained as a diver in the Navy, settled in Orkney and worked for salvage firm Metal Industries not as a diver but in the dockyard before becoming the company's sign-writer giving him ample scope to develop his very considerable artistic talents. He then entered government service again this time as Customs Officer at Lyness.

An accomplished amateur artist he specialised in detailed and vivid oil paintings of the Longhope Lifeboats in action on their hazardous rescue operations, which paintings he donated for fund-raising purposes.

He was a born raconteur with the gift of spinning yarns including one in which he made himself a set of false teeth using fibre-glass for he was also a talented handyman - and he could, and often did turn these tales into short stories. Orkney Sound Archive RO157.

Bews, Professor John William, MA, DSc, FIS, FRS (SA) - b.1884 St Ola, Orkney d.1938 Natal, South Africa. Botanist. Educ. Kirkwall Burgh (Grammar) School, Edinburgh University.

Appointed Assistant Professor of Botany, Edinburgh University 1908; Professor of Botany, Natal University College, 1910; Botanist-in-Charge Eastern Area for Botanical Survey of South Africa 1918; Dean of Faculty of Science, University of South Africa 1921; Chairman of Senate of University of South Africa 1922-24; Principal of Natal University 1934.

Researched and wrote papers on vegetation and ecology of Natal and South Africa in general. Contributed section on botany to first 'Orkney Book' 1909. Books include 'Grasses and Grasslands of South Africa', 'Flora of Natal and Zululand', 'Plant Forms and their Evolution in South Africa', 'Human Ecology', 'Life as a Whole', 'The World's Grasses'. Orc 17/11/1938, OH 16/11/38.

Bignold, Sir Arthur - b.1839 Norwich d.1915 London. Qualified in law
   Cambridge University but did not practise.
   Entered Stock Exchange 1861 making considerable fortune largely
   through investments in property. MP for Northern Burghs (including
   Kirkwall) 1900-1910. An accomplished linguist he learned Gaelic after
   becoming a Ross-shire laird. Founder member of Kennel Club and
   Chief of Gaelic Society 1910. Made many substantial donations to
   projects in his constituency notably Bignold Park in Kirkwall and
   hospital in Wick.   44, OH 31/3/1915.

Birsay, Lord - see Leslie, Harald Robert.

Bjarni Kolbeinsson - Bishop of Orkney. 1188-1223. 2nd s. of *Kolbein
   Hruga (Cubbie Roo) of Wyre and Herbjorg, grt grd dau. of Earl *Paul
   I. Poet, diplomat and man of letters (Jomsvikinga Drapa and Proverb
   poem Malshatta Kvardi); succeeded *Bishop William II 1188;
   continued the building of St Magnus Cathedral begun by *Kol in 1137.
   May have inaugurated Kirkwall Grammar School. Accompanied Earl
   *Harald II Maddadsson and Orkney delegates to Bergen to make
   peace with *King Sverre after defeat of the Eyjarskeggjar (Island
   Beardies) at Florvåg 1193. Given papal permission to translate body of
   Earl (St) *Rognvald II from Caithness, where he was murdered, for
   burial in St Magnus Cathedral. Described in OS as 'greatest of
   chiefs'.   1,2,3,21,35(7),100.

Bjarni Thorleifsson - Governor of Iceland. On way home to Denmark
   1486 with royal and ecclesiastical rents was forced by press of weather
   to seek shelter in Orkney and was imprisoned with his wife and
   followers. Possibly an attempt by Earl *William to delay discussions
   between Scotland and Denmark over payment or non-payment of
   Annual of Norway, the tax agreed at Treaty of Perth 1266 when
   Norway ceded Hebrides to Scotland but retained control of Orkney
   and Shetland.   2.

Black, Henry - Constable of Kirkwall Castle c1604 onwards, under Earl
   *Patrick Stewart.   13.

Black, Thomas - d.1615 Edinburgh. Chamberlain of Orkney under Earl
   *Patrick Stewart. Supported *Robert Stewart, Patrick's illegitimate son,
   in his unsuccessful attempt to regain Earldom 1614 for his father then
   being held in Dumbarton Castle on charges including treason. In the
   attack on Kirkwall he led rebel party which secured the tower of the
   Cathedral covering the nearby Castle. Also led party which
   intercepted the herald on his way from Shapinsay via Carness to
   deliver ultimatum by *Earl of Caithness, whose force with artillery

was anchored in Elwick Bay, demanding Robert's submission. When Cathedral position was surrendered he was taken prisoner with his party, tried, condemned and hanged in Edinburgh, along with Robert and others 1615. 2,13.

Blair, Patrick, of Little Blair - Sheriff Depute during Commonwealth. Recorded as holding courts in Kirkwall 1664. 2,4,69.

Bligh, Captain William RN - b.1754 Plymouth d.1817. Joined Royal Navy 1770 and sailed on Captain Cook's last Pacific Ocean expedition. After Cook was killed in Hawaii 1779, his ships returning to Britain with Bligh on board, called at Stromness.
   As Captain of HMS *Bounty* 1787 on voyage to collect bread-fruit in the Pacific some of the crew mutinied and set him adrift in mid ocean. One of his officers, Orcadian Lieutenant *Stewart of Massater, was kept on board by the mutineers and later released and put ashore in Tahiti. 35(6),96.

Bonot - Sheriff and Commissioner of Orkney 1543-c1558. French favourite of Dowager Queen *Mary of Guise. 1,2.

Borrow, George Henry - b.1803 Norfolk d.1881. Novelist, travel writer, eccentric. Deeply interested in gypsy lore. While on walking tour of Scotland visited Orkney during winter 1858 taking in Dwarfie Stone, Ring of Brogar, St Magnus Cathedral and the Palaces having walked from Stromness to Kirkwall. Author of 'Lavengro', 'Romany Rye' 'The Bible in Spain' and many other publications. Orc 11/2/54.

Bothwell, Bishop Adam - b.c1536 Edinburgh d.1593 Edinburgh; s. of Francis Bothwell, Lord Provost of Edinburgh and *Katherine Bellenden; cousin of *Patrick Bellenden of Evie and Stenness; bro.-in-law of *Gilbert Balfour of Westray; m. Margaret Murray.
   Educ. St Andrews and in France. Judge in Court of Session. Appointed Bishop of Orkney 1559 by Pope Paul IV - the last Orkney Bishop to be appointed by the Vatican - but becoming Protestant adhered to Reforming Party in Scotland. Arrived Orkney 1560 bringing some Reforming order to a confused diocese, 'planting' ministers in the various parishes and prebends. Feued Bishopric lands to his family and friends but was eventually in acrimonious dispute with cousin, *Sir John Bellenden, Justice Clerk in Edinburgh, bro. of Patrick Bellenden of Stenness, believing him to be too greedy in many of these transactions. Travelled to France to put the matter before Queen Mary and returned to Scotland in her train 1561. Officiated at ill-starred marriage of Queen to *James Hepburn, Earl of Bothwell 1567 and also at coronation of her son James VI by previous husband, Darnley.

Was member of expedition which pursued Earl of Bothwell northwards to Orkney and Shetland when Mary was deposed, only just escaping with his life when his ship was wrecked in Bressay Sound, Shetland.

Exchanged what remained of Orkney Bishopric estate for Earl *Robert Stewart's Holyroodhouse estate 1570. Scholarly but did not enjoy good health which he claimed accounted for his long and frequent absences from Orkney.   2,12,21,101.

Bothwell, Francis - Nephew of *Bishop Adam Bothwell who left affairs of diocese in his hands while he was absent in France 1561. Treasurer of St Magnus Cathedral, Parson of Stronsay and in charge of Bishopric revenues 1562. Disapproved of the extent of Bishop Adam's distribution of Bishopric lands by feuing to relations and other interested parties after the Reformation and, in fact, headed a Kirkwall mob rioting on the matter during the Bishop's absence. But accepted funding himself from Church revenues 1592.   2,4,21.

Bothwell, 4th Earl of, - see Hepburn, James.

Bothwell, Margaret - Half-sister of *Bishop Adam Bothwell; m. *Gilbert Balfour.

Bough, Samuel RSA - b.1822 Carlisle d.1878. Artist. Worked as theatre scene-painter before becoming one of Scotland's leading landscape artists. Elected to Royal Scottish Academy 1875. Painted number of landscapes in Orkney.   51.

Brand, Sir Alexander - Edinburgh arms-dealer; rapacious tacksman of Orkney and Shetland during 1693-5 famine which became known as 'Brand's Years'.   2.

Brand, Rev. John - Minister in Bo'ness. Wrote 'A Brief Description of Orkney, Zetland, Pightland Firth and Caithness' published 1701. Member of General Assembly of Church of Scotland Commission appointed to visit and enquire into the 'state of religion and morals of these parts' 1700 and which investigated ministers of Jacobite or Episcopalian sympathies leading eventually to the removal of every single Orkney minister. He gave himself an even wider remit for this 'Description'.   2.

Bremner, Rev. James - b.1740 d.1836 Edinburgh. Educ. Edinburgh University and Marischal College, Aberdeen. Minister of Walls and Flotta 1772-1814, tutor to Moodies of Melsetter; m. Isabella Mowat. A mechanical genius, he designed a new lock for naval guns and improvements in signalling equipment. Finding his manse in North Walls inconveniently sited he started to build himself a new one in a better position but it was never completed. 6(p.226).

Bremner, John - b.1793 d.1852. Surgeon; s. of *Rev. James Bremner; m. Sibilla Guthrie. Surgeon in Royal Navy and then in Kirkwall. Was one of the four physicians appointed to share attendance in the new Balfour Memorial Hospital 1845 and undertook the first three-month stint free-of-charge. Liberal in politics and an Elder in the Free Kirk he was friend of *Professor T. S. Traill. Lived in house on Broad Street. 4.

Bridei mac Bile - Pictish king. Attacked and devastated Orkney c.682. 2.

Bridei mac Maelchon - Pictish King. Inverness c.561 granted safe conduct to St Columba's missionaries sailing in Orkney waters. Also present in Inverness was 'the subject-king of the Orcades', who was apparently being held by Bridei as hostage. 2.

Broadfoot, Rev. William - b.1775 Whithorn d.1837 London. First Secession minister in Kirkwall 1798-1817. Ordained at open-air service in Kirkwall 1798. His regular Sunday congregation numbered 1250. 6.

Brown, George Mackay, MBE - b.1921 Stromness d.1996 Orkney. Poet, author, playwright; s. of postman and part-time tailor, his mother was a Gaelic speaker from Bettyhill in Sutherland across the Pentland Firth and from both of them he absorbed his life-long sense of identification with the north and the islands.

Educ. Stromness Academy, Newbattle Abbey Adult Education College, where he studied under Orkney-born poet and writer *Edwin Muir, Edinburgh University. Apart from student days hardly ever left his native Orkney, its Norse history and sagas along with his conversion to Roman Catholicism, providing the main influence and inspiration for his work. He never enjoyed good health having suffered from tuberculosis in his 20s.

In addition to his poetry, novels and short stories which earned him international renown he was columnist and reporter for both local newspapers, first the *Orkney Herald* and after it folded in 1961, *The Orcadian*. Collaborated with composer Sir Peter Maxwell Davies in many works including libretto for the music-drama 'The Martyrdom of Magnus' based on his novel 'Magnus' which launched the St Magnus Festival in 1977. His volumes of poetry include among many others, 'The Storm', 'Loaves and Fishes', 'The Year of the Whale', 'Fishermen with Ploughs', and his novels, 'Greenvoe', 'Magnus', 'Hawkfall'. 65, Orc April 1996.

Brown, James and Robert - Orkney-based pirates captured in Wales 1590
and imprisoned.   2.

Brown, James Donald, CBE, DL - b.1902, Stromness d.1978 Stromness.
Agriculturist, colonial administrator, Convener Orkney County
Council; s. of James Brown, solicitor, Town Clerk of Stromness. Educ.
Stromness Public School. Aberdeen Grammar School, Aberdeen
University, BSc (Agric) 1924; swimming and athletics blue.
   Appointed Superintendent, Dept of Agriculture, Nigeria 1924;
Deputy Director 1945; Director of Agriculture, Northern Nigeria 1950-
53 when he retired to Orkney and became a prominent pig-breeder.
During World War II served as Major in Royal West African Frontier
Force.
   Member of Orkney County Council for Stromness Parish 1958;
Convener 1970-75 seeing the advent of North Sea oil and the
reorganisation of local government when OCC became Orkney Islands
Council. He was a keen gardener and trout fisher.   Orc 4/5/78.

Brown, Thomas - 17th century Writer (lawyer) and Notary Public,
Kirkwall. Probably member of Brown family which owned lands of
Weyland near Kirkwall at this period. m. (1) Margaret Simme 1667 (2)
Marjorie Taylour 1671. Surviving fragments of his diary, published
1898, provide a valuable record of individuals and events of the
period.   4,69.

Brøgger, Professor A. W. - Norwegian archaeologist, specialised in viking
period including Norse colonisation of Orkney. Author of 'Ancient
Emigrants', 1929.

Bruce, James - Earldom estate factor 1809-1825. Former over-seer of
slaves in West Indies. Earned himself reputation of being a hard task-
master in dealing with Orkney tenants on the estate. His main sport
and amusement was said to be cock-fighting.   2.

Bruce, Robert the - see Robert I, King of Scotland.

Brunton, Mary - b.1778 Burray d.1818 Edinburgh. Novelist; dau. of
*Thomas Balfour and Frances Ligonier, sister of Earl Ligonier; m. Rev.
Alexander Brunton. They first met when, as a divinity student he was
preacher in Shapinsay, tutor to her bros *Edward and *William Balfour
and chaplain of the North Lowland Fencibles raised by her father.
Later, having been taken to Edinburgh by her mother in order to be
launched into fashionable society she eloped with him. After their
marriage 1798 he became successively Minister of Bolton, East
Lothian, Greyfriars Kirk and the Tron Kirk in Edinburgh, Professor of

Oriental Languages at Edinburgh University 1813 and subsequently Moderator of the General Assembly of the Church of Scotland 1823.

She played an active part in the literary life of Edinburgh writing 3 novels, 'Self Control' 1810, 'Discipline' 1814 and 'Emmeline' published posthumously 1819. Orc 23/7/1987.

Brusi Sigurdsson - Earl of Orkney 1014-c.1035; s. of Earl *Sigurd II The Stout; bro. of *Hlodver, Earls *Somerledi, *Einar II Wrymouth and half bro. of Earl *Thorfinn II; father of Earl *Rognvald I.

Joint earl 1014 with bros. Somerledi and Einar II, Hlodver having predeceased his father, and after their deaths and a power-struggle, shared the Earldom with Thorfinn II being granted two-thirds by King Olaf of Norway 1020 Thorfinn retaining one third, but Brusi being 'A mild man and peacemaker' (OS) handed his second third over to Thorfinn on condition that he undertook defence of the entire Earldom against attack. 1,2,3,35(7),76.

Buchanan, Capt. Angus, MC, FRSGS - b.1897 Kirkwall d.1954 Edinburgh. Explorer, naturalist, architect. s. of Angus Buchanan, Kirkwall banker and sportsman, mother was dau. of Sandison whisky family.

Educ. Kirkwall Grammar School. Practised as architect in Canada and in 1914 was member of zoological expedition to the Arctic Barren Lands. Joined Legion of Frontiersmen 1915 and saw 3 years active service in East Africa before being invalided back to UK. On expedition exploring central Sahara 1919-20. Made successful 18-month-long crossing of Sahara from south to north collecting new species of animals and birds 1922-24. Wrote and lectured on his experiences in the desert. In World War II served in the 1940-43 Abyssinian campaign. Orc 11/2/54.

Buchanan, Arthur, of Sound - m. Margaret Buxtoun. With *Hugh Craigie of Gairsay represented Orkney in Commonwealth Scottish Parliament and supported move to unite the Scottish and English Parliaments half a century before the unification actually took place in 1707.

Owned land throughout the West Mainland as well as most of Shapinsay, including Sound which he bought from *Sir John, most of Stronsay and all of North Ronaldsay. Also owned a number of houses in Kirkwall including his own Great Lodging in what is now Albert Street with an open space in front reaching down to the Peerie Sea. 4.

Buchanan, Lieut. Col. Fred - b.1880 Edinburgh d.1962 Kirkwall. Soldier, solicitor, sportsman; s. of Angus Buchanan, agent for National Bank of Scotland who moved to Orkney with his family on taking over the Kirkwall branch when Fred was 4 years old; bro. of *Angus Buchanan.

Educ. Kirkwall Burgh (Grammar) School, George Watson's College,

Edinburgh. Studied law and entered Kirkwall law firm started by his father who, incidently, played rugby for Scotland in the first Calcutta Cup international against England.

Back in Orkney he began his long military career by joining the Orkney Garrison Artillery 1909 serving on Scapa Flow Defences in Flotta and later in France during World War I. After war was active in ex-servicemen's organisations such as British Legion. In 1939 commanded Orkney Heavy Regiment (Coast Artillery) serving again on Flow defences in Flotta until retired on reaching age-limit in 1942 after which served in Orkney Home Guard. Continued work with British Legion after war and took command of Army Cadets.   Orc 3/1/62.

Buchanan, Janet - d.1756. Inherited Eday and Sound in Shapinsay from her grt uncle, *Arthur; m. *James Fea, 6th of Clestran. Present at Carrick House, Eday when her husband organised capture of *Gow the Pirate 1725. Forced to witness burning of her mansion house of Sound 1746 by Hanoverian troops as reprisal for her husband's Jacobite activities during the '45 Rising.   11.

Buchanan, Sir John - d.1643 of Scotscraig, Fife; grt uncle of *Arthur Buchanan. Was involved in scandal when his wife Margaret Hartsyde was convicted of theft of jewels from her mistress, Ann of Denmark, Queen of James VI and I. He was apparently cleared of the offence but accompanied his wife when she was banished to Orkney where in due course he acquired lands in Eday from John, Earl of Carrick who died without male issue 1652, and the estate of Sound in Shapinsay which he later sold to *Arthur Buchanan. Jointly with *Sir George Hay of Kinfauns, later 1st Earl of Kinnoull, he obtained tack of the Earldom c1620, was knighted and became Sheriff of Orkney 1622-4.   2,4.

Burroughs, General Sir Frederick William Traill, b.1831 India d.1905 London, of Rousay and Viera (Wyre) - s. of General Frederick William Burroughs from Ireland and Anglo-French Caroline de Peyron. Aged 9 came to UK from India with distant relative, honorary 'uncle' *George William Traill of Viera who retiring from Bengal Civil Service, became his guardian and made him his heir; m. Eliza (Lizzie) d'Oyley Geddes.

Educ. Blackheath and Hofwyl, Switzerland. Commissioned into 93rd Foot (Sutherland Highlanders) 1848. Fought in Crimean War 1854-6 and later distinguished himself during Indian Mutiny 1857-8. Disappointed at not being awarded Victoria Cross for his part in relief of Lucknow although recommended for it. Promoted Lieut. Col. 1864 commanding regiment in Northwest Frontier campaigns before returning UK and Rousay 1870. Retiring from army 1873 lived in Rousay and managed the estate inherited from 'uncle' *George William Traill. Having built Trumland House moved there from

Westness; also built Trumland Pier 1871. Founded Rousay, Evie & Rendall Steamship Company, ss *Lizzie Burroughs* making first voyage to Kirkwall 1879. Knighted 1904.

A strict disciplinarian in the army he carried a high-handed authoritarian attitude into civilian life continuing the system of 'clearances' in Rousay started by his 'uncle'. This, with raising of rents and evictions, caused bitter resentment and discontent among his tenants and crofters coming to a head during visit of Napier Royal Commission whose findings led to the Crofters' Act of 1886. He evicted tenants who gave evidence to the Commission and, having come to regard all crofters with enmity, would have cleared them all from his estate had not the passing of the Crofters' Act prevented him from doing so. As a result he earned himself the reputation of being 'the worst of the 19th century lairds in Orkney'.   9,70.

C

Calder, James Traill - b.1794 Caithness d.1864 Shapinsay; historian, teacher; s. of George Calder, gardener to *James Traill of Hobbister and Rattar. Crippled from boyhood. Academically brilliant. Schoolmaster Canisbay 1815. Retired 1856 on annual pension of £25. Published 'Poems from John o'Groats' 1856 and 'History of Caithness' 1861. Stayed with bro. Peter in Stronsay 1861-3 and died at home of bro. *Marcus, Shapinsay.   Memoir in 2nd edition of his *History* 1887.

Calder, Marcus - b.c1814 Caithness d.1881 Shapinsay. Factor 1846-81 for Balfour and Trenaby estates covering lands in Westray, Stronsay, Sanday and especially Shapinsay where he carried out agricultural improvements including division of holdings on a 10-acre grid system increasing the arable acreage from 750 to 2250. Also raised quality of livestock, cattle, sheep, horses and pigs by selective breeding. Served on a number of local bodies including 4 School Boards, Commissioners of Supply and was Major in Orkney Artillery Volunteers. Bro. of *James Calder, the Caithness historian.   2,79,85, OH 6/7/1881.

Campbell, Very Rev. Andrew James, MA, DD - b.1878 Crathie, Aberdeenshire d.1950 Edinburgh. Moderator of the General Assembly of the Church of Scotland. Educ. Fettes College, Edinburgh, St John's College, Cambridge, Divinity Hall Edinburgh University; m. (1) Caroline Cumming Spence (2) Anne Mary Robertson. Minister,

Lerwick 1902; Glasgow 1910; Chaplain 52 Division, Gallipoli, Egypt, during World War I; Clerk of Glasgow Presbytery 1929-36; Minister of Evie, 1936-1948 during which time became the only serving Minister from Orkney ever to be appointed Moderator of the General Assembly 1945. Publications include 'Two Centuries of the Church of Scotland' 1929, 'The Church in Orkney' 1936.   OH 9/5/50, 49(1941-50).

Carnegie, Andrew - b.1835 Dunfermline d.1919 Mass,. USA. Millionaire American industrialist, ironmaster, philanthropist; s. of weaver who emigrated with family from Fife to USA 1848. Made his fortune first in oil but particularly in steel later. On retirement returned to Scotland where for a time was Laird of Skibo Castle, Sutherland. Formed Carnegie Trust which founded educational projects, especially public libraries throughout English-speaking world, including what became Orkney County Library building in Laing Street, Kirkwall which he opened in person 1909 being made Freeman of the Burgh.
Orc & OH Sept 1909, *Collins Biographical Dictionary etc.*

Carrick, Alexander, RSA - b.1882 Musselburgh d.1966 Galashiels. Sculptor. m. Elizabeth Harold Leith, St Margaret's Hope, whose family ran a tailoring business there. Educ. Musselburgh, Edinburgh, London.
Carried out restoration work on St Magnus Cathedral 1912-13 before serving in Royal Artillery during World War I. Among his many commissions were the Royal Artillery and Royal Engineer panels for the Scottish National War Memorial, Edinburgh Castle. Also sculpted figures of kilted Highland soldiers for over 20 war memorials throughout Scotland one of the earliest of which was acquired by St Margaret's Hope for the South Ronaldsay memorial.
One of Scotland's leading sculptors of his day, he was Head of Sculpture at Edinburgh College of Art.   49.

Carrick, John, Earl of - see Stewart, John, Master of Orkney.

Childe, Professor V. Gordon, DLitt, DSc, FBA, FRAI, FSA Scot - b.1892 Sydney, Australia d.1957 Australia. Archaeologist. Educ. Church of England Grammar School, New South Wales, Sydney and Oxford Universities.
Private Secretary to Premier, NSW, 1919-21. Travelled widely studying archaeology in Middle East, Greece, the Balkans and Eastern Europe. Appointed Professor of European Pre-historic Archaeology, Edinburgh University 1927-1946 and Director of Institute of Archaeology, London University, 1946-56. Excavated Stone Age village of Skara Brae, Bay of Skaill and also Midhowe Broch with the stalled cairn and Rinyo in Rousay during late 1920s and early 1930s. After World War II carried out excavations at Maeshowe, the stalled cairn at Quoyness, Sanday and elsewhere in Orkney.

Being a Communist gave him comparatively easy access to museums and sources in Eastern Europe and the Soviet Union both before and especially after WWII, a facility not enjoyed by most archaeologists from the West. Numerous publications including 'Skara Brae' 1931 and 'Prehistoric Scotland' 1935.

Orc 24/10/57, OH 22/10/57, 49(1951-60).

Chiocchetti, Domenico - b.1910, Moena, Trento. Italian artist and craftsman. Studied art of painting statues and church decoration. Captured in Libya by 8th Army while serving with an Italian anti-aircraft unit and held in British Prisoner-of-War Camp 60 on Lambholm with several hundred other Italian POWs 1942-44. Engaged on work connected with construction of Churchill Barriers.

Leading spirit and inspiration behind construction of Italian Chapel on Lambholm made from 2 Nissen huts and whatever scrap material was available. Painted the interior himself including altarpiece and also crafted nearby statue of St George and the Dragon. Repatriated to Italy after the war but returned twice to carry out restoration work on the chapel. 31.

Christian I - b.1426 d.1481. King of Denmark 1448-81 and Norway 1450-81. In 1468 pledged his lands and sovereign rights in Orkney for 50,000 Rhenish florins as part payment of the 60,000 florins of his dau. Margaret's dowry on the occasion of her marriage to *James III of Scotland (The Impignoration). His Shetland rights and possessions were similarly pledged the following year for the sum still outstanding. The pledges were never redeemed and Orkney and Shetland remained henceforth under control of the Scottish Crown despite periodic attempts by Denmark to negotiate their return.

1,2, *The Pawning of Orkney and Shetland* - Barbara Crawford,
Scottish Historical Review xlviii 1969 and *Saga Book* 1968.

Churchill, Sir Winston Spencer - b.1874 d.1965. Statesman, politician, wartime Prime Minister. First visited Orkney 1911 when First Lord of the Admiralty to assess Scapa Flow's potential as wartime naval base. Accompanied by Prime Minister *Asquith. Next visited Scapa September 1939 immediately after outbreak of World War II again as First Lord to assess need for reinforcing woefully inadequate defences of Naval Base. Returned March 1940 to welcome Home Fleet back after its dispersal to other anchorages following the submarine and air attacks on the base in October 1939; also to inspect build-up of defences and give go-ahead for building permanent barriers to block the eastern entrances to the anchorage which would eventually bear his name.

As Prime Minister, came to Scapa again 1941 to see Lord Halifax off aboard HMS *King George V* on his way to be Britain's ambassador to the United States. A few months later he himself embarked at Scapa for an Atlantic crossing in the ill-starred HMS *Prince of Wales* to meet President Roosevelt of the United States in Placenta Bay, Newfoundland from which historic conference emerged the Atlantic Charter. His return voyage via Iceland was also to Scapa Flow.   26,44,95.

Clere, Vice Admiral Sir John - Landed Kirkwall August 1557 on expedition with 13 English warships ostensibly to protect English fishing fleet from the Scots while returning from northern fishing grounds. Burned part of town, captured St Magnus Cathedral and landed guns to bombard castle. Made a second landing the following day intending to capture Bishop's Palace but was driven off by force of 3,000 Orcadians led by Summerdale veteran *Edward Sinclair of Strom at 'Battle of Papdale' with loss of 97 men including three ships' captains and was himself drowned in Kirkwall Bay trying to regain his ship.   2.

Clouston, Rev. Dr. Charles - b.1800 Sandwick, Orkney d.1884 Orkney. Physician, botanist, meteorologist; s. of *Rev. William Clouston. Educ. Edinburgh University where in addition to qualifying for the Ministry studied meteorology, botany and obtained degree in medicine. Ordained 1825 and became assistant to his father succeeding him as Minister of Sandwick and Stromness 1832. Made detailed study of Orkney's weather and of Gulf Stream temperatures publishing a paper on the subject for the British Association and contributed similar chapter in *Encyclopaedia Britannica*. Continued botanical studies adding several new species to Orkney list and followed his father's example by writing section for Sandwick in Second Statistical Account 1839. Was first President of Orkney Natural History Society 1837-84 which founded Stromness Museum. Also used his medical expertise, treating patients free of charge.   6.

Clouston, Dr. David, CIE. FRSE, FRSGS - b.1872 Deerness d.1948 Heathfield, St Ola. Agriculturalist; as a boy, brought up and gained 'hands on' agricultural experience on an Orkney farm; m. Ida Spence, dau. of *Magnus Spence.
Educ. Edinburgh University graduating in Arts and Science. Appointed by Indian Agricultural Service 1905 to Pusa Institute, Bihar with its fully equipped laboratory and cattle-breeding farm, an Institute of which he became Director 1923 and Agricultural Advisor to the Indian Government, Pusa Institute being the agricultural research and development nerve-centre for the entire sub-continent. Left India 1929 and lived in Edinburgh until 1947 when he returned to Orkney. Author of 'From Orcades to Ind' 1936 and 'Let the People Laugh' 1946.   OH 20/4/48.

Clouston, Joseph Storer, OBE, JP, FSA Scot - b.1870 Cumberland d.1944 Orkney. Novelist, historian; s. of *Sir Thomas Clouston; m. his cousin Winifred Clouston. Educ. Merchiston Castle, Edinburgh, Magdalen College, Oxford; called to the Bar 1895; Sub Commissioner National Service Department (Scotland) Agricultural Section 1917-18; County Councillor for Orphir becoming County Convener 1930; Chairman Orkney Harbours Commissioners 1935.

Specialised in Orkney's Norse history and saga background. Novels include 'Vandrad the Viking', 'The Spy in Black', 'Lunatic at Large', 'Beastmark the Spy'. Edited 'Records of the Earldom' 1914, wrote 'History of Orkney' 1932, and 'The Orkney Parishes' in which he collected, edited and wrote introductory comments on all the chapters relating to Orkney in the First (Old) Statistical Account as well as contributing numerous papers to learned societies on Orkney's past. Founder member of Orkney Antiquarian Society and prolific contributor to its Proceedings.   49(1941-50), Orc 21/5/70.

Clouston, Robert Stewart - b.1857 Sandwick, Orkney d.1911 Sydney, Australia. Artist; s. of *Rev. Charles Clouston and Margaret Clouston of Smoogro, Orphir. Educ. St Andrews, Edinburgh University 1876 and studied art at Royal Scottish Academy College of Art, Edinburgh.

Exhibited at both Royal Academy, London and Royal Scottish Academy, Edinburgh, mainly portraits and mezzotints, an art form in which he was recognised as a leading exponent in the country and for which he devised a new method of preparing the plates.

Interested in archaeology he carried out first excavation of Onston cairn in Stenness. Also produced book on 18th century furniture and biography of artist Arthur Melville. Moving to New Zealand for health reasons continued painting, mostly portraits.   35(4).

Clouston, Sir Thomas Smith, MD, LLD - b.1840 Harray d.1915 Edinburgh. Mental health specialist. Youngest s. of Robert Clouston, Nisthouse, Harray; m. Harriet Segur Storer, Boston, USA; father of *J. Storer Clouston.

Educ. Harray Parish School. Aberdeen, Edinburgh University, which he entered aged only 15. Specialised in study and treatment of mental illness. Appointed Superintendent Cumberland and Westmorland Asylum at age of 23 and Physician Superintendent Royal Edinburgh Asylum, Morningside 1873, a position he held with distinction for nearly 40 years until his retirement 1911. Pioneered methods of treating mental illness which have since become the norm but at the time were far in advance of current medical thought and practice.

Lecturer in Mental Diseases, Edinburgh University, President of Royal College of Physicians, Edinburgh, President of Medical Psychological Society and wrote many books on his subject which became standard works. Retained contacts with Orkney spending summers at his home, Holodyke, Harray. Made Freeman of Kirkwall 1908.   Orc 20/4/15, OH 28/4/15.

Clouston, Rev. William - b.1747 d.1832 Sandwick, Orkney. m. Isabella Traill of Holland. Father of *Charles Clouston. Ordained 1773. Minister of Cross and Burness, Sanday for 20 years until translated to Sandwick and Stromness 1793. Wrote accounts for both twin parishes in Old Statistical Account c1790. With his very thorough knowledge of his parishes these are among the best accounts produced anywhere in Scotland.   6,7.

Colville, Rev. Henry - Parson of Orphir 1580-1596 having declined presentation to Provostry of St Magnus Cathedral. Early convert to Protestantism, appointed to promote Reformation in Orkney. Favourite of Earl *Robert Stewart. Supervised interrogation under torture of *Alison Balfour, a reputed witch implicated with *John Stewart, Master of Orkney and Heir Apparent to Earldom, in unsuccessful plot to kill his brother Earl *Patrick Stewart. He was present at her execution where she renounced her confession. Colville himself was murdered in Shetland 1596 probably by followers of the Master who had been acquitted of attempted fratricide.   2,6,31.

Colville, Vice Admiral Sir Stanley - Admiral Commanding Orkney and Shetland (ACOS) during World War I becoming virtual 'Governor' of the islands for the duration. Had been former shipmate of King *George V who invested him with the Grand Cross of the Victorian Order (GCVO) in Longhope Hotel (Base HQ) during royal visit to Grand Fleet in Scapa Flow, 1917.   26,95.

Copland, Sir William Robertson, M Inst CE, JP, LLD. - b.1838 Stirling d.1907 Glasgow. Educ. Stirling and Edinburgh University. Expert in water supply and drainage. Engineer for Stromness Water Works and Consultant Engineer to Kirkwall Town Council. Family originated in Orkney.   35(1).

Cormac, Saint - Early voyager and hermit saved from death in Orkney by intervention of St Columba who was visiting *King Bridei at Inverness.   84, *Adomnan's Life of Columba* - A.O. Anderson.

Cormack, Frederick, CIE - b.1891 Edinburgh, where his father, who left Orkney in 1870s, was a pharmacist, d.1948 Newcastle-upon-Tyne; Civil Engineer, road-builder; m. Elspeth Linklater, sister of *Eric Linklater. Educ. Edinburgh University after which appointed to Public Works Department, (PWD) India until 1914 when during World War I served with the Army Engineers in Middle East. After war returned to PWD in India where he became celebrated for his road building achievements notably in Assam where his road through the jungle-clad Khasi Hills from Shillong, where he was based, to Sylhet became known as 'Freddie's Road'. During World War II he worked with the Army building the Manipur Road, a vital link connecting the Dimapur railhead with the 14th Army forward base at Imphal again through extremely difficult jungle and mountain terrain. He was appointed Chief Engineer, Assam in 1943 and was later made CIE (Commander of the Order of the Indian Empire, the equivalent of the CBE).

An accomplished horseman he played a prominent part in the race meetings in Shillong and had, indeed, been a jockey himself. He retired to Orkney, Hobbister House, Orphir, after the war but came out of retirement to work for the newly-formed National Coal Board in Newcastle where he died. Orc 30/9/48.

Corrigal, Betty - Young Hoy girl who committed suicide early 19th century when she became pregnant by her sailor lover. Refused burial in consecrated ground she was buried on the boundary between the parishes of Hoy and Walls. Her body, well preserved in the peaty soil was discovered during trench-digging in World War II and a fibre-glass headstone made by *Harry Berry erected over the grave.

Corsie, Netta (nee Pratt) - b.1904 Edinburgh d.1973 Kirkwall. Early life spent in Orkney; Educ. Kirkwall Grammar School; m. William (Bill) Corsie, India 1932 where he was on the staff of Calcutta sugar milling and distilling firm, Lyall Marshall & Co. Became active in All-India Women's Conference setting up and managing a shop in Calcutta to sell craft-work from all over the sub-continent to raise funds for many women's charities and organisations. The shop was called 'The Good Companions' a name she later used for the Old Folks Club she established in Kirkwall on returning to UK after World War II.

During that war she organised and ran a large Canteen for the Forces serving in the Far East. In their own home the Corsies ran what was, in effect, an informal club and meeting place for Orkney servicemen on their way to or from the war fronts in Burma. For her efforts in these varied fields the Indian Government awarded her the Kaiser i-Hind (First Class). Returning to Orkney after partition of India 1948 she was tireless in her support of good causes notably care of the elderly. Orc 21/6/73.

Costie, Christina (Chrissie) - b.1902 d.1967 Kirkwall. Dialect poet and short story writer. Her father coming from Rousay and her mother from Longhope she was steeped from childhood in the lore of both North and South Isles while with all her working life spent with the

law firm of Macrae and Robertson in Kirkwall she had close contact
with the farming community and country life of Orkney as a whole.
From this background emerged the collection of poems with authentic
Orkney dialect and feeling, published under the pen-name Lex, 'But-
end Ballans' 1949 followed by the short stories of 'Benjie's Bodle' and
many other newspaper and magazine features and stories. To help her
gain even deeper insight into Orkney's Norse traditions she taught
herself Norwegian and Icelandic which, of course, was also of great
value in the consular work of her employers.   Orc 29/6/67.

Countrywoman - see Grieve, Bessie.

Coventrie, John, d.1742, of Newark, Deerness - s. of David Coventrie of
Eynhallow.
      Tacksman of Bishopric estates 1727-31; Provost of Kirkwall 1718-30.
'Very astute and not over-scrupulous merchant laird'. Made bid for the
Bellenden Stenness estate (William Bellenden was deeply in debt to
Honyman of Graemsay) but was thwarted by *Christian Crawford,
Bellenden's widow.   11.

Cox, Ernest - b.1885 d.1959. Brilliant if autocratic engineer and salvage
expert. Head of salvage firm Cox & Danks. In 1924 bought 26
destroyers and 2 battleships of German High Seas Fleet scuttled Scapa
Flow in 1919. From HQ Lyness raised all destroyers by May 1926. Then
began work on battleships using new compressed air technology to
refloat them from depths of up to 100 feet (30 m.). By 1932 had raised
total of 32 ships including 8 of over 20,000 tons in 8 years - one of
world's greatest salvage feats. Slump in scrap metal prices during
1930s forced him to abandon the Flow salvage work but he continued
to run scrap business in England and still carried out some salvage
work there. Was rated as greatest salvage expert of his time although
prior to 1924 he had never raised a ship.
      To facilitate his frequent journeys between Orkney and destinations
in the south he bought a 1st Class season ticket between Thurso and
London for £267 probably the season ticket for the greatest mileage in
the history of British railways.   26,78.

Craigie, David, of Oversanday - Provost of Kirkwall 1681. Elected
Commissioner to represent Kirkwall at Scottish Parliament 1669 but
unable to attend owing to ill health.   69.

Craigie, Hugh, - d.c1670 of Gairsay. Member of Commonwealth Scottish
Parliament 1652. Commissioner to Charles II Scottish Parliament 1660.
Bought Wyre 1659 from *David MacLellan of Woodwick.   2,69.

Craigie, John, of Sands - On committee of gentry appointed during Commonwealth to administer justice and maintain order 1653.   4.

Craigie, Magnus - Flourished as merchant and money-lender, Kirkwall 1616. m. Elizabeth Paplay.   1,2.

Craigie, Patrick, b.c1620 d.1682 Kirkwall, of Wasdale - Prominent merchant, Provost of Kirkwall; s. of *William Craigie; m. Anne Bellenden of Stenness. Bailie, Kirkwall Town Council 1649.
    Kirkwall Town Council became inactive during Commonwealth but resumed operation 1654 when Bailie Craigie spent a year in Edinburgh negotiating with the Commonwealth Scottish Parliament. After Restoration when Earl of Morton attempted to deprive Kirkwall of its rights and privileges as a Royal Burgh for having allegedly collaborated with Commonwealth authorities, Craigie, along with other Councillors, was declared a rebel on grounds of disloyalty. His goods and property were ordered to be confiscated but he refused to comply and in Edinburgh rebutted the Morton charges of contempt and disobedience both on his own behalf and that of the Burgh. He was successful in that Charles II confirmed the Burgh's Royal Charter but at considerable expense to himself and the Burgh. Was Provost of Kirkwall 1662 and 1672 but ran into debt and died in Kirkwall Tolbooth 1682.   15,69.

Craigie, William, d.pre-1652, of Gairsay - s. of *Magnus Craigie. Prosperous merchant and money-lender. m. Margaret Halcro; father of *Hugh Craigie. Bought Papdale 1627; Gairsay 1640.   2.

Craigie, Sir William d.1712, of Gairsay - MP 1681 and 1689-1700. Knighted 1690 by King William III. Stewart Principal and tacksman of Earldom estates 1686-1691 and also farmed Bishopric rents; m. (1) Anne Graham, widow of *John Buchanan of Sandside, Deerness (2) Margaret Honyman (3) Anne Hamilton. His eldest son was killed at battle of Blenheim 1704. The family lost much of its importance falling on evil days financially when trade slumped due to series of bad harvests at the end of 17th century and he was jailed for debt to *Sir Archibald Steuart of Burray 1703.   2,46(p.238),69.

Craven, Venerable Archdeacon Rev. Dr. James Brown - b.1850 d.1924. Rector of St Olaf's Episcopalian Church, Kirkwall, 1876-1924. Educ. Aberdeen Grammar School and University. Historian; author of 'History of the Church in Orkney'. Founder member and first President Orkney Antiquarian Society 1923. Having acquired the greater part of the Kirkwall Bibliotheck he bequeathed the books to Aberdeen University Library.   20(1).

Crawford, Andrew - Master of Works for Earl *Patrick Stewart c1600. In charge of building Earl's Palace, Kirkwall and Scalloway and Muness Castles, Shetland where he died and is buried in Tingwall Kirkyard. His Earl's Palace is reckoned to be the finest Renaissance building in Scotland.   13.

Crawford, Christian or Christiana, - Probably originally from Ayrshire, widow of William Bellenden of Stenness being life-rented in half the estate; m. (2) Captain *James Moodie snr RN of Melsetter on his retiral from Navy 1718. Mother of *Benjamin Moodie of Melsetter for whom she managed estate and over which they fell out until on reaching his majority he was able to take control himself.

Present in Kirkwall when second husband Capt. James Moodie snr was murdered on Broad Street by Steuart of Burray faction 1725. She charged *Robert Honyman of Graemsay, Stewart and Depute Justiciar of Orkney, who had been accompanying her husband to a meeting of the Justices in St Magnus Cathedral when the fatal shot was fired, accusing him of aiding the Steuarts and conniving at the murder, but without success. Notoriously headstrong and sometimes accused of insobriety she continued the long-running feud with the Steuarts which had existed even before the murder and with the Honymans of Graemsay who had claims on the Bellenden estates in Stenness and Evie. She frequently abused and threatened Rev. John Keith, Minister of Hoy and Walls, refusing to pay his stipend. Immortalised in *Walter Traill Dennison's story 'The Heuld-horn Rumpis' in his 'Orcadian Sketchbook'.   11.

Cubbie Roo - see Kolbein Hruga.

Currey - Fought, probably unwillingly, at battle of Carbisdale 1650 under Marquis of Montrose and was one of the few to escape after the defeat. On return to Orkney led an insurrection of his fellow survivors to oppose royalist gentry and officers sent north to recruit for the Scots army which was to fight at battle of Worcester 1651. Taken prisoner when insurrection was suppressed.   2,11(p.59).

Cursiter, James Walls - d.1939 Edinburgh. Banker, businessman, antiquarian, archaeologist; s. of John Cursiter who after sojourn in Edinburgh returned to his native Orkney to set up his own wholesale and general merchant business in partnership with his 3 bros; uncle of *Stanley Cursiter RSA.

Educ. Kirkwall, Aberdeen Grammar and Edinburgh Royal High Schools he then served apprenticeship with Union Bank in Kirkwall before working as accountant in London. Owing to ill-health returned to Orkney and joined the family firm eventually becoming sole partner. Commissioned into Volunteers. Keenly interested in Orkney's past, particularly its pre-history, he was involved in many of the archaeological investigations of his day. He campaigned successfully for the preservation of parts of St Magnus Cathedral threatened by 'restoration' projects of the time especially the rose-window in the south transept which was in danger of destruction to make way for 2 pointed windows to match those of the north transept.

A keen collector of local artefacts he bought many antiquities at West Brough sale in Sanday after *Walter Traill Dennison's death. Also acquired artefacts from Skaill Hoard 1854. His collection was donated to Hunterian Museum, Glasgow after his death where it is known as the Cursiter Collection.   Orc 24/8/39, OH 22/8/39.

Cursiter, Stanley RSA, CBE - b.1887 Kirkwall d.1976. Artist. Educ. Kirkwall Grammar School, apprenticed to Edinburgh printing firm for design and attended Edinburgh College of Art. Commissioned into 7th Scottish Rifles, 1914, and served throughout World War I in France being seconded to Survey Unit to produce front-line maps. Twice mentioned in dispatches and made OBE. After war returned to Scotland and resumed painting career.

Was first secretary of Royal Fine Arts Commission for Scotland. Made ARSA (Associate of Royal Scottish Academy) 1927, full Member RSA 1937. President of SSA (Society of Scottish Artists). Appointed Director of National Gallery of Scotland being particularly interested and involved in restoration of Old Masters. During World War II worked with Ordnance Survey again on military mapping. Appointed Queen's Painter and Limner for Scotland and CBE 1948 when he was also made Freeman of his native Kirkwall. Specialised in portrait painting and landscapes particularly of his native islands to which he returned to live in Stromness on his retirement. Author of 'Scottish Art' and biography of Samuel Peploe, the Scottish painter.   52.

Cutt, William Towrie - b.1898 Sanday d.1981 Edmonton, Canada. Teacher, author; 7th s. of John Cutt and Betsy Muir; m. Margaret Nancy Davis. Educ. Sanday Central and Kirkwall Grammar Schools; emigrated Canada 1926. Taught in frontier country at Beaton Creek until 1941 when attended Alberta University, Edmonton and then worked in Alberta's government correspondence school until retirement 1960 after which embarked on career as writer of children's books, 'On the Trail of Long Tom' 1970, 'Message from Arkmae' 1972, 'Carry my Bones North West' 1973, 'Faraway World' 1977 and in collaboration with his wife, 'The Hogboon of Hell and other Strange Orkney Stories' 1979.   Orc 17/9/81, *Orkney View* No.36.

D

Dagfinn Hlodvarsson - held estate in Fair Isle where Earl *Paul II appointed him warden and keeper of the beacon 1135-6. 'A man of honour' (OS).   1,3.

Daniell, William, RA - Prolific landscape painter, exhibited overall total of 168 pictures at Royal Academy during his lifetime. Elected RA 1822. Spent 10 years in India and Far East with his uncle Thomas, also an RA, producing collection of prints entitled 'Oriental Scenery'. Made voyage round north of England and Scotland 1814 resulting in four volumes of prints including 12 of Orkney published 1825.   44.

David Haraldsson - Earl of Orkney 1206-1214. s. of Earl *Harald II Maddadsson. Joint Earl with bro. *John.   1,2,3.

Defoe, Daniel - b.1659 London d.1731 London. Novelist, journalist, travel writer, political pamphleteer. Author of 'Robinson Crusoe', 'Moll Flanders', 'Journal of the Plague Year' among many publications including his report on trial of *Gow the pirate. Visited Orkney in 1720s during which, writing in 'Atlas Maritimus & Commercialis' 1728 claimed to have seen reflection of the Icelandic volcano Hecla eruption in the night sky.   Orc Jan/Feb 1967.

Dennison, Jerome, of Noltland - Well-connected man living in Noltland Castle, Westray in 18th century; m. (1) Katherine Traill of Holland (2) Helen Traill of Westove, Sanday. Was present with his father when pirate *Gow was captured in Eday 1725, his father being bro-in-law of *James Fea of Clestran who master-minded the arrest.
    After the '45 he supplied the 4 rebel Jacobite lairds in hiding in Westray's sea-caves with food and drink and was taken prisoner by *Benjamin Moodie's government troops but released probably at the instance of his 1st bro-in-law *George Traill of Holland. Later taught navigation at Noltland and traded to ports in the south in his own ship.   11,64.

Dennison, Brigadier Malcolm Gray - b.1924 Nyasaland (Malawi) d.1996 Orkney; s. of John Reid Dennison, Shapinsay and Margaret Gray, Roeberry, South Ronaldsay. RAF Navigator, soldier, military and political advisor to Sultan of Oman; Lord Lieutenant of Orkney 1990-96. Educ. Lincoln School, Edinburgh University. Joined RAF 1942 serving in Bomber Command 1944-45 in raids over Germany. After

World War II studied Arabic at Centre for Arab Studies in Lebanon then posted to HQ Middle East Air Force Command for Intelligence duties 1948-51. Joined Sultan's Armed Forces, Oman 1955 as political officer becoming Director of Intelligence and finally Advisor on Security to the Sultan with rank of Brigadier, taking part in a number of desert operations. Retired 1983 to Orkney residing at Roeberry House, home of his mother's family for over 300 years. Appointed Lord Lieutenant of Orkney 1990.   Orc 20/9/96.

Dennison, Walter Traill - b.1825 Sanday, d.1894 Sanday. Farmer, historian, short story writer especially in Orkney dialect, poet, folklorist, religious leader; s. of James Dennison and Jane Traill; m. Elizabeth Robertson, dau. of Customs & Excise Officer, Kirkwall 1870.
    Progressive agriculturist farming West Brough, Sanday with bro, Jerome; founder member of Sanday Agricultural Society. Gave evidence to Napier Commission on farming and crofting in the North Isles. Served on Parochial Board and School Board of Cross and Burness.
    Deeply religious, he was a member of the Free Kirk in Sanday but when the congregation disapproved of the Minister, Rev. *Matthew Armour's style of preaching during the 'Sanday Revival' movement 1860, he, with his bro. Jerome, led a break-away group to form a separate congregation nearby in what became known as the Station or 'Dennison's Kirk'.
    Author of 'Orcadian Sketch Book' and numerous essays, papers to learned societies, poems and short stories many of which have been collected in 'Orkney Folklore and Sea Legends.'   7,36,53,70,79.

Dick, Alexander - Last Provost of St Magnus Cathedral before the Reformation being appointed pre-1561. Sold Provost's Lodging opposite Cathedral to William Gude and his wife Margaret Cumming 1571.   2,4.

Dick, Captain Andrew - Stewart Principal Orkney and Shetland 1669, Chamberlain of Stewartry 1675; s. of *Sir William Dick; bro. of *John Dick. Farmed Bishopric rents 1675-81. Accused of '. . . many malversations and oppressions' and banished from Orkney 1686 going to Shetland where he had acquired lands.   2,4,69.

Dick, John - d.1596. Sheriff Depute to his father *Sir William Dick 1628 becoming Sheriff 1630. Wealthy Edinburgh merchant and money-lender. Earl *Patrick Stewart owed him £26,000 when Dick died. 2,4.

Dick, Sir William, d.1653 London, of Braid - Provost of Edinburgh. Farmed Bishopric rents 1638-1646 but apparently never resided in

Orkney. Knighted 1646. Reputedly Scotland's richest man of his day. Claimed he could ride from North Berwick to outskirts of Linlithgow without leaving his own lands. A Covenanter he lent large sums of money to Scottish Convention of Estates to prevent the disbandment of their army. Later 1641, lent £20,000 Scots to support Charles I for which, when Cromwell came to power, he was fined £65,000 and imprisoned in Westminster where he died possibly of starvation. 2,4.

Dishington, Rev. Andrew - d. pre 1627. Minister, teacher; s. of *John Dishington. Schoolmaster Dunbar and Haddington before being appointed schoolmaster Kirkwall Grammar School 1591. Subsequently Minister in Stromness 1599 though still schoolmaster KGS; Minister Rousay and Egilsay 1601, Walls and Flotta 1613.   6.

Dishington, John - Sheriff Depute under Earl *Patrick Stewart. Compiled 1595 Rental.   2.

Douglas, Alexander - d.1699, of Spynie - Appointed factor and Chamberlain for Earl of Morton's trustees 1662. Authorised to feudalise Crown estates and to offer feu charters to udallers which he did but only at a price to his own advantage. The scheme was received with understandable hostility. Occupied the Palace, Birsay for a time and also the Earl's Palace in Kirkwall. Provost of Banff when he died. 2,4.

Douglas, Sir Alexander, 2nd of Egilsay - Stewart of Orkney and tacksman of Bishopric rents 1705-1714.

Douglas, Egidia - d.1420. Grd-dau. of Robert II of Scotland; m. Earl *Henry II Sinclair; mother of Earl *William Sinclair.   2.

Douglas, Elizabeth - grd dau. of Robert III of Scotland; m. Earl *William Sinclair.   2.

Douglas, Lieut. Col. George, b.1662 d.1738, 13th Earl of Morton - Succeeded bro. *Robert as Earl 1730-38. MP for Orkney from 1722 until his succession to the Earldom. After Union of Parliaments 1707 became one of the 12 representative Scottish Peers in House of Lords 1730-38. Supporter of Walpole government.   2,11,83.

Douglas, James, d.1686, 10th Earl of Morton - formerly Sir James Douglas of Smithfield. Succeeded as Earl 1681. Suppressed Orkney insurrection 1651 led by *Currey who, with the survivors of Carbisdale, was resisting attempts to recruit Orcadians for the Scots army.   2,83.

Douglas, James, d.1715, 11th Earl of Morton - Succeeded his father, also

*James 1686. Member of Queen Anne's Privy Council and one of the Commissioners for the Union which he strenuously supported in Parliament. Having previously held only the tack of Orkney and Shetland his grant of the Earldom was re-instated in 1707 after the Union of Scottish and English Parliaments. In 1706 floated an unsuccessful company in London aimed at encouraging fishing and whaling in the islands. He was unmarried and succeeded by bro. Robert.   2,11,83.

Douglas, James, b.1702 d.1768, 14th Earl of Morton - Lord Aberlour, heir apparent to Earldom 1730 to which he succeeded 1738-1768; m. Agatha Halyburton of Pitcur. Educ. Marischal College, Aberdeen, Kings College, Cambridge; President of the Royal Society 1763-68. Representative Peer for Scotland 1739-68.

Deeply involved in the long-drawn-out Pundlar Process 1733-59 when a cabal of mainly pro-Jacobite Orkney lairds headed by *Sir James Steuart of Burray, alleged that he and his ancestors, or their factors, had falsified the ancient Orkney system of weights and measures in such a way as to exact higher superior dues in kind from them. Disillusioned by this Process, which he actually won, and other disagreements and disputes with the lairds before, during and after the Process, his grant of the Earldom lands being, since 1742, irredeemable by the Crown, he sold the estate to *Sir Lawrence Dundas 1766 in order to pursue his scientific interests with the Royal Society of which he was active President 1764 until his death. Was largely responsible for choice of Captain Cook, a fellow amateur astronomer, for the Tahiti expedition 1766, to observe the transit of the planet Venus across the face of the sun. He died 7 weeks after Cook sailed.   2,11,83.

Douglas, Admiral Sir James, of St Ola - MP for Orkney and Shetland 1754-68. Member of Morton family. Seldom if ever in constituency as most of his life spent on active service in the Navy. Knighted 1759 for having brought to London first news of capture of Quebec and death of General Wolfe that year.   4,14.

Douglas, Robert, d.1649, 8th Earl of Morton - Succeeded as Earl 1648. Gave only reluctant support to his nephew the *Earl of Kinnoull and the *Marquis of Montrose when they arrived in Orkney 1649 to raise troops to fight for the Stuart cause at battle of Carbisdale 1650. Both he and his nephew died that same year 1649.   2,83,86.

Douglas, William, b.1582 d.1648, 7th Earl of Morton - Lord High Treasurer of Scotland 1630-36. A strong supporter of Stuarts he received pension 1632 from payments to Crown by *Sir William Dick for his tack of the Orkney Earldom. In the Civil War loaned substantial sums to Charles I who by Royal Charter granted him Orkney and Shetland 1643 redeemable by the Crown for £30,000 sterling, so beginning the long association of Morton family with Orkney. 2,83,86.

Douglas, William, d.1681, 9th Earl of Morton - Succeeded as Earl 1649. Regained control of Orkney Earldom lands 1662 after Restoration, again in form of mortgage redeemable by Crown. Held Earldom until 1668 when Charles II again annexed it to Crown owing to dispute over gold salvaged from Dutch East Indiaman, *Kennermerland*, wrecked 1664 on Out Skerries, Shetland.   2,83,86.

Douglas, William, 1st of Egilsay - s. of *Alexander Douglas of Spynie for whom he acted after 1669. Bought greater part of Egilsay.   4.

Drever, David, of Newark and Huip - Farmed Newark, Sanday and Huip, Stronsay where he established herring fishery 1814. Bought land in Upper St Catherine's Quoy, Kirkwall 1804 on which he built workmen's houses.   2,4.

Drever, Professor Harald FRSE - b.1912 d.1975. Geologist; s. of Professor *James Drever snr; bro. of Professor *James Drever jnr. Educ. Edinburgh High School, Edinburgh and Cambridge Universities. Joined Geology department of St Andrews University being appointed to its Chair. Led several expeditions to Greenland and served on Commission for Arctic affairs. Was chosen to carry out investigation of lunar rocks brought back by American astronauts 1971.   Orc 9/10/75.

Drever, Professor James, MA, BSc, DPhil, FRSE - b.1873 Shapinsay d.1950 Edinburgh. Psychologist, educationist; s. of James Drever, building contractor; m. Annie May Watson, Stromness.

Educ. Stromness Public School where he was pupil teacher for 2 years before going to Edinburgh University where graduated MA 1893 then studied medicine for 2 years. Returned Stromness to teach before being appointed assistant headmaster Tain, headmaster Stronsay PS and then took teaching post at George Watson's Boys College, Edinburgh until being appointed Assistant to Professor of Education at Edinburgh University 1905 and in 1908 graduated BSc (1st Class Hons) in Psychology, London University. Took charge of and reorganised Pedagogical Laboratory at Moray House Teachers Training College, first of its kind in Great Britain, obtaining his Doctorate 1916. After being Reader in Psychology at Edinburgh University he was appointed its first Professor of Psychology 1931-45. President British Psychological Society 1935-38; Chairman of Royal Blind Asylum and School, Edinburgh and Scottish National Institute for Blinded Ex-Servicemen 1941-44. Made Knight (1st Class) of Norwegian Order of St Olav 1938.

Author of many books on his subject in particular 'The Psychology of Everyday Life' and the Penguin 'Dictionary of Psychology' aimed at making psychology intelligible to the lay reader. President of the Twelfth International Congress of Psychology in 1948. Contributor to first 'Orkney Book' 1909. Keen sportsman enjoying sailing, football, cricket and bowls.

Two of his sons also became Professors, *James jnr succeeding him in the Chair of Psychology at Edinburgh University later becoming 1st Principal and Vice Chancellor of Dundee University; and *Harald, Professor of Geology, St Andrews.   Orc 2/7/31, 49(1941-50), *A History of Psychology in Autobiography* Vol II.

Drever, Professor James jnr, MA, LLD, FRSE. - b.1910 Edinburgh d.1991 Dundee. Philosopher, psychologist; s. of Professor *James Drever snr; bro. of Professor *Harald Drever.

Educ. Edinburgh Royal High School, Edinburgh and Cambridge Universities. Appointed Assistant, Department of Philosophy. Edinburgh University later Lecturer in Philosophy at Newcastle followed by service in Royal Navy during which time he developed major interest in psychology to such an extent that he succeeded his father as Professor in the Chair of Psychology at Edinburgh 1944. Became increasingly involved in principles and practice of higher education becoming member of the Robbins Committee for Higher Education 1961.

When Queens College, Dundee separated from St Andrews University to become the independent Dundee University in 1967 he was appointed its first Principal and Vice Chancellor, a position he held until retirement 1978.   *Contract* Vol 9 No.3, Dec 1991.

Dryden, 7th Bt. Sir Henry - b.1818 d.1897 Canons Ashby, Northants. Antiquarian, archaeologist. Lineal descendant of English poet John Dryden. Educ. Shrewsbury, Trinity College, Cambridge MA 1839. Specialising in church architecture he spent 10 summers 1845-55 in Orkney drawing and measuring St Magnus Cathedral the result of his researches being published by Architectural Institute of Scotland 1868 with a shorter 'Description' 1871.   OH 2/8/1897, *Saga Book of Viking Society* Vol II.

Duffus, Lord - see Sutherland, Capt. James.

Dundas, Charles - b.1751 d.1832. 2nd s. of Thomas Dundas of Fingask; created Baron Amesbury 1832. MP for Orkney & Shetland 1781-4 although having first been successfully opposed by *Robert Baikie 1780. On appeal, however, Baikie's election was declared void on grounds of malpractice at the poll and Dundas took the seat.   2,4,14.

Dundas, Sir Lawrence, b.1712 d.1781, of Kerse. Merchant, army contractor, entrepreneur. Owner of Orkney Earldom estate 1766; 2nd s. of Thomas Dundas of Fingask, Perthshire who, after failure of family fortune, became successful Edinburgh merchant. His son Lawrence was even more successful; starting in the drapery business he became merchant contractor to the British army in the '45 Jacobite Rebellion from the profits of which bought his way into Parliament as MP for Burgh of Linlithgow but was unseated on grounds of corruption. Using sometimes devious means as Commissary General during the Seven Years War in Europe (1757-63) he added to his already great fortune through extremely lucrative contracts to supply the allied armies with food, forage and horses. Was reputed to be wealthiest man in Scotland.

Having sold his interests in Linlithgow bought the estate of Aske in Yorkshire which included the 'rotten borough' of Richmond and through influence was elected MP for Newcastle-under-Lyme becoming a baronet in 1762. Badly wanted a peerage which he decided could best be achieved by becoming a major land-owner with ready access to the right political patronage, so built up his influence by purchase of estates in Stirlingshire, Clackmannan, Fife and in Ireland adding the Earldom of Orkney and the Lordship of Shetland which he bought for £63,000 from the *14th Earl of Morton in 1766 so becoming feudal Superior of the islands with control of who represented the constituency in Parliament. Never resided in Orkney leaving its management to members of his family, his lawyers and his 'man of business', *Col. James Masterton MP for Stirling Burghs.

Also held controlling interest in Forth-Clyde Canal running through his lands. He was Director of the Royal Bank of Scotland, involved in plate glass manufacture, shipping and finance as well as owning two slave-operated plantations in the West Indies. Had houses in the fashionable parts of London and Edinburgh and a country mansion and estate, Moor Park, in Hertfordshire which as a patron of the arts he embellished with fine furniture and paintings. He died in 1781 - without a seat in the Lords although his descendants were elevated to the peerage, his son *Thomas becoming a Baron and his grandson the 1st Earl of Zetland.   2,14,17.

Dundas, Lawrence John Lumley, b.1876 d.1961, Lord Ronaldshay and later 2nd Marquis of Zetland - was given the Orkney and Shetland estate 1914 while his father was still alive.

Aide-de-camp to Lord Curzon, Viceroy of India 1900; Conservative MP for Hornsey 1907-16; Governor of Bengal 1917-22; Secretary of State for India 1935-40; President of the Royal Geographical Society and the National Trust; Steward of the Jockey Club. An absentee Superior he had little involvement in the management of his island estates. Author of biography of Lord Curzon and several books about India. 83.

Dundas, Thomas, b.c1708 d.1786, of Fingask - Bro. of *Sir Lawrence. MP for Orkney and Shetland 1768-71. 2,14,17.

Dundas, Col. (later Major General) Thomas, d. 1794, of Fingask and Carron Hall - nephew of *Sir Lawrence. MP for Orkney and Shetland 1771-80 and 1784-90.

Dundas, Thomas, b.1741 d.1820, of Castlecary MP - s. of *Sir Lawrence whom he succeeded as 2nd Baronet of Aske 1781; created Lord Dundas of Aske 1794. 2,17.

Dundas, William - nephew of Henry Dundas, Viscount Melville. MP for Northern Burghs (including Kirkwall) 1796-1802.

Dungad - Caithness chieftain occasionally styled as 'Earl' but apparently exiled in Orkney when m. Groa, grd dau. of *Aud the Deep Minded. Father of Grelod who m. Earl *Thorfinn I Skullsplitter. His name survives in the modern place-name Duncansby. 2,35(7),76.

Dunn, Robert - Self-styled 'naturalist' who also described himself as 'animal preserver' ie taxidermist. Visited Orkney and Shetland 4 times between 1831 and 1835 spending up to 9 months on each visit before returning to his native Hull. In his 'Ornithologist's Guide to Orkney and Shetland' he reported that there were 88 species of birds in Orkney but that he had not been able to collect specimens of quite all of them. He had nonetheless done quite well for his business by shooting large numbers of great northern diver, red-throated diver, red-necked phalarope, eider and long-tailed duck, merganser, great crested grebe and storm petrel as well as collecting their eggs. He even managed to secure 8 white-tailed eagles and with one shot, 6 gannets. In Orkney based himself and his son in Stromness where he bought a boat in order to cover the islands. 47, Orc 25/5/12.

E

Einar Hardkjoptr (Hard-chaps) - Grd s. of Earl *Thorfinn I. Orkneyinga Saga tells how *Ragnhild promised him herself and the Earldom of Orkney if he would kill his cousin *Einar Buttered-bread whom she had already employed to kill her husband *Havard Harvest-Happy which he did but she went back on her word and married *Ljot instead who became Earl of Orkney and put him to death.   2,3,35(7),76.

Einar Klining (Buttered-bread) - Grd s. of *Earl Thorfinn I. Orkneyinga Saga claims he was persuaded by *Ragnhild to kill her husband Earl *Havard Harvest-Happy with herself and the Orkney Earldom promised as reward. He forced a fight with Havard in Stenness and killed him but did not get either Ragnhild or the Earldom. Instead she conspired with his cousin *Einar Hard-chaps who killed him for the same promised reward but he did not get Ragnhild or the Earldom either being killed by her third husband, *Ljot, who became Earl.
                                                              2,3,35(7),76.

Einar I Rognvaldsson (Torf-Einar) - Earl of Orkney c892-946. Thrall-born s. of *Rognvald, Earl of Møre in Norway; half-bro. of Earl *Hallad and Hrolf the Ganger who was ancestor of the Dukes of Normandy including William the Conqueror; father of Earls *Erlend I, *Arnkel and *Thorfinn I Skullsplitter.

According to OS Rognvald of Møre was granted Orkney Earldom by *King Harald Fairhair of Norway as compensation for his son Ivar's death in battle while serving the king. Rognvald handed it on, first to his bro. *Sigurd I whose son *Guthorm succeeded but died without heir, the Earldom thus reverting to Rognvald who handed it to his own son *Hallad who ruled ineffectually for a year then returned to Norway. Rognvald then gave it to his illegitimate son Einar with the title of Earl who became known as Torf-Einar. The Saga claimed that he acquired this name having introduced the use of peat (torf) to Orkney but there is no evidence to support this myth.

When *Halfdan Long-legs, *Harald Fairhair's son killed Torf-Einar's father Rognvald of Møre in Norway and fled to Orkney to escape his father's wrath Torf-Einar retired temporarily to Caithness but returning to Orkney killed Halfdan in North Ronaldsay. Harald Fairhair then descended on Orkney seeking revenge or compensation for his son's death and Torf-Einar again prudently retired to Caithness. Harald fined the Orkney bonder 60 gold marks which Torf-Einar himself paid in full in return for the bonders' udal rights. He then ruled Orkney for many years and, unusually for a Norseman of his time and status, died in his bed. '. . . a tall man and ugly, one-eyed but of all men the most keen-sighted.' (OS) 1,2,3,30,35(7),76.

Einar II Sigurdsson (Wrymouth) - Joint Earl of Orkney 1014-c1020; s. of *Sigurd II The Stout: bro. of *Hlodvar, and Earls *Somerledi and *Brusi; half bro. of Earl *Thorfinn II The Mighty.

Described in OS as '. . . stern, grasping, unfriendly and a mighty man of war,' he oppressed the bonder of Orkney in order to fund his annual viking forays but, the OS says '. . . was unfair in the distribution of plunder'. Reluctantly, however, he responded to appeals by Deerness chieftain *Thorkell Amundisson Fostri to ease this burden by halving his demands on the bonder for one year but on a second attempt to get similar relief for them twelve months later he refused forcing Thorkell to quit Orkney whereupon he crossed to Caithness, joined Einar's half bro. Thorfinn II becoming his foster-father.

When *Sigurd II died at the battle of Clontarf 1014 his 3 oldest sons, *Sumerledi *Einar II, *Brusi, inherited the Orkney Earldom ruling jointly. His youngest son Thorfinn, by a 2nd marriage to a dau. of Scots King Malcolm II, had been granted Earldom of Caithness and Sutherland by his royal grd father. On Sumerledi's death Einar II seized his share of Orkney thus controlling two-thirds of the Earldom but Thorfinn claimed what he considered to be his rightful share also. With very bad grace Einar eventually acceded to his claim and an accord was arranged between him and Thorfinn's chief adviser and counsellor, *Thorkell Fostri, to be cemented with a feast at each of their head-houses. The first took place at Skaill in Deerness where Thorkell was host. They were then to travel to Einar's feast but Thorkell justifiably suspecting treachery struck first and Einar was killed in the drinking hall of Skaill c.1020. 1,2,3,30,35(7),76.

Eindridi Ungi (the Younger) - Troublesome Norwegian chieftain. Caused delay in start of Earl *Rognvald II's Crusade to the Holy Land 1151 although he had been prominent in encouraging the Earl to take up the challenge in the first place. In the event he commanded one of the 15 ships involved.

Was one of the leaders in the attack on a castle in Galicia, but Godfrey, Keeper of the Castle got away and Eindridi was suspected of having assisted his escape. Then, when passing through the Straits of Gibraltar into the Mediterranean, he deserted the expedition taking six ships with him. Some years later he was killed during the civil war in Norway. 1,3.

Eithne (Edna) - Dau. of Irish King Kjarval. m. Earl *Hlodver Thorfinnsson c978; mother of Earl *Sigurd II The Stout. Seamstress of the enchanted

Raven Banner carried by Sigurd when he was killed at battle of
Clontarf 1014.   1,2,3,35(7),76.

Elphinstone, Euphemia - b.c1509. Mother of Earl *Robert Stewart by
*James V of Scotland. Dau. of Lord Elphinstone; m. John Bruce of
Cultmalindie.   12,13,75.

Elphinstone, Gavin - Earl *Robert Stewart's 'maister household'. Went to
Denmark 1572-4 apparently committing treason by offering Danish
Crown dominion over Orkney and Shetland.   12.

Elphinstone, Rany - 1579. Servitor of Earl *Robert Stewart. May have
been related to Robert's mother, *Euphemia Elphinstone. Granted
lands in Cairston 1590; m. Janet Halcro dau. of *Magnus Halcro of
Brough.   12.

Elphinstone, Col. Robert, of Lopness - Came to Orkney 1690 and lived in
Earl's Palace, Kirkwall having obtained tack of both Earldom and
Bishopric. Was autocratic and overbearing. Tried to alter local weights
in order to extract higher rents but muddled his affairs and was said to
have fled the country insolvent. Made bid for a continuation of the
tack but lost to wealthy arms dealer, *Sir Alexander Brand.   4,12.

Elphinstone, William, of Tresness - Sheriff Depute 1576. Kinsman of
*Euphemia Elphinstone. Granted Tresness 1589 by Earl *Patrick
Stewart.   12.

Erburie, Harry - Cromwellian soldier posted to Orkney during Commonwealth 1653-59; m. (1) Barbara Garden (2) Anna Moncrieff, an Orcadian.
Remained in Orkney when garrison withdrew after the Restoration.
Became prosperous merchant and Bailie on Kirkwall Town Council.
When the spire of St Magnus Cathedral was struck by lightning 1671
and went on fire he helped save some of the bells by placing hides
from his store below them to break their fall.   4,35(6),69.

Erik Bloodaxe - King of Norway 942-47 and York 948-54. Eldest s. of
*Harald Fairhair; m. Gunnlaug, sister of Harald Bluetooth, King of
Denmark; father of *Ragnhild; succeeded to Norwegian throne 942 on
abdication of his 80-year-old father. After brief reign characterised by
violence was deposed by youngest bro. Hakon the Good, 947. Left
Norway for the British Isles using Orkney from time to time as a
raiding base. Became King of York in the viking realm of Northumbria
from which he was subsequently expelled. Accompanied by the
Orkney Earls *Arnkel and *Erlend I attempted to regain York at battle
of Stainmore 954 where all three were killed.   1,2,3,30,76,100.

Erlend I Einarsson - Earl of Orkney c946-954. s. of *Torf-Einar; bro. of Earls *Arnkel and *Thorfinn I Skullsplitter. Ruled Orkney jointly with bros. Killed at battle of Stainmore 954 along with Arnkel while supporting *Erik Bloodaxe of Norway. 1,2,3,30,35(7),100.

Erlend II Thorfinnsson - Joint Earl of Orkney with bro. *Paul I c1065-1099; s. of *Thorfinn II; m. Thora dau. of Icelander Sumerledi Ospaksson; father of St *Magnus and *Gunnhild, wife of *Kol Kalisson.

Both bros. accompanied *Harald Hardrada of Norway on his expedition to England in 1066 and survived battle of Stamford Bridge. They returned to Orkney and ruled the Earldom amicably for several years. Then their sons (St) *Magnus Erlendsson and *Hakon Paulsson fell out over the possible division of the Earldom and the two fathers were inevitably drawn into the dispute with civil war only averted by the intervention of the Orkney gødings. The sons left Orkney for a time and the quarrel was patched up, Erlend and Paul again ruling in peace until *Magnus Barelegs, King of Norway on his way to war in the Western Isles stopped off in Orkney and seized the two Earls Erlend and Paul sending them to Norway where they died. 1,2,3,30,35(7),102.

Erlend III Haraldsson - Earl of Orkney 1151-1154; s. of Earl *Harald I Smoothtongue. Last in the male line of *Torf-Einar. Close friend of *Sweyn Asleifsson. Brought up in Sutherland with *Frakokk, *Thorbjorn Klerk and *Olvir Rosta. Later lived mainly in Caithness with *Anakol as adviser. Granted title of Earl and half Caithness by Scottish Crown and half Orkney Earldom by Norwegian Crown jointly with *Harald II Maddadsson; but with support of *Sweyn Asleifsson he claimed *Rognvald II's share of Orkney as well. Norwegian King Eystein, however, rejected this claim but granted him Harald's share instead. On *Rognvald II's return from his Crusade to Holy Land the dispute developed into what became known as the War of the Three Earls with Sweyn Asleifsson acting as adviser and supporter of Erlend who was still in his teens. In 1154, however, he left Erlend temporarily unguarded in his galley moored off Damsay in Bay of Firth where he was surprised, lying drunk, by Harald and Rognvald who killed him. His remains are immured in the south wall of the choir of St Magnus Cathedral just across from those of St Magnus himself. 1,2,3,35(7).

Erlend Ungi (The Younger) - Shetland chieftain who eloped with *'Countess' Margaret, Earl Harald II Maddadsson's mother. They took refuge in the Mousa broch, Shetland where they were besieged by Harald who objected strongly to the liaison but eventually agreed to their marriage 1153 in return for Erlend's support in the War of the Three Earls against Erlend III and Rognvald II.   1,2,3.

Ermingerd - 'Entertained' Earl *Rognvald II and his Crusaders in France (Narbonne?) 1152 on their way to the Holy Land. 'The snow white lady' and 'A chief among maidens this lady of the bracelets' (OS).   1,2,3.

Erngisl Sunesson - Swedish nobleman. Claimant 1353 Orkney Earldom through his marriage to Agneta, dau. of Earl *Malise of the Strathearn line.   1,2.

Erskine, John - Linen manufacturer at Scapa late 18th century.   2.

Eunson, George - b.c1756 Kirkwall d.1796 drowned when HM Cutter *Curlew* foundered in Sumburgh Roost.
    One of Orkney's most colourful characters. A notorious firebrand, smuggler-turned-exciseman, poet, shipmaster, pilot for Northern Lighthouse Commissioners during building of North Ronaldsay lighthouse, one of the first in Orkney; produced chart of Orkney waters which was accepted and published by the Admiralty.
    Smuggled mainly for local lairds but cheated and lost their confidence. Joined pirate ship at Kirkwall but deserted in Dunkirk where he was pressed and saw some active service in the Royal Navy against the Dutch but again deserted and made his way back to Orkney. Here, on the principle of 'set a thief to catch a thief' he was employed by *Robert Baikie of Tankerness who in 1782 had formed an anti-smuggling association in order to embarrass the Kirkwall merchants, supporters of the Dundases of Kerse. Most of these merchants and officials were guilty of illicit trading and their prosecution would hurt their political patrons who had twice frustrated Robert Baikie's attempts to win the Orkney Parliamentary seat. In order to cover his own connection in the plot Baikie had Eunson nominated as 'Extraordinary Officer of Customs' so that he could prosecute whomsoever he alleged was guilty of smuggling. Eunson petitioned the authorities with the names of several merchants he alleged were smuggling but there was some confusion over the charges and in attempting to retrieve the 'charge sheets' he assaulted the Town Clerk and was deprived of his 'Extraordinary Officer' status and his job. He was also involved in another affray in 1786.
    Author of 'The Ancient and Present State of Orkney' published in Newcastle 1788 attacking the local authorities.   4,14(4),31.

Eunson, Magnus - A renowned 18th century Orkney smuggler and 'moonshiner' who produced illicit whisky in his bothy outside Kirkwall on a site now occupied by Highland Park Distillery. The most

northerly in Britain, it was established in 1798 and still produces fine malt whisky from water out of the same spring that Magnus used.
Highland Park Distillery 1798-1952 - Anon 1952.

Eunson, Reynold - b.1932 Kirkwall d.1978 Kirkwall. Joiner, woodcarver, Orkney chairmaker. Educ. Kirkwall Grammar School and after apprenticeship as joiner served 2^1_2 years in Fleet Air Arm before being discharged on health grounds, returning to his trade in Kirkwall; m. Maureen Cromarty, Kirkwall 1954 and in 1956 bought undertaking firm of D. M. Kirkness, Kirkwall reviving and expanding the Orkney straw-back chair-making side of the business where he not only used his joinery expertise but taught himself the straw-plaiting craft as well. He also developed his skill as a woodcarver recognised and encouraged by *Stanley Cursiter RSA who produced designs for the decoration and furnishing of St Rognvald's Chapel in St Magnus Cathedral with Eunson using his craftsmanship to achieve the finished works of art. Out of this fruitful partnership emerged the three Norse figures at the east end, the carving of the choir stalls and the organ screen, the Provost's and the County Convener's chairs, two figures for the Cameronian's Regimental Museum and many other works both in Scotland and overseas. 52, Orc 3/3/78.

Eyvind Melbrigdason - Orkney chieftain possibly of Celtic extraction; kinsman of *Sweyn Asleifsson. Member of Earl *Paul II's hird providing him with a fully manned ship at battle of Tankerness 1135 and later that year at Paul's Yuletide feast in Orphir acted as his Master of Ceremonies and cup-bearer. At that feast he encouraged Sweyn Asleifsson to kill his namesake *Sweyn Breastrope and after the killing helped him to escape. 1,3,35(7).

Eyvind Urarhorn - Killed 1018 by Earl *Einar II while storm-stayed in Osmondwall, South Walls while on voyage from Ireland to Norway. He had been part of the Irish king's force which defeated Einar in Ireland the previous year. 1,2,3,30,76.

F

Farrer, James - d.1879. Antiquarian, MP for Durham. Spent vacations in Orkney excavating archaeological sites including Maeshowe 1861 and the Knowes of Trotty in Harray where the famous gold discs were found. His amateur excavations were recorded by *George Petrie and the finds donated to what is now the National Museum of Scotland, Edinburgh. He published a record of the 'digs' himself in 'Maes-Howe' 1862.

Fea, Alan - Author of 'The Real Captain Cleveland' published 1912, an account of how one of his ancestors, *James Fea, 6th of Clestran, organised the capture of *Gow the Pirate after his ship, *Revenge*, ran ashore on the Calf of Eday 1725. Sir *Walter Scott after learning of Gow when he visited Orkney in 1814 based his novel 'The Pirate' on the story as it was then known calling his eponymous hero Captain Cleveland instead of Gow. The book also covers the history of the Fea family generally.   39.

Fea, Barbara - b.1689 d.1739. Dau. of Patrick Fea 1st of Whitehall and Barbara Traill of Holland. After an affair with, and disputed promise of marriage by her cousin, *Patrick Traill, eldest son of John Traill 2nd of Elsness, he deserted her and was sent to Edinburgh by his father to complete his education. She followed him to the University, had him arrested and imprisoned until he repeated his promise of marriage - this time in writing. On his release he again absconded and on this occasion joined the Navy.

   She returned to Orkney now claiming that the written promise was in Scots law the equivalent of actual marriage and eventually styled herself 'the lady Elsness', a title repudiated by the Elsness family. With her baby son she twice attempted to occupy Housby in Stronsay, a property owned by her 'husband' but was repelled. She fought for her 'rights' through the courts in a series of litigations which continued long after the main protagonists were dead.   20(10&11),73.

Fea, James, b.c1694 d.1756, 6th of Clestran - Eldest s. of James Fea 5th of Clestran and Barbara Traill of Elsness; m. Janet Buchanan of Sound 1720.
   Educ. Edinburgh, France, Holland; returned UK 1717. Owned estates in Eday, Sanday (Stove), Stronsay and, after his marriage, Sound in Shapinsay. Captured erstwhile school-fellow, *Gow the pirate, whose ship, *Revenge*, grounded on Calf of Eday, part of the Fea estate opposite his mansion, Carrick House, Eday 1725 after which

spent much time in Edinburgh and London engaged in litigation. some of it connected with the capture. Leading figure in opposition to *Earl of Morton over Pundler Process.

An extreme Jacobite he met the Young Pretender during the '45 and offered to raise troops for his cause in Orkney but received little support in the islands not even from the known Jacobite lairds. In the event Culloden was fought and lost before he could raise any volunteers and he went into hiding in Caithness emerging only after the passing of the Act of Indemnity 1747. Even so his Eday lands were pillaged by Government troops and his Shapinsay mansion at Sound was looted and burned by the Navy. Died in London and there being no issue of his marriage Clestran estate passed to his bro. *John.   11,20(10,11),39,40.

Fea, James, 2nd of Whitehall - Eldest s. of Patrick Fea 1st of Whitehall and Barbara Traill of Holland; m. (1) Jacobina Forbes, dau. of Bishop Forbes (2) Jean Manson of Kirkwall.

Introduced kelp industry to Orkney c1720. Assisted his cousin *James Fea, 6th of Clestran in capture of pirate *Gow 1725.   5,39,48,79.

Fea, John, d.1760, 7th of Clestran - Bro. of *James Fea 6th of Clestran from whom he inherited the estate which he had been managing on his bro's behalf during his frequent absences from Orkney. Having no legitimate heir when he died 1760, the last of the direct Clestran line, the estate passed to his 2nd cousin, *Dr. James Fea of Whitehall who thus became also the 8th and as it happened, the last laird of Clestran.   20(11),39,48.

Fea, Patrick, b.c1710 d.1796, of Airy - Eldest s. of Charles Fea of Airy, Stronsay and Barbara Mein; grd s. of Patrick Fea 1st of Whitehall; m. Barbara Traill of Westove.

Spent early days as merchant in Kirkwall being granted his Burgess Ticket as Freeman 1732. Strongly anti-Mortonian, prominent in Pundlar Process 1733-59 where he was described as 'a hot-headed Jacobite'. Before and after the '45 was factor for the Burray and South Ronaldsay estates of another staunch Jacobite, Sir *James Steuart. Engaged in clandestine negotiations with Caithness Jacobites and after Culloden 1746 was forced into hiding, successfully using a sea-cave near Airy in Stronsay to escape capture by Government troops commanded by *Benjamin Moodie of Melsetter sent to apprehend dissident Orkney lairds. Emerged from hiding 1747 after restrictions on Jacobite sympathisers were lifted he continued for a few years as factor of the Burray estates now owned by the *Earl of Galloway who inherited them following the death of Sir *James Steuart in a London jail awaiting trial for supporting the Stuart cause.

Took over farm of Stove after death of his uncle *John Fea 7th of

Clestran. A progressive farmer he worked it until his death in 1796 and from 1766 kept a day-to-day diary of his farming routine and social life in Sanday and in Orkney generally.   20(11),48.

Findan, Saint - d.878 AD. An Irishman captured by vikings and while being transported into slavery escaped in Orkney (Papa Westray?) receiving help from a bishop apparently still active in this early Norse period. The rest of his life was spent in continental Europe.   46,84.

Finlayson, John - Sheriff Depute and agent for Lord *Ochiltree, Royal Chamberlain of Earldom, for whom he collected rents 1613. Described as '. . . hated to the death by all sorts of men'. With 200 men tried and failed to put down rebellion raised and led by *Robert Stewart 1614 on behalf of his imprisoned father, Earl *Patrick Stewart to regain the Earldom. He was later captured and sent south by the rebels during their brief occupation of Kirkwall.   2,13.

Finn Arnisson - Norwegian chieftain. Father of *Ingibjorg, wife of Earl *Thorfinn II; bro. of *Kalf Arnisson; grd father of Earls *Paul I and *Erlend II.   1,3,76.

Firth, John - Finstown carpenter and wheelwright. Author of 'Reminiscences of an Orkney Parish' (Firth) 1920 which appeared as a series of papers in the 'Old Lore Miscellany' of the Viking Club from 1910 onwards for several years having first been basis of talks on folklore, customs, ceremonies etc given locally.   35(3).

Flett, James - b.1881 Kirkwall d.1960 Kirkwall. Printer, bookseller, local historian. Educ. Kirkwall Burgh School; served apprenticeship as printer with *The Orcadian*. After brief period in Glasgow returned to Orkney and joined *Orkney Herald* 1912 moving back to *The Orcadian* 1921-30 when he bought shop of David Spence, newsagent and bookseller, Broad Street, Kirkwall. Elected Kirkwall Town Council 1928 for 3 years but returned 1940 when co-opted topping the poll at all subsequent elections and was Provost from 1954-57 when he retired. During his term as Provost he was largely responsible for persuading the Council to buy Tankerness House, now the town's museum, which was in danger of demolition to make way for developers. He had a deep-felt sense of Kirkwall's history and especially of its cathedral of which congregation he was an elder. He was a dedicated Freemason writing a history of the local Lodge in which he held high office. He was an early member and secretary of Orkney Antiquarian Society in the 1920s and 30s contributing a series of informed papers on the Incorporated Trades Guilds of Kirkwall to its Proceedings.   OH 20/9/60, Orc 22/9/60.

Flett, Sir John Smith, KBE, MA, CM, MD, DSc, LLD, FRS - b.1870 Kirkwall d.1947 Saffron Walden, Essex. Geologist; s. of Bailie James Ferguson Flett, ironmonger, Kirkwall. Educ. Kirkwall Burgh (Grammar) School, Watson's College, Edinburgh and Edinburgh University graduating in Arts, Science and Medicine; m. Mary Jane Meason, Kirkwall.

One of Britain's leading geologists. Assistant to Director of HM Geological Survey in charge of Scottish Survey 1911-1920, Director of Geological Survey of Great Britain and of Museum of Practical Geology 1920-1935. Lecturer in Petrology, Edinburgh University, geological adviser to Services in World War I. Knighted 1925. Author of many standard works on geology, those on his native islands being 'Trap Dykes of Orkney' and 'Old Red Sandstone of Orkney'. Contributed section on geology to first 'Orkney Book' 1909. 49, Orc and OH January 1947.

Flosi Thordarson - Icelandic chieftain, leader of the 'Burners' of *Njal for which murder he was outlawed at the Althing and forced to leave Iceland. According to Njal's Saga his ship was wrecked on the Orkney Mainland then ruled by Earl *Sigurd II (c991-1014). Flosi had also killed *Helgi Njalsson, son of the 'Burnt Njal', who had been one of Sigurd's hird, but having lost everything in the wreck, Flosi had no alternative but to give himself up to the Earl who was about to have him killed to avenge his retainer's death when Thorstein, also of Sigurd's hird whose sister was married to Flosi, interceded on his behalf. Sigurd relented, spared his life and, in fact, he joined the Earl's hird himself and served him for some time. 38.

Forbes, Admiral Sir Charles - C-in-C Home Fleet in Scapa Flow during World War II and from where he conducted naval side of the 1940 Norwegian campaign. 26, 95.

Fortesque, Archer Irvine - b.1810 d.1907. Landowner, farmer; s. of Rev. William Fortesque, Minehead. Educ. Aberdeen University.

A Devon man, bought 3000-acre Swanbister estate, Orphir 1845. Progressive agricultural improver, abolished runrig on his estate carrying out enclosures, drainage and building of roads. Employed deep ploughing methods, heavy manuring with Peruvian guano, bonemeal, seaweed and town dung brought from Stromness in his own sloop as well as composting dogfish and sillocks. Owned another estate in Kincardineshire where he wintered and finished sheep and two-year-old cattle from Orkney. Hunted his pack of hounds round Orphir which with his insistence on herding cattle on the hill and imposing penalties on tenants who let their stock stray earned him the nickname of 'Devil of the Hills.'

Director, North of Scotland Bank, North of Scotland Orkney & Shetland Steam Navigation Company. Deputy Lieutenant Orkney and Kincardineshire.   2,35(1),70,79.

Foulzie, Gilbert - d.c1595. Last Roman Catholic Archdeacon and Provost of St Magnus Cathedral under Catholic Bishop *Adam Bothwell before Reformation and first Protestant priest in Kirkwall after it under the same but now Protestant Bishop Adam Bothwell. Acquired church lands, the Archdeaconry and Sub-Chantry on Broad Street and with extensions in 1574 converted them into a mansion now known as Tankerness House and used as Kirkwall's Museum. His arms and those of his wife with their initials, MGF and EK (probably Elizabeth Kinnaird), are over the gateway to the courtyard. Appointed Commissioner 1576 to 'plant' churches in Orkney and Shetland where required.   4,21.

Fox, Charles James, MP - b.1749 London d.1806. Brilliant statesman but erratic in political judgement and although twice Foreign Secretary never achieved full potential. Elected MP for Northern Burghs (including Kirkwall) 1784 but being also elected for Westminster constituency at the same election chose the latter seat. Never visited Orkney.   44.

Frakokk - d.c1141; dau. of Caithness chieftain Moddan of the Dales; m. Ljot Niddering of Sutherland; mother of *Olvir Rosta (the Unruly), grandmother of *Thorbjorn Klerk. Her sister Helga was mother of Earl *Harald I. According to OS the 2 sisters prepared the poisoned shirt which killed Harald although it had been intended for his half bro. Paul II. Banished from Orkney she retired to home near Helmsdale, Sutherland where she died when it was burned over her during an attack by *Sweyn Asleifsson.   1,3,35(7).

Franklin, Sir John - b.1786 d.1845 Northern Canada. Naval officer and Arctic explorer. Took part in naval battle of Copenhagen 1801 and Trafalgar 1805. Commissioned to map and chart coasts of Australia and explored feasibility of North West Passage linking Atlantic and Pacific Oceans round the northern ice-bound coast of Canada where he spent several years in exploration. After taking part in the Greek War of Independence 1821-8 was given command of expedition to northern Canada again searching for the North West Passage and with his two ships, *Erebus* and *Terror*, called at Stromness 1845 for supplies and water from Login's Well. It was his last port of call and later in the year the expedition disappeared until some years later when relics were found by another Arctic explorer, the Orcadian, *Dr. Rae.   23,44.

Fraser, Eliza - d.1858. Wife of Stromness sea-captain. Leaving her 3 children in the care of the minister, she sailed with her husband for Australia where his ship, the *Stirling Castle*, was wrecked on the Barrier Reef 1836. The crew mutinied, some of them taking Eliza and her husband in one of the ship's boats which after several days, during which they subsisted on little more than water, beached on an island 200 miles north of Brisbane. Captured by local tribesmen they were treated as slaves, beaten, tortured and starved. Her husband was killed and 2 other men died. Eliza, passed from one tribe to another, was taken to the mainland but after negotiation was freed by the search party, consisting largely of convicts deported from UK, who found her.

Married again she returned to London where she acquired celebrity status and, not admitting the existence of her children and second husband and by other dubious means, benefited from the proceeds of appeals launched by the Lord Mayor of London and others. She also published a successful book describing her ordeal 1838. Later she emigrated to New Zealand and is believed to have died in a traffic accident in Melbourne, Australia.   81.

Fremantle, Vice Admiral Sir Sydney - b.1867-d.1958. Commander 1st British Battle Squadron in Scapa Flow after World War I when interned German High Seas Fleet scuttled its 74 ships 1919.   26,55,95.

Fresson, Captain Edward OBE - b.1891 d.1963. Pioneered air services in north of Scotland particularly to Orkney and Shetland during early 1930s. Started first scheduled passenger air services (Highland Airways) flying 8-seater twin-engined biplanes, De Havilland Dragons and Rapides, between Inverness, Wick and Kirkwall 1933 and flew first UK internal air mail service on the same route 1934. Continued operating these services throughout World War II and until 1948 when they were taken over by the nationalised British European Airways.   60.

Frobisher, Sir Martin - b.c1535 d.1594. Elizabethan sailor and explorer who became obsessed with the idea of finding North West Passage linking Atlantic and Pacific Oceans by way of the ice-bound northern coast of Canada. His 1575 expedition called in at Orkney for water and supplies.   12.

Fullarton, John - b.early 18th century, Orkney d.c1765 Firth of Forth. Master Mariner, smuggler, privateer, pirate.

After commanding his own merchant ship fell on hard times and took to smuggling in the Channel Islands with such success that he was able to fit out a ship and set up as privateer probably during Seven Years War 1756-63.

Again he was financially successful to such an extent that he was able to fit out several pirate ships operating mainly in the North Sea where as the 'Orkney Pirate' he earned reputation for ruthlessness and extreme cruelty while amassing a fortune with which he is said to have bought an estate in Orkney where he lived for a time with his mother. However the call of the sea under the Jolly Roger drew him back to piracy this time mostly in the Firth of Forth area where he met his end. Attacking a heavily-laden merchantman, the *Isabella*, he met unexpected resistance from her crew who returned his broadside. Eventually, however, he boarded her and in a fit of frustrated rage shot and killed the captain. He turned to haul down the colours whereupon the grief-stricken captain's wife, Mary Jones, now a widow, in turn shot him through the head and killed him.   31.

G

Gaius - Mythical king of Orkney said to have been defeated by the Romans and taken as prisoner to Rome.   80.

Galloway, 6th Earl of - see Stewart, Alexander.

Gander Dower, Eric Leslie, MA - b.1894 d.1987. Actor, playwright, aviator, politician. Educ. Brighton College, Jesus College Cambridge, Royal Academy of Dramatic Art, London.

Established Dyce (Aberdeen) Airport, Founded Allied Airways (Gander Dower Ltd) 1934 operating Aberdeen, Wick/Thurso, Kirkwall/Stromness, Shetland air service in competition with *Fresson's Highland Airways. Conservative MP for Caithness and Sutherland 1945-50.   49 (1981-90).

Garden, Robert - b.1846 Rayne, Aberdeenshire d.1912 Kirkwall. Merchant; s. of a slater he became Master Slater himself, but having commercial ambitions started a travelling-shop business in Orkney with a horse-drawn van. This was soon followed, not only by many more vans but also by so-called shop boats, firstly in sailing ships then using small steamers such as the *Cormorant*. The vans, eventually motorised, covered the Mainland of Orkney and the floating shops ranged round the outer isles, Shetland and down the west coast of Scotland as far as Ullapool establishing branches in many of the small ports they used. And so he built up a commercial empire based on the extensive retail and wholesale business complex established in Bridge Street, Kirkwall, buying and selling everything from farm seeds and fertilisers through to groceries, crockery, hardware, drapery and much else besides as well as operating a very successful bakery and a mineral water factory. *The Orcadian* accurately described him as 'Orkney's premier merchant prince'.

He played an active part in public life being Bailie on Kirkwall Town Council. Also served on Orkney County Council, Parish Council and Orkney Harbours Commissioners.

He built several blocks of dwelling houses for working people still known as Garden Street and was involved in restoration work on St Magnus Cathedral of which congregation he was a staunch and active member. Left money for the building of a large modern extension of the Balfour Hospital but after his death in 1912 the 1914-18 war prevented such a project going ahead at that time but when peace came his widow and family made offer to Balfour Hospital Trustees to build a new hospital in Kirkwall in his memory. The Robert Garden Memorial Hospital was opened in 1926.   Orc 7/9/12.

Gilbert I - Earl of Orkney; obscure 2nd representative of the Angus line, succeeded *Earl Magnus II c1239.   2.

Gilbert II - Earl of Orkney; obscure 3rd representative of the Angus line, succeeded *Earl Gilbert c1256.   2.

Gilli of Coll - Hebridean chieftain, bro.-in-law of Earl *Sigurd II and his viceroy in the Western Isles. Together they raided down the west coast of Scotland into Irish Sea probably conquering Kingdom of Man, 986-989.   2,3,76.

Gils - tenant and friend of *Sweyn Asleifsson 1154.   3.

Gladstone, William Ewart - b.1809 d.1898. Leader of Liberal Party 1867, Prime Minister 1868-74, 1880-85, 1886, 1892-94. Visited Kirkwall 1883 accompanied by Poet Laureate *Alfred Lord Tennyson when both were made Honorary Freemen at a ceremony in the Paterson (now East) Kirk. Visited the Cathedral, the Palaces and the Ring of Brogar.   Orc Sept 1883 & Jan/Feb 1967.

Godfrey - Galician chieftain whose castle in Spain was attacked and captured by Earl *Rognvald II during his Crusade to the Holy Land 1152.   1,2,3.

Gold, Andrew - b.1810 Fife d.1907 Edinburgh. Chamberlain of Earldom estate for Marquis of Zetland 1845-1898. Played prominent part in

Orkney public life becoming Vice-Convener of County Council; served on a number of other bodies including 5 school boards.   2,35(1).

Gordon, Miss - dau. of Stromness merchant James Gordon. Engaged to marry pirate *John Gow during his visit to the town 1724/5. According to legend their 'troth was plighted' with hand-shake through the hole in the Odin Stone then standing between the Harray and Stenness Lochs and as this was binding unless their hands met again she was said to have travelled to London to touch his fingers in Execution Dock after he had been hanged.   4.

Gow, John - b.1697 Wick d.1725, London. Pirate; s. of William Gow, Wick merchant and Margaret Calder. Family moved from Caithness to Stromness where they built a house 1716 and where John grew up before running away to sea.

Led mutiny on board *The George* in Mediterranean 1724 taking command, turning pirate and renaming the 200 ton, 26-gun ship, *Revenge*. Intercepted and robbed several ships in Atlantic off Spain, Portugal and France without finding booty of much value.

Sailed to Orkney 1725 believing there could be rich pickings from some of the isolated island mansion houses of the gentry. Anchored off Stromness and with crew enjoyed hospitality of the town. Contracted to marry *Miss Gordon, but rumours spreading as to his true character, attempted to evade capture by making for the open sea again but not before his crew had sacked the *Honyman mansion, Hall of Clestrain, opposite Stromness. Then, while on passage through the North Isles apparently intending to rob Carrick House, Eday, home of former school-friend *James Fea 6th of Clestran, his ship grounded on Calf of Eday immediately opposite Fea's mansion. Fea by rather devious means effected his capture and he was tried, sentenced and hanged with several of his crew at Execution Dock on the Thames.

Gow was inspiration for Captain Cleveland in *Sir Walter Scott's novel 'The Pirate'.   20(7),39,40.

Graeme, Admiral Alexander, b.1741 Greenwall, Holm d.1818 Edinburgh, 6th of Graemeshall - 2nd s. of Mungo Graeme, 4th of Graemeshall and Jean Chancellor.

Joined Royal Navy and commissioned Lieutenant by 1760 seeing service mainly in West Indies and North American stations though visiting Orkney on several occasions with his ship. Promoted Captain 1776. Lost right arm in Battle of Dogger Bank 1781 against the Dutch while commanding 44-gun HMS *Dolphin*. Retired on half-pay to Edinburgh but often visited Orkney staying with his older bro. Patrick, 5th of Graemeshall then Sheriff of Orkney, inheriting the estate himself when Patrick died without issue 1786.

Recalled to Navy 1795 to command HMS *Glory* in Channel Fleet but during temporary lull in the French Revolutionary War the same year she was taken out of commission and he was retired once again on half-pay but with rank of Rear Admiral. Promoted Vice Admiral 1799 and appointed Commander-in-Chief Nore where became an intimate acquaintance of Nelson. Became full Admiral on seniority 1804 living in retirement for rest of his life in Edinburgh visiting Orkney only occasionally, the day-to-day running of the estate being left in the hands of his factor, *David Petrie. He was unmarried. 2,43,56,57.

Graeme, Alexander Malcolm Sutherland, b.1845 d.1908, 8th of Graemeshall - s. of Alexander Sutherland 7th of Graemeshall who had assumed name of Graeme on succeeding to Graemeshall estate following death of his cousin *Admiral Alexander Graeme 1818. Also served in Royal Navy succeeding to estate himself 1894. m. Margaret Isobel Neale 1874, dau. of Rev. John Mason Neale the hymnologist. Father of *P. N. Sutherland Graeme.

Graeme, Sheriff Patrick, b.1739 d.1786, 5th of Graemeshall - Advocate; s. of Mungo Graeme. Educ. St Andrews University.

Called to Scottish Bar 1763; appointed Sheriff Depute for Orkney and Shetland 1767 but continued to practice at the Edinburgh Bar as Advocate until the 1770s, visiting his Sheriffdom and Graemeshall only during vacations, delegating his judicial functions in the islands to local Substitutes until he became resident. Strong supporter of Dundas regime. 14(3).

Graeme, Patrick Neale Sutherland, CBE, DL, JP, b.1877 Graemeshall, Holm d.1958 Graemeshall, 9th of Graemeshall - Barrister-at-Law; s. of *Alexander Malcolm Sutherland Graeme and Margaret Isabel Neale; m. Bethea Hamilton Maclean, St Leonards, Sussex 1903.

Educ. Malvern College, Pembroke College, Cambridge. Called to Bar 1903; Secretary to Lord Chief Justice of England 1902-13; Legal Assistant to Judge-Advocate-General 1914-18; Deputy Judge Advocate 1918; Deputy Judge-Advocate-General 1932-38; Lord Lieutenant of Orkney 1948.

After taking up permanent residence in Orkney on retirement from his legal career was elected County Councillor for Holm 1938 and Vice-Convener, County Council from 1944; Hon. Sheriff Substitute; Member and subsequently Chairman of Orkney War Emergency Committee during World War II and active in many other local organisations including Kirkwall and St Ola Community Association which developed from his close friendship with Rev. T. B. (Tubby) Clayton of Toc H who established canteens etc for troops in Orkney during WWII.

President of Orkney Record and Antiquarian Society he contributed many papers to its *Proceedings* and to the local Press drawing extensively on his family archives dating back to his ancestor *Bishop George Graham in the 17th century.

A keen sportsman he played cricket and football as a young man and was member of the MCC.   49(1951-60),57, Orc 12/9/58, OH 10/9/58.

Graham, Alexander - d.1783. Stromness merchant. Led campaign against taxes and trading restrictions imposed on Stromness merchants by Kirkwall as a Royal Burgh. Litigation dragged on through local courts, Court of Session and House of Lords for 16 years from 1742. He succeeded in relieving Stromness and other small burghs in similar circumstances throughout Scotland from the 'thralldom' of the Royal Burghs, in this case Kirkwall, but was himself financially ruined.

Kirkwall had claimed that as a Royal Burgh it had the right to pass some of its taxation to the 'unfree traders' of Stromness. Graham's case was based on conflicting clauses in the 1707 Act of Union which promised continuation of the privileges enjoyed by Royal Burghs in restricting the right of foreign trading to themselves while also stating that all Scots had the same trading rights as the rest of British citizens.   2,66,67.

Graham, Bishop George - b.c1565 probably Perthshire d.c1643 - 2nd s. of George Graham, 2nd Baron of Incolbrackie and a grt grd s. of 1st Earl of Montrose. Bishop of Orkney 1615; m. Marion Crichton. Founder of Breckness and Skaill estate and Graham/Graeme of Graemeshall dynasty though not classed as its 1st laird. Had previously been Bishop of Dunblane from 1604. Was accompanied to Orkney by his ward and future son-in-law *Patrick Smythe of Braco, a shrewd businessman who was associated with him in feuing and parcelling out substantial portions of Bishopric estate to friends, relatives and themselves.

On abolition of episcopacy in Scotland 1638 he resigned after 23 years as Bishop expressing contrition to the Presbyterian General Assembly for his episcopal career, so avoiding excommunication and/ or deposition and in retirement acquired lands of Breckness and Skaill, building up an extensive estate in the name of his youngest son, *John, who thus became named as 1st Laird of Breckness.   1,2,21,56,67,69.

Graham, Henry (Harie), b.1648 d.1718, 2nd of Breckness - Grd s. of *Bishop George Graham; s. of *John Graham 1st of Breckness; m. (1) Euphemia Honyman, dau. of *Bishop Andrew Honyman 1669 (2) Jane Law of Anstruther (3) Ann Coult. Educ. Kirkwall Grammar School, St Andrews University. Tutored by his uncle James Stewart of Graemsay.

Succeeded to Breckness and Skaill estate 1666. For various periods as tacksman managed Bishopric estate for his father-in-law Bishop

Honyman. Appointed Sheriff and Admiral Depute of Orkney, Member of Scottish Parliament for Orkney and Shetland 1685-6. Became one of principal landowners in Orkney but got into financial difficulties incurring heavy debts. 2,67.

Graham, James, b.1612. d.1650, Marquis of Montrose - Came to Orkney 1650 on invitation of Robert 8th Earl of Morton to continue his struggle for the Royalist cause. Had originally supported the Covenanters but disagreeing with certain aspects of their policies transferred his allegiance to Charles I. At the head of the Royalist army won a number of spectacular victories before his defeat at Philiphaugh 1645. He fled to Continent but returned to Scotland via Orkney to avenge death of Charles I. On the way from Gothenburg, however, lost most of his fleet in North Sea gales. In Orkney raised some 2000 men by levy and crossed with them from Holm to Mainland of Scotland where they were decisively routed and dispersed by the Covenanter army at Carbisdale in Sutherland 1650. Montrose was later captured, tried, condemned and hanged in Edinburgh. Few of the Orkney levies survived to return home. 1,2,44.

Graham, John, b.c1615 d.1666, 1st of Breckness - Youngest s. of *Bishop Graham; m. Barbara Stewart, dau. of Harie Stewart of Graemsay.
Bailie of Sandwick and JP. Expanded Breckness estate, main part of which he acquired in settlement of money owed him by Patrick Moodie of Melsetter - money which had originally been lent to Moodie by his father Bishop Graham. 2,67.

Graham, Margaret Manson, b.1860 Orphir d.1933 Nigeria, of Calabar. Nurse and missionary. Educ. Orphir Public School where she became pupil-teacher at age of 16 and subsequently qualified as a teacher.
She then trained as nurse in Glasgow and on ordination volunteered for Mission service in Calabar, Nigeria where she was one of its pioneer nurses. When the Government built a hospital at Duketown for its officials and white traders she was asked to take over as sister-in-charge but in addition she treated the sick of the native population. She also saw active service with the army up-country and was decorated with the Africa General Service Medal and the Order of St John of Jerusalem for devotion to duty during an up-rising in northern Nigeria.
Retired 1919 but after two years returned to West Africa as a missionary-nurse based on the Calabar Slessor Memorial Home opening her own private dispensary or clinic near Duketown for treatment of native population. OH 25/10/33, *Islander* 1994.

Graham, Patrick, b.c1600 d.1675, of Rothiesholme and Greenwall, 1st of

Graemeshall - s. of *Bishop George Graham. Acquired Meall, Holm (later renamed Graemeshall) from his nephew, *Patrick Smythe of Braco and Meall, grd s. of Bishop Graham.   57.

Graham, Thomas - b.1840 Kirkwall d.1906 England. Artist. Closely associated with the Orchardson/Pettie Group in both Edinburgh and London. Painted landscapes in Orkney where his father and grandfather had both held post of Crown Chamberlain.   51.

Grant, Walter Gordon FSA(Scot) - b.1886 Elgin d.1947 Orkney; distiller, company director, amateur archaeologist; s. of James Grant, Highland Park, Kirkwall; m. Florence Davidson, Kirkwall.

Associated with father and other local owners in Highland Park Distillery, Kirkwall, becoming a Director of James Grant & Co and later a Director of Highland Distillers Co. Ltd. Glasgow after they acquired Highland Park.

Owner of most of Rousay, living at Trumland House in summer, Hillhead, St Ola in winter, he became keen amateur archaeologist financing excavation and preservation of a number of ancient monuments in Rousay in close association with *Gordon Childe, notably the Midhowe Broch and Stalled Cairn.

A keen angler he was President of Orkney Trout Fishing Association carrying out trout hatchery experiments. Was active in encouraging establishment of air service between Orkney and Scottish mainland in early 1930s.   22, Orc 17/4/47.

Grelod - c940. dau. of *Dungad and *Groa; grd. dau. of *Thorstein the Red; grt grd dau. of *Aud the Deepminded; m. Earl *Thorfinn I Skullsplitter; mother of Earls *Arnfinn, *Hlodver, *Ljot and *Havard Harvest-Happy.   3,35(7),71,76.

Grieve (nee Skea), Jemima Bessie - b.1923 Shapinsay d.1996 Shapinsay. Columnist under pen-name Countrywoman for *Orkney Herald* 1958 and from 1961 *The Orcadian*. Born and brought up on family farm in Shapinsay and lived there during World War II during which met her husband stationed there in one of the batteries. Lived in Harray after the war where she wrote on a wide variety of subjects mainly relating to Orkney life past and present, its land and seascapes, natural history and her cats - widely read by Orcadians at home and overseas.

Her first book, 'A Countrywoman's Calendar', appeared in 1962 to be followed by 'Waves and Tangles' 1964, 'A Countrywoman's Diary' 1983 and 'Island Journeys' 1996.   Orc 96.

Grim Njalsson - Icelander. Bro. of *Helgi Njalsson. Member of Earl *Sigurd II's hird for a time.   38.

Grimble, Dr. Ian - b.1921 Hong Kong d.1995 Bettyhill, Sutherland. Historian specialising in inter-action between Norse and Gaelic cultures, lecturer, broadcaster, television personality. Educ. Balliol College, Oxford, Aberdeen University. Served in Intelligence Corps in India, World War II then after spell as a Librarian in the House of Commons joined BBC Scotland from where in 1960, based on Aberdeen, he set up and was producer of the first local broadcasting programme in the country making frequent visits to Orkney. Called 'Town and Country' it was broadcast twice a week covering local events and matters of interest to Orkney and Caithness on VHF slotted into the Scottish national programmes. For a time before the Islamic revolution was lecturer in English at Tehran University in Iran.

Publications include 'Scottish Islands' 1985, complementing one of his many television documentary series on BBC TV and ITV; 'Clans and Chiefs' 1980, 'Robert Burns' 1986.

Grimond, Jo - b.1913 St Andrews, Fife d.1993 Kirkwall, Lord Grimond. MP for Orkney and Shetland 1950-83; Leader of the Liberal Party 1956-67; s. of a Dundee jute manufacturer; m. *Laura Bonham Carter, grd dau. of *Lord Asquith 1938.

Educ. Eton, Balliol College, Oxford. Served with Fife and Forfar Yeomanry World War II; staff officer 53rd Division; after D-Day served with UNRRA (United Nations Relief and Rehabilitation Administration). On demobilisation appointed Secretary to National Trust for Scotland. Standing for the second time was elected MP for Orkney and Shetland 1950 continuing to represent the constituency with increased majorities at each election until his retirement 1983. After winning the seat in 1950 the Grimonds made the Old Manse of Firth their family home.

On elevation to the Lords he continued to press Orkney's case where necessary and went on playing an active part in island affairs.   58.

Grimond, Lady Laura Miranda - b.1919 d.1994 London; grd dau. of *Lord Asquith; dau of Sir Maurice and Lady Violet Bonham Carter; m. Jo *Grimond 1938. Made their home in Old Manse of Firth after he was elected MP for Orkney and Shetland 1950 playing an active part both in his political career and generally in the public life of the constituency. Represented Firth and Harray on Orkney Islands Council 1974-80 being convener of its Social Work and Housing Committees. Very involved in conservation matters she was founder member of Orkney Heritage Society single-handedly raising funds to buy the Strynd Houses for Kirkwall which she dedicated to the memory of her mother. A strong supporter of *Evan MacGillivray in the establishment of Corrigall Farm Museum she also headed the Hoy Trust and campaigned for the preservation of Papdale House, once home of

*Samuel Laing. She served on the Bench as Hon. Sheriff Substitute. In a unique ceremony on steps of St Magnus Cathedral 1987 was given Freedom of Kirkwall jointly with her husband.   Orc 17/2/94.

Groa - dau. of *Thorstein the Red; grd dau. of *Aud the Deepminded; m. *Dungad of Caithness.   2,71,76.

Groat, John Malcolm Freswick, (Jackie) - b.1923 Longhope d. 1998 Longhope; merchant, Hon. Secy. Longhope Lifeboat; e.s. of John M. F. Groat, founder of Longhope firm J. M. F. Groat & Sons, general merchants; m. Edna Yule. Educ. South Walls School and at 14 entered family business. During World War II joined RAF, piloting Lancasters of Bomber Command in missions over enemy territory finishing his service in the Far East as Officer in charge air transport S.E. Asia. After war returned to family business taking it over with his brother on their father's death. Appointed Hon. Secy. of Longhope Lifeboat 1962, a position he held for the next 33 years - becoming the RNLI's longest serving Hon. Secy. in the British Isles. During that period he had to cope with many emergencies but none more harrowing or exacting than the loss of the station's own Lifeboat, the *TGB*, with all hands during a severe gale 1969 while going to the assistance of a drifting cargo ship. He was awarded the MBE 1985 and the RNLI Gold Badge 1993. He was Postmaster 1964-98, served on the School Management Committee, the Orkney Health Board and was Director of the Orkney Islands Shipping Company.   Orc 27/8/98.

Groundwater, Rosetta - b.1901 Stromness d.1976 Kirkwall. Teacher, Provost Stromness Town Council; dau. of John Bain, Mason's Arms Hotel, Stromness; m. *William Groundwater.
    Educ. Stromness, Glasgow University BSc (Agric): Taught Rural Science, Roxburghshire; elected Kirkwall Town Council 1945 and moving to Stromness on her husband's appointment as Rector of the Academy became member of that Town Council and subsequently, for 6 years, its first and only woman Provost.
    As a girl she had been aboard the *Flying Kestrel* on a school outing in Scapa Flow sailing through the 74 ships of the interned German High Seas Fleet when they scuttled and sank on Midsummer Day 1919.   Orc 23/12/76.

Groundwater, William MA - b.1906 Stromness d.1982 Kirkwall. Teacher, naturalist; m. *Rosetta Bain. Educ. Stromness Secondary School, Edinburgh University.
    Taught English Stromness, Westray, Wigtown, Kirkwall Grammar School before being appointed Headmaster Stromness Academy 1948-69. Major in Royal Artillery World War II serving on Scapa Defences

and in India. Keen on sport, football, golf, angling. An enthusiastic birdwatcher he contributed Nature Notes to *The Orcadian* and was author of 'Birds and Mammals of Orkney' 1974 and co-editor of 'New Orkney Book' 1966. President of Orkney Natural History Society (Stromness Museum) 1971-76.   Orc 15/4/82.

Gunn, Professor James Andrew, CBE, MA, MD, DSc (Edin), DM(Oxon), FRCP - b.1878 Kirkwall d.1958 Oxford. Pharmacologist, Professor Emeritus Oxford University. Bro. of Professor *John W. C. Gunn. Educ. Kirkwall Burgh (Grammar) School, Edinburgh University.
   Appointed Reader in Pharmacology when that Department was first formed Oxford University 1912 and its first Professor when Chair established there 1917 and the first Director of the Nuffield Institute for Medical Research when it was founded 1936 and its Professor of Experimental Therapeutics shortly afterwards. President of Pharmacopoeia Revision Commission 1939/40 and President of Therapeutic Section of Royal Society of Medicine. Fellow of Balliol College, Oxford.
   During World War II was one of those responsible for selection and despatch of drugs to Russia for medical purposes.
   Lectured extensively in UK and USA and wrote 'Introduction to Pharmacology and Therapeutics' as well as being joint editor of Cushing's standard textbook on Pharmacology and for relaxation was a keen golfer and angler.   49(1951-60), Orc 13/11/58.

Gunn, Dr. John MA DSc - b.1859 Stromness d.1939 Edinburgh. Author and publisher. Educ. Stromness Academy, Edinburgh University.
   Joined Edinburgh publishing firm Thomas Nelson & Son 1899 becoming Chief Editor before which had been schoolmaster and Inspector of Schools. Editor of first 'Orkney Book' 1909. Author of 'Orkney the Magnetic North', 'Sons of the Vikings', 'The Boys of Hamnavoe' among others.   Orc and OH March 1939.

Gunn, Professor John William Cormack, MA, MB, ChB, FRSS Af - b.1889 Kirkwall d.1941 Cape Town, South Africa. Pharmacologist; bro. of Professor *James Gunn. Educ. Kirkwall Burgh (Grammar) School, Edinburgh University.
   Assistant in Materia Medica, Edinburgh University 1912; Assistant in Pharmacology Dept, University College, London 1913; served in RAMC during World War I, when Major in charge Medical Division 19th General Hospital 1917-19; mentioned in dispatches. Lecturer in Pharmacology, Queens College, Belfast 1919. Appointed Professor of Pharmacology Cape Town University 1920.   OH 28/5/41.

Gunnar Lambasson - Icelander. One of the 'Burners' of Njal in Iceland.

According to Njal's Saga killed by *Kari, Njal's son-in-law 1014 while giving a biassed account of the 'Burning' at Yuletide feast hosted by Earl *Sigurd II in Orkney.   38.

Gunnhild - wife of *Erik Bloodaxe, King of Norway; mother of *Ragnhild; grd mother of Earls *Arnfinn, *Havard Harvest-Happy and *Ljot. Came to Orkney after Erik was killed at battle of Stainmore 954.   3,35(7),76.

Gunnhild Erlendsdotter - Dau. of Earl *Erlend II; m. *Kol Kalisson 1103; mother of Earl St *Rognvald II.   3,35(7).

Gunni of Westray - Claimed St Magnus had appeared to him in a vision and had ordained that his relics should be moved from Christ Church, Birsay to Kirkwall.   2,3.

Gunni Olafsson - s. of Olaf Hrolfsson; bro. of *Sweyn Asleifsson; father of illegitimate child c1150 by 'Countess' *Margaret, widow of Maddad Earl of Atholl, mother of Earl Harald II Maddadsson.   1,3,35(7).

Guttorm Sigurdsson - c890. Earl of Orkney; s. of Earl *Sigurd I whom he succeeded but ruled Orkney for one year only and dying without issue Earldom reverted to his grandfather *Rognvald, Earl of Møre, who passed it to his own son, *Hallad.   3,35(7).

Gwyn, Captain David - 1590. English pirate, captured and robbed ship carrying Earl *Patrick Stewart and his treasure in money, jewellery and movables valued at some £3,000 sterling.   13.

H

Hagart, Patrick - Replaced *William Balfour as factor of the Dundas estates and Chamberlain of Earldom 1780-92.   17.

Hakon IV Hakonsson, The Old - 1204-63. King of Norway. Grd s. of King *Sverre Sigurdsson. Called at Orkney late summer 1263 with fleet of over 100 ships on expedition intended to strengthen hold on possessions and boost waning Norse influence in Hebrides and west of Scotland having annexed Iceland and Greenland to the Norwegian Crown the previous year. After landfall in Shetland sailed south to Orkney concentrating his fleet in Elwick Bay, Shapinsay and then in St

Margaret's Hope (Rognvaldsvoe) before sailing out through the Pentland Firth, down west coast of Scotland to Clyde estuary where he fought the Scots at the indecisive battle of Largs, real victors being early autumn gales which scattered and mauled his ships forcing him to retire to Orkney, still a Norse possession. Laying up what remained of his fleet round Scapa Flow he took up winter quarters himself in the Bishop's Palace, Kirkwall where he died at Yule and was buried in St Magnus Cathedral until Spring 1264 when his body was taken back to Norway for interment in Bergen.   1,2,3,30.

Hakon Jonsson - 1364 sysselman and governor in Orkney for King Hakon VI of Norway with whom he had family connections.   1,2.

Hakon Kló Havardsson - Orkney gøding based in Stenness; grt grd s. of Earl *Paul I; s. of Havard Gunnasson and Bergliot, grd dau. of Paul I.
      Supported his bro.*Magnus Havardsson in killing *Thorbjorn Klerk for his murder of Earl *Rognvald II in Caithness 1158.   2.

Hakon Paulsson - Earl of Orkney c1103-c1123. s. of Earl *Paul I; grd s. of *Thorfinn II; cousin of (St) *Magnus with whom he was joint Earl from c1105 until c1114 when, with Magnus out of Orkney for a time, he seized control of the Earldom for himself. When Magnus returned the resultant dispute between them was temporarily patched up by their followers among the leading men on either side and it was arranged that ratification of the agreement should take place at a 'peace conference' in Egilsay on Easter Day 1117 (or possibly 1116, the actual year is uncertain). The two parties were each to have only 2 ships. Magnus complied reaching Egilsay with his 2 galleys the night before the scheduled meeting but next morning Hakon came with 8, fully manned with armed men. Their followers refused this time to negotiate terms between them stipulating that only one Earl should rule Orkney. Magnus offered to submit himself to banishment, imprisonment or mutilation but none of these choices was acceptable and he was duly killed by an axe-blow on the head delivered unwillingly by Hakon's cook, *Lifolf.
      Hakon later went on pilgrimage to Rome, receiving absolution from the Pope for the murder before going on to the Holy Land where he bathed in the Jordan. Returning to Orkney he ruled the Earldom well and peacefully for the rest of his life. In all probability the Round Church in Orphir based on a plan of the Church of the Holy Sepulchre which he had visited in Jerusalem, was built to his instructions.   1,2,3,35(7),100.

Halcro, Magnus of Brough - Chantor in charge of music in St Magnus

Cathedral 1561, and Prebendary in Orphir. Illegitimate s. of Malcolm Halcro onetime Provost of St Magnus Cathedral under *Bishop Reid. While Precentor of the Cathedral he was one of the mob led by *Francis Bothwell protesting at *Bishop Bothwell's feuing of bishopric lands and Protestant innovations. Bought Brough in Rousay and obtained lease of extensive bishopric lands also in Rousay 1560. Already father of 3 illegitimate children; m. Margaret Sinclair, dau. of *James Sinclair of Brecks, she having to obtain divorce before the marriage could take place. Feued lands in Flotta and Burray 1566 in name of his wife and her mother.

Along with *William Moodie was sworn enemy of Earl *Robert Stewart when he came to Orkney and signed undertaking to support Earl of Caithness should he wish to pursue his claims on Orkney, but later changed his mind. Robert imprisoned them, deposed Magnus as minister of Orphir 1572 confiscating much of his property and banishing Moodie. In 1584, after Magnus was dead, Robert seized his lands in Rousay alleging unpaid debts.   2,12.

Halcro, Patrick - s. of *William Halcro of Aikers; kinsman of *Magnus Halcro. Supporter of Earl *Patrick Stewart and his s. *Robert. Played prominent part in latter's 1614 rebellion on his father's behalf, taking and occupying the Palace at Birsay. Having possibly previously served as a soldier he planned and led attack on Kirkwall during the rebellion with the resultant capture and occupation of the Castle and St Magnus Cathedral. But was also involved in subsequent negotiations with *Bishop Law and the Earl of Caithness for the surrender of the Castle which led to the imprisonment and execution of Robert in Edinburgh. Halcro himself escaped execution probably for his part in the surrender.   2,13.

Halcro, William, b.c1545 d.c1593, of Aikers - Onetime Bailie of Firth and Harray but deprived of this position on arrival of Earl *Robert Stewart who regarded him as an enemy on account of his family connection with *Magnus Halcro who was anti-Stewart. William, however, subsequently appears to have supported the Stewarts.   12,13.

Haldane, James Alexander - b.1768 Dundee d.1851. Evangelist. During his evangelical tour of Scotland 1798 he and his party preached to open-air congregations throughout Orkney in an 18-day 'crusade' with numbers attending in Kirkwall during the Lammas Market varying from 1800 to 2500. He condemned lax condition of the Established Church and the visit resulted in a vigorous revivalist movement throughout Orkney and the establishment of the Secession Church.

He had previously served in the Navy 1785-94 rising in rank from midshipman aboard an East Indiaman to command of the *Melville*

Castle. Ordained Edinburgh 1799 and preached gratuitously for 50 years leading his congregation into Baptist fold. 4,6,7.

Halfdan Longlegs - d.c894 North Ronaldsay; s. of *Harald Fairhair, King of Norway; bro. of Kings *Erik Bloodaxe and *Magnus the Good. Killed *Torf-Einar's father *Rognvald of Møre, close friend of Harald Fairhair. Fled to Orkney to escape his father's wrath, and tried to make himself master of the islands. Torf-Einar, then Earl of Orkney, withdrew to Caithness c894 but returned the same year and defeated Halfdan in a sea fight off North Ronaldsday. Halfdan jumped from his ship and swam ashore but Torf-Einar caught and killed him next day and according to the Orkneyinga Saga, carved a ritual 'blood-eagle' on his back in revenge for the killing of his father. 1,2,3,35(7),76,100.

Hallad Rognvaldsson - Earl of Orkney for a year c892/3; s. of *Rognvald Earl of Møre; bro. of Hrolf the Ganger, ancestor of the Dukes of Normandy including William the Conqueror; half bro. of *Torf-Einar. Sent by his father to be Earl of Orkney following death of *Guttorm son of Earl *Sigurd I but proving ineffectual renounced his title and returned to Norway after only a year in the west. 1,2,3,35(7),76,100.

Hamilton, Lord George, b.1666 Lanark, d.1737 London. Earl of Orkney - 5th s. of William, Earl of Selkirk, later Duke of Hamilton. General serving under William of Orange and the Duke of Marlborough, being present at all the latter's major battles. Married his cousin, Elizabeth Villiers, a former mistress of the king - the marriage is said to have been arranged by William himself, full of remorse on the death of his wife, who had always deplored the liaison. Shortly afterwards Lord George was created Earl of Orkney, Viscount Kirkwall and Baron Dechmont. However, it appears that neither he nor his 8 successors in the present line ever took much interest in the islands that still give them their title. 83.

Hamilton, Sir Robert William - b.1867 d.1944. Liberal MP for Orkney and Shetland 1922-35; m. Gertrude Williamson, Kirkwall 1925. Educ. St Pauls, Trinity College, Cambridge.
   Called to Bar 1895; entered Colonial Service 1902; Judge of High Court, East Africa 1904 and became Justice of East African Protectorate and President of Court of East Africa; knighted 1918. Retired from Colonial Service 1920.
   Member of Round Table Conference on India 1930; Parliamentary Under-secretary for Colonies in Ramsay Macdonald's 2nd National Ministry 1931 but resigned 1932 over Free Trade issues. Scottish Liberal Chief Whip 1934. Did not seek re-election 1935. 49(1944), Orc 15/7/44.

Hammer, Dr. Armand - b.1898 New York d.1990 Los Angeles. American oil entrepreneur and art collector of Russian extraction. In 1961 acquired Occidental Petroleum Corporation (Oxy) which brought oil age to Orkney with the establishment of Flotta oil terminal for the reception, storing and processing of North Sea oil from Piper and Claymore fields. As its Chairman and Chief Executive visited Orkney on several occasions including the official opening of the terminal 1977.   Orc 13/12/90.

Hanef Ungi (Younger) of Wyre - Probably grt grd s. of *Kolbein Hruga and nephew of *Bishop Bjarni. Had been member of Royal Hird in Norway. Royal sysselman of Orkney c1230 when *John Haraldsson was Earl. With cousin *Snaekoll involved in killing of John during drunken brawl in Thurso c1231 after which they took refuge from the Earl's men in Cubbie Roo's Castle in Wyre. A truce was arranged so that the matter could be put before *King Hakon VI in Norway. No decision was reached and Hanef was possibly pardoned after being spirited away by some of his former comrades in the Royal Hird. The Earl's men were all drowned when their ship (later known as the Gøding Ship) foundered while returning to Orkney 1232. Hanef died later in Norway.   1,2.

Harald Fair-Hair - c860-933 (dates very uncertain). King of unified Norway after his victory at battle of Hafrsfjord traditionally 872 but may have been later. According to the saga's account he sailed to Orkney to subdue and root out vikings who were using the islands as base from which to continue their resistance to him by raids on Norway. *Ivar, son of *Rognvald of Møre, close friend of Harald, accompanying the king was killed on this expedition and Harald granted Orkney and Shetland to his father in compensation for the loss of his son. Rognvald passed the island Earldom to his bro. *Sigurd who thus became first Earl of Orkney. When Harald's own son, *Halfdan Longlegs, killed Rognvald of Møre he fled to Orkney to escape his father's anger and was himself killed by *Torf-Einar, Rognvald of Møre's illegitimate son now Earl of Orkney, in revenge for his father's murder. According to the Saga Harald then made a 2nd expedition to Orkney seeking retribution in turn for his own son's death. He imposed a fine of 60 gold marks on the islanders which Torf-Einar paid himself making a bargain with the Orkney land-holders that they make over their udal rights to him in exchange.   1,2,3,30,76,100.

Harald Gilli(christ) - King of Norway 1130-36; s. of King *Magnus Bare-legs. Confirmed *Kali Kolsson in his share of Orkney with the title of Earl *Rognvald II previously granted him by the late King Sigurd Magnusson.   1,2,3,30.

Harald I Hakonsson Smoothtongue - Earl of Orkney c1123-1128; s. of Earl *Hakon Paulsson and *Helga Moddansdottar; father of Earl *Erlend III. Joint Earl with half bro. *Paul II but they did not agree and so divided Earldom between them. He also held Caithness from the Scottish Crown and spent considerable periods there and in Sutherland where he had many friends and kinsmen. One of his close associates was the flamboyant Norwegian chieftain *Sigurd Slembi who accompanied him to Orkney with some of his Scots kinsfolk and where, fearing he might stir up trouble for them, they killed *Thorkell Somerledisson Fosterer, uncle of St *Magnus and close friend of Paul II who was outraged by the killing. But a reconciliation between the two Earls was planned for a Yule feast in Orphir 1127. The OS account tells how on arrival there Harald found his mother, *Helga and her sister *Frakokk, stitching a fine shirt for Paul to wear at the feast but Harald demanded that he should wear it not Paul. Seizing it from them he put it on - and dropped down dead. It was a poisoned garment they had prepared for Paul. And so, having survived the murder attempt Paul became sole Earl of Orkney and not surprisingly promptly banished his 2 would-be murderesses.   1,2,3,35(7).

Harald Hardrada - b.1015 d.1066 Stamford Bridge. King of Norway 1047-1066; half bro. of King (St) *Olaf and was saved from death by Rognvald Brusisson (subsequently Earl *Rognvald I) after battle of Stikkelstad 1030 where Olaf was killed. They met again later in Russia where Harald and his nephew Olaf II had sought refuge with their kinsman, Prince Jaroslav the Wise. Harald and Rognvald later served as mercenaries in Varangian Guard of Constantinople. Returning to Norway Harald demanded and received half share of the kingdom becoming sole king on his nephew's death 1047. Conducted relentless campaigns against Denmark until 1066 when after the death of Edward the Confessor he laid claim to the English Throne and mounted an expedition to the west. Sailing by way of Orkney 1066 and leaving his queen and daughters in the islands went on to England accompanied by the joint Earls, *Paul I and *Erlend II, sons of *Thorfinn II, where he was killed at the battle of Stamford Bridge. Paul and Erlend survived and returned to Orkney.   1,2,3,30,76,102.

Harald II Maddadsson - Earl of Orkney 1138-1206. s. of *Maddad, Earl of Atholl and *Margaret, dau. of Earl *Hakon Paulsson; m.(1) *Afreka (2) Hvarflod, dau. of MacHeth Earl of Moray.

Succeeded to Orkney Earldom at age of 5. Fostered in Orkney by Earl (St) *Rognvald II and ruled with him for his first 20 years as joint Earl. While Rognvald was absent on his Crusade 1151-3 he left Harald, still in his teens, in charge of the Earldom. That same year 1151 King Eystein of Norway on a raiding expedition surprised and captured

him in Thurso. Harald was forced to yield Orkney and ransom himself
for 3 gold marks whereupon Eystein restored the Earldom to him in
return for a vague promise of his support in the future. Eystein then
continued his viking raid down the east coast of Britain and
apparently played no further direct part in Orkney affairs.

Harald now became involved in the so-called 'War of the Three
Earls' (Harald II himself, *Erlend III and *Rognvald II) 1152-54 when
the Scottish Crown granted half Caithness to Erlend III Haraldsson, grd
s. of Earl Hakon Paulsson while the King of Norway granted him half
Orkney. Erlend was supported by *Sweyn Asleifsson. On Rognvald's
return from his Crusade he first formed an alliance with Erlend in an
attempt to deprive Harald of his share of Orkney but later switching
sides and teaming up with Harald together they surprised and killed
Erlend who was lying drunk on his galley off Damsay during a
temporary absence of Sweyn who had been his adviser and protector.

But while hunting together in Caithness 1158 Rognvald was
ambushed and killed by an old enemy, *Thorbjorn Klerk, grd s. of
*Frakokk and one-time chief adviser and close friend of Harald who
now became sole Earl of Orkney.

He was disastrously involved in an attempt to put Sigurd
Magnusson, son of late King Magnus Erlingsson, on the Norwegian
throne in place of King *Sverre by lending support to the Norwegian
aristocratic opposition to the King who they dubbed 'the Imposter'. He
gave approval to an anti-Sverre expedition of leading men in Orkney
and Shetland, known as the Island Beardies (Eyjarskeggjar), one of
whose chief proponents was his son-in-law Olaf Jarlsmagr. This island
force optimistically invaded Norway 1193 and after initial success was
utterly routed by Sverre in sea-battle of Florvåg 1194 near Bergen.

With *Bishop Bjarni Harald crossed to Norway and made peace
with Sverre by abject submission. Sverre imposed harsh terms
separating Earldom of Orkney from Lordship of Shetland, placing a
sysselman in Orkney to look after his royal interests, collect revenue
and administer forfeited 'Island Beardie' estates. Harald was
reinstated as Earl of Orkney 1196 but across the Pentland Firth had to
submit to Scottish King, William the Lion, who invaded the north of
Scotland. Harald was allowed to retain half Caithness on condition
that he hand over to William the 'king's enemies' there. This he failed
to do and so forfeited his share of Caithness as well as being
imprisoned in Edinburgh. He was later released when his son
Thorfinn was seized and taken hostage in his place. At battle of Wick
1198 Harald defeated and killed the rival claimant to Orkney Earldom,
*Harald Ungi (the Younger).

1,2,3,35(7), *Harald Maddadsson Earl of Orkney and Caithness*
- P. Topping in *Scottish Historical Review* lxii 1983,
B. Crawford in *Northern Scotland*.

Harald Ungi (the Younger) - s. of Erik Stagbrell and Ingirid. dau. of Earl (St) *Rognvald II and so his grd s. Claimant to Orkney Earldom and recognised as heir to Rognvald II's share of it by Norwegian Crown. Invaded Orkney in pursuit of claim but was defeated and later killed in battle near Wick 1198 by Earl *Harald II Maddadsson.

Credited with several miracles and revered locally as saint although never officially canonised. 1,2,3,35(7).

Hartsyde, Margaret - Married to *Sir John Buchanan and while in service of Queen Anne of Denmark, wife of James VI & I, was charged 1608 with stealing some of the Queen's jewellery. Tried and found guilty on a reduced charge in Edinburgh she was banished, along with her husband, to Orkney where her father was said to be a merchant in Kirkwall. It was a *cause celebre* at the time and there is some doubt as to whether she did actually steal the jewellery or did she perhaps pass confidential information to James about the Queen? At all events her husband was later knighted by the King and given the tack of Orkney along with *Sir George Hay of Fauns, Chancellor of Scotland. 2,4,13.

Harvie-Brown, J. A. - b.1844 d.1916. Naturalist; s. of Stirlingshire landowner. Acknowledged authority on birds and mammals of Scotland spending long periods in Orkney being particularly interested in bird migration, study of which was then in its infancy. In 1887 launched Fraserburgh-built yacht, *Shiantelle*, giving him increased access to the isles accompanied by the ornithologist W. Eagle Clarke.

With T. E. Buckley, an English ornithologist who had also spent long periods in Orkney, especially in Rousay, produced the classic work, 'A Vertebrate Fauna of the Orkney Islands', containing three illustrations by *J. G. Millais, and in which were listed 225 species of birds found in Orkney at that time. 47.

Havard Gunnisson - Leading Orkney gøding of his day; c1090-c1117; kinsman of the Earls; m. Bergljot, grd dau. of *Paul II, with estates in West Mainland (Stenness, Ireland). Councillor-in-Chief to Earl *Hakon Paulsson and leader of gødings who tried to maintain peace between Earls *Paul I and *Erlend II and their respective sons, *Hakon and (St) *Magnus, in dispute over division of Earldom.

Also prominent in arranging the fateful meeting between Hakon and Magnus on Egilsay 1117. It was only when en route for this meeting in Hakon's war galley that he learned of Hakon's treacherous intent and wishing no part in it jumped overboard and swam to the nearest uninhabited island, probably either Sweyn Holm or Boray Holm. 1,3,35(7).

Havard Thorfinnsson Harvest-Happy - Earl of Orkney for some years between 976-991; 2nd s. of Earl *Thorfinn I Skullsplitter; m. *Ragnhild, dau. of King *Erik Bloodaxe. Was considered lucky during brief rule as Earl when Orkney enjoyed good harvests. He was not so lucky in marriage as Ragnhild had him killed probably in Stenness. 1,2,3,35(7).

Hay, Sir George, b.1572 d.1635, of Kinfauns, later 1st Earl of Kinnoull - Chancellor of Scotland. Granted feu of Orkney jointly with *Sir John Buchanan c1620. Non-resident Superior.   2.

Hay, George, d.1649 Orkney, 4th Earl of Kinnoull - Nephew of Robert, 8th Earl of Morton. Of strong Royalist persuasion joined his uncle in Orkney with small force of Danish troops to await arrival of *Marquis of Montrose from Sweden to launch his second and ill-fated campaign to re-instate the Stuart monarchy which ended in disaster at Carbisdale 1650. Both Kinnoull and his uncle died within weeks of each other before Montrose reached the islands.   2.

Hay, John, of Balbithan - Chamberlain of Earldom, tacksman of bishopric lands 1732-41 and Earl of Morton's factor. His dispute with *Sir James Steuart of Burray over alleged alteration and manipulation of Orkney's ancient weights and measures by the Mortons led to Pundlar Process litigation 1733-59.   2,11.

Heddle, Charles William Maxwell - b.1812 Sierra Leone d.after 1888 France. Merchant, trader, shipowner; natural s. of *John Heddle by native Senegalese woman probably Sophy Bouchier by whom he had several other sons. Educ. Kirkwall Grammar School, and Edinburgh Academy. Returning to Sierra Leone he very successfully developed business started by his uncle *Robert Heddle, pioneering the ground-nut trade and owning half-a-dozen ships. Became leading trader in Sierra Leone - a true merchant prince. Bought property in Freetown including his own house where *William Balfour Baikie died 1864.

Perhaps because of his mixed blood he seemed impervious to the deadly diseases of what was called 'The White Man's Grave' and completely independent of official favours he was a fearless critic of government in the legislative council.

Crippled and lame he retired to France 1870 with fortune estimated at £$\frac{1}{2}$ million which in a will dated 1888 he left to his son with the proviso that if the son predeceased him the residue of his estate was to go to the Burgh of Kirkwall. But the son survived him and in any case having married a French-Canadian woman he made another will leaving everything to her. The will was unsuccessfully contested the court finding in her favour but she gave £120,000 to the son. Kirkwall got nothing.   87,88.

Heddle, John - b.1776 Orkney d.1812 Sierra Leone. Surgeon, soldier, administrator; s. of John Heddle, Town Clerk of Kirkwall 1788-1801.

Assistant Surgeon, 2nd Dragoon Guards 1797; Surgeon, Royal African Corps 1800; Staff Surgeon 1804, wounded in action against the French on island of Goree off Senegal coast during Napoleonic Wars. Described as 'a very gallant officer'; mentioned in dispatches for staff work and for negotiating surrender of French forces in Senegal itself 1809; Colonial Secretary of Council of Sierra Leone and Chief Surgeon 1811. Committed suicide Freetown 1812.   4,87,88.

Heddle, Robert, b.1790 d.1842, of Cletts and Melsetter - Writer, Army Paymaster, trader; s. of John Heddle, Town Clerk of Kirkwall; trained as Writer in Kirkwall then followed his bro. *John Heddle who was trading in Senegal, West Africa. Appointed Deputy Assistant Commissary General, Senegal 1810.

On bro's death 1812 succeeded to family properties in S. Ronaldsay. As merchant had been very successful and when Senegal was given back to France 1817 he returned to Orkney with a fortune of £90,000, using £24,000 of it to buy the Melsetter estate from the Trustees of the bankrupt Major John Moodie at public roup 1818. Later that year he married Henrietta, 2nd dau. of the bankrupt Major Moodie, by whom he had 10 children. She had previously been engaged to Rev. Thomas Bremner, Minister of Walls and Flotta.   88.

Heddle, William John - b.1865 Kirkwall d.1952 Edinburgh. Solicitor, Town Clerk of Kirkwall 1902-45. By raising action on behalf of Kirkwall Town Council in Court of Session 1911 retained adequate finance (£9,000) from *Sheriff Thom's Bequest to provide Maintenance Fund for preservation of fabric of St Magnus Cathedral. Closely associated with establishment of Kitchener Memorial on Marwick Head 1926 and organisation of the Cathedral Octo-centenary celebrations 1937. During 43 years as Town Clerk of Kirkwall saw introduction of gas and electricity supplies to Burgh and introduction of council housing schemes. Made Freeman of Kirkwall 1948.   Orc 22/6/52, OH 20/5/52.

Helga - dau. of Moddan of the Dales; mother of Earl *Harald I by Earl *Hakon Paulsson; sister of *Frakokk with whom she was embroidering the poisoned shirt intended for *Paul II but which by mischance killed his half bro. her son *Harald 1127.   1,2,3,35(7).

Helgi of Hofn - Chieftain in north end of Westray including present-day Pierowall (Norse Hofn). 'Wise and powerful' (OS). Submitted to *Rognvald II when he invaded Orkney 1136 landing in Westray from Shetland in successful pursuit of his claim to share of Earldom.   1,3.

Helgi Njalsson - Icelander. s. of Njal of Njal's Saga fame. On voyage abroad with bro. *Grim they were attacked and hard pressed in the Minches by a larger fleet of viking raiders when *Kari Solmundsson, one of Earl *Sigurd II's retainers returning to Orkney from the Hebrides, came to their assistance dispersing the vikings. He then invited the bros. to Orkney where they were well received by Sigurd and joined his hird in Orkney, fighting with him against the Scots. 38.

Henderson, William - d.1592. Churchman and lawyer. Dingwall Pursuivant, Treasurer of Orkney, Vicar of North Ronaldsay. Came to Orkney c1563 with *Patrick Bellenden as factor for Orkney lands of Bellenden's bro. John, Justice Clerk of Scotland. Associated with and from time to time served Earl *Robert Stewart who granted him tack of land in North Ronaldsay. Was also presented to parsonage of Stronsay 1578. Was on Commission 1577 to hear Shetland complaints against Lawrence Bruce of Cultmalindie.   12.

Henry I, - Bishop of Orkney - d.c1269. Consecrated in Norway 1248. After disastrous battle of Largs 1263 *Hakon IV Hakonsson took up winter quarters in the Bishop's Kirkwall Palace where he died at Yuletide with Bishop Henry present. After the king's death he headed an unsuccessful peace mission to Alexander of Scotland.   1,21.

Henry II - Bishop of Orkney 1394 probably succeeding *Bishop William. 21.

Hepburn, James - b.c1535 d.1578 Denmark, Earl of Bothwell - Protestant but supported Catholic Mary of Guise. Involved in murder of Darnley, husband of Mary Queen of Scots and having divorced his first wife married the Queen himself 1567 being created 'Duke' of Orkney by her. After Mary was deposed by the Scottish nobles following battle of Carberry he fled north hoping for sanctuary in his Orkney 'Dukedom' but being denied refuge by *Gilbert Balfour went on to Shetland where he was also refused shelter. Although pursued by four warships, in one of which was *Bishop Adam Bothwell, he escaped to Norway where he fell into the clutches of the kinsmen of Anna Throndsen, a Danish noblewoman whom he had seduced, taken to Denmark and imprisoned for the rest of his life.   2,12,44.

Herbjorg - Grt grd dau. of Earl *Paul I; m. *Kolbein Hruga c1142; mother of *Bishop Bjarni.   1,3.

Hewison, Capt. William - b.1744 Westray d.c1797 probably France; m. Ann Balfour 1769. Skipper and sometimes part-owner of sloops and cargo vessels operating out of Orkney for merchant firm of *William Watt Jnr & Company, trading to Scandinavian, Baltic and British ports often carrying cargoes of kelp to Tyne. Was master of *Peggy and Isabella*, *Castle Carey* among others. Occasionally engaged in smuggling runs.

His fate is uncertain as when homeward-bound, 1797, presumably in the English Channel his brig, *Pomona*, owned by *Thomas Balfour, was captured by a French privateer, taken to Dieppe where he and his crew were imprisoned and never heard of again.   48,59.

Hlodver Sigurdsson (Hundi) - s. of *Earl Sigurd II The Stout. Taken hostage by *King Olaf Trygvasson at Osmondwall 995 as guarantee that his father would adhere to his forced conversion to Christianity imposed by Olaf. Died in Norway.   1,3.

Hlodver Thorfinnsson - Earl of Orkney for some years between 976-c991. 4th s. of Earl *Thorfinn I Skullsplitter and *Grelod, dau. of *Dungad of Caithness; m. *Eithne, dau. of King Kjarval of Ireland. Father of Earl *Sigurd II The Stout.   1,2,3,35(7).

Holdbodi of Tiree - Hebridean chieftain, said to have been one of leading men with *St Magnus and witness of his martyrdom in Egilsay 1117. May have been the Holdbodi Hundison of Tiree with whom *Sweyn Asleifsson took refuge after killing *Sweyn Breastrope at Yule feast in Orphir 1135.   1,3,35(7).

Honyman, Bishop Andrew - b.1619 St Andrews, Fife d.1676 Kirkwall. m. (1) Euphemia, dau. of Rev. Samuel Cunninghame of Ferry-Port-on-Craig (2) Mary Stewart, dau. of Sir James Stewart and lady of Graemsay in her own right; his son *Robert Honyman inherited Graemsay. Consecrated Bishop of Orkney 1664; arrived Orkney 1665.

Had been wounded in assassination attempt on life of Archbishop of St Andrews in Edinburgh when he intercepted bullets fired by an anti-Episcopalian zealot. Poisoning from the bullets led to his early death. Made last appearance in Scottish Parliament 1669.

Was in Kirkwall when spire of St Magnus Cathedral destroyed by lightning 1671. Saved the bells and was instrumental in ordering their repair and restoration. Organised first Register of Deaths in Orkney. 'Much loved and respected by all classes' (Wallace).   4,21,69.

Honyman, Robert, b.1676 d.1737, 1st of Graemsay - s. of *Bishop Honyman and 2nd wife Mary Stewart who had inherited Stewart estates including Graemsay; m. Catherine Graham, dau. of *Harie Graham of Breckness.

Stewart and Sheriff Depute of Orkney 1725. Farmed bishopric estate 1722-26 and had claim on the Bellenden Stenness estate and parts of the Moodie lands in Walls. His mansion, Hall of Clestrain, Orphir, plundered by pirate *Gow 1725.

Was accompanying *Capt. Moodie snr on his way to an official meeting in St Magnus Cathedral when Moodie was shot by the Steuart of Burray faction on Broad Street and later died 1725. Honyman prepared report to the Magistrates on the murder but did not pursue the matter further. Moodie's widow, *Christiana Crawford, formerly married to *Bellenden of Stenness, had Honyman charged with being an accomplice of the murderers and to having failed to arrest them. He was detained in Edinburgh Tolbooth but was acquitted at the subsequent trial.   11.

Honyman, Sir William, b.1756 d.1825, Lord Armadale - Court of Session Judge; grt grd s. of *Robert Honyman 1st of Graemsay; m. dau. of Lord Braxfield. Prominent lawyer and landowner whose Orkney estate, including Graemsay, was second largest after the Earldom. On appointment as Judge assumed title of Lord Armadale. A shrewd businessman he was also a Director of the Bank of Scotland and was first Orkney laird to divide the commonty in his Stenness estate 1802-17.   2.

Hossack, Buckham Hugh - b.1832 Stronsay d.1902 Kirkwall; s. of Hugh Hossack, Hunton, Stronsay; m. Sibla Monteith.
     Educ. Kirkwall, Edinburgh. Schoolteacher in Edinburgh until he retired, returned to Orkney, built Craigiefield House near Kirkwall, and after prodigious research produced the outstanding history of the burgh, 'Kirkwall in the Orkneys' published 1900 with its detailed house by house account of the town's development and personalities through the centuries. Hon. Sheriff, JP and member of Orkney County Council.   4,46.

Hrafn the Red - Follower of Earl *Sigurd II. Refused to carry the raven banner of ill-omen at battle of Clontarf 1014.   1,2.

Hutton, Thomas - factor Earldom estate 1825-1845.   2.

Hvarflod - dau. of arch-rebel Malcolm MacHeth who had claims on the earldom of Ross; 2nd wife of Earl *Harald II Maddadsson m. c1170. The marriage allied Harald to the *MacWilliam pretenders to the Scottish throne. This brought him into conflict with King William the Lion and ultimately led to the imposition of Scottish rule over Caithness.   1,2,3,35(7).

I

Ingarth - m. St *Magnus. '. . . of the most noble family in Scotland.' Said to be buried in Egilsay.   3,20(6).

Ingibjorg - Dau. of Norwegian nobleman *Finn Arnisson; m. Earl *Thorfinn II; mother of Earls *Paul I and *Erlend II and perhaps ancestor of the *MacWilliam claimants to the Scottish throne. However, it has been suggested that there were two Ingibjorgs, the first who married Thorfinn, and a dau. of the same name who married Malcolm Canmore, King of Scotland.   1,2,3,35(7),76.

Ingigerd - sister of *Sweyn Asleifsson; m. *Thorbjorn Klerk.   1,3,35(7).

Ingigerd - dau. of Manx chieftain Thorkell, kinswoman of *Erlend II; 2nd wife of *Sweyn Asleifsson.   1,3.

Ingigerd - dau. of Hakon the Elder of Paplay; 2nd wife of *Thorbjorn Klerk he having divorced his 1st wife, also *Ingigerd, *Sweyn Asleifsson's sister, after he had fallen out with her brother.   3.

Ingirid - dau. of Earl (St) *Rognvald; m. Sutherland chieftain Erik Stagbrell; mother of *Harald Ungi who claimed unsuccessfully his grd father's share of Earldom.   1,2,3,35(7).

Inglis, Thomas - factor of Bishopric estate for *Bishop Andrew Pictoris during 15th century.   2.

Irving, Oliver - Servant of *Alexander Steuart, bro. of Jacobite *Sir James Steuart of Burray. Fired the shot on Broad Street, Kirkwall which killed *Captain James Moodie snr 1725. Escaped with Alex Steuart after the murder and never returned to Orkney. Had been one of the party with Alex Steuart which trespassed on Moodie's land in Walls earlier in 1725 in pursuit of game and was intercepted by the Moodies who, it is alleged, had them flogged with tangles from the shore.   11.

Irving, Washington - 1783-1859. American author ('Rip Van Winkle', 'Legend of Sleepy Hollow', 'The Alhambra' etc); born New York of Orcadian and Devonian parents. Father came from Quholm, Shapinsay.
     Paid one visit to Orkney including Shapinsay where he met *Col.

David Balfour who presented him with documents referring to his
family.   21.

Isabella - dau. of *Malise, Earl of Strathearn and Orkney by 2nd marriage;
m. *Sir William Sinclair of Roslin; mother of Earl *Henry I Sinclair, first
of the Strathearn line of Orkney Earls. Returned to Orkney in her old
age and, having outlived her sisters who died without issue, inherited
all the divided Strathearn properties including Orkney, except
*Alexander of Ard's portion, which she passed to her grd son Earl
*Henry II Sinclair.   1,2.

Isbister, James - First civilian air-raid casualty in Great Britain during
World War II. Killed, aged 27, at his home near Brig o' Waithe, Stenness
during attack on Scapa Flow by German bombers March 1940.   26.

Isbister, Joseph - d.1771 Canada. Son of Stromness merchant. Joined
Hudson's Bay Company as sailor 1726. Appointed Chief Factor of
Albany Fort 1740. Introduced the York boat based on Orkney yole
design to the Canadian fur trade. Expanded Company's influence far
inland and eventually became independent fur-trader himself in
competition with his old Company.   2, *The New Orkney Book.*

J

Jakobsen, Dr. Jakob - b.1864 Faroe d.1918 Copenhagen. Faroese
philologist who made study of Orkney/Shetland dialects and place-
names especially their relation to the Norn language still spoken in the
18th/19th centuries. Visited Orkney 4 times 1909,1910,1912,1915
meeting and discussing his studies with *Dr. Hugh Marwick who was
working in the same field.
    Published a number of volumes on Shetland dialect and several
papers on related matter. He intended producing similar volumes on
the old Orkney tongue but died before it was completed although his
copious notes on the subject are preserved in Torshavn.   82.

James III - b.1452 d.1488. King of Scots 1460-1488. m. *Margaret, dau. of
*Christian I of Denmark who pledged his Orkney rights and
possessions in part payment of her dowry 1468 and Shetland was
pledged a year later for the remainder of the dowry. The pledges

were never redeemed. Granted Kirkwall its first Royal Charter in 1486. 1,2,10,22,28,75,96.

James V - b.1512 d.1542; King of Scots 1513-1542; m. (1) *Madeleine de Valois (2) *Mary of Guise; father of *Mary Queen of Scots and, by *Euphemia Elphinstone, dau. of Lord Elphinstone, fathered illegitimate son *Robert Stewart who became Earl of Orkney.

Authorised invasion of Orkney by *George Sinclair Earl of Caithness to put down rebellion instigated by Sinclair faction and led by *James Sinclair of Brecks which ended in rout of the invaders at battle of Summerdale 1529 in which the Earl was killed. Later 1535 he not only pardoned James Sinclair but knighted him.

Visited Orkney 1540 accompanied by *Oliver Sinclair of Pitcairns and Cardinal Beaton with fleet of 17 ships on voyage round Scotland with its main aim to restrict activities and ambitions of chieftains in Hebrides and western Scotland. 'Nobly entertained' in Kirkwall by Bishop *Robert Maxwell during his visit.

Dubious legend has it that this was his second visit to Orkney, the first having been incognito c1530 when he was said to have worked herding geese on the farm of Stove in the West Mainland conferring a sort of honorary knighthood on the Kirkness family who had befriended him before his cover was blown. There is another and equally doubtful story that he held a session of parliament in Kirkwall just off the present Albert Street. 2,75,96.

James, Richard - b.1592 Isle of Wight. Educ. Newport Grammar School and Oxford University. Wrote first recorded English 'Description' of Orkney. Travelled in Britain, Greenland and Russia. 14.

Jellicoe, Admiral Sir (later Earl) John - b.1859 d.1935. Took over as Commander-in-Chief Grand Fleet in Scapa Flow just before outbreak of World War I June 1914 until November 1916 when he became First Sea Lord. He built up the woefully inadequate defences of the Flow from which the Navy maintained its blockade of Germany throughout the war and from where he sailed in his flagship HMS *Iron Duke* to engage the German High Seas Fleet at Jutland May 1916. Promoted Admiral of the Fleet 1919 and became Governor General of New Zealand after the war.

The troop train running nightly between Euston, London, and Thurso, Caithness, for embarkation of servicemen at Scrabster for ships in the Flow and army units on the defences was known as 'The Jellicoe' in both World Wars. 26,44,95.

Jofreyer - Bishop of Orkney c1224-c1247 probably succeeding *Bishop Bjarni. Building of St Magnus Cathedral continued during his

episcopate including some of its best masonwork. A sick man he was
paralysed during his later years.   21.

John I Haraldsson - Earl of Orkney 1206-30. 3rd s. of Earl Harald II
   Maddadsson. Ruled Earldom jointly with bro. *David who died 1214
   after which he ruled alone pledging allegiance and loyalty to King of
   Norway at whose Court he was a frequent visitor.
      Implicated in murder of Bishop Adam of Caithness though played
   no active part in the actual killing but it earned him the anger of
   Scottish King Alexander who deprived him of some of his estates on
   mainland Scotland. Was in competition for the Orkney Earldom with
   *Snaekoll Gunnisson, grt grd s. of Earl *Rognvald II. Snaekoll and his
   followers killed John during a drunken brawl in Thurso, then took
   refuge in Cubbie Roo's Castle in Wyre where they were ineffectually
   besieged by John's followers.   1,35(7).

John II Magnusson - Earl of Orkney 1284-c1301. s. of *Magnus II; bro. of
   Magnus IV. Was betrothed 1300 to Ingibjorg the 2-year-old dau. of Erik of
   Norway and his 2nd wife, Isabella, sister of *Robert the Bruce. 2,35(7).

John the Wode - Probably the Irish name for *Sweyn Asleifsson (Wode =
   mad).   2.

Johnston, Alfred Wintle, FSA (Scot) - b.1859 Orphir d.1947 Welwyn
   Garden City; s. of James Johnston; m. Amy Leslie 1905. Founder of
   Viking Club now the Viking Society for Northern Research.
      Educ. privately Orkney and Edinburgh, Dollar Academy,
   Edinburgh College of Art, some training in law before apprenticeship
   to Edinburgh firm of architects. Became increasingly interested in
   Norse saga studies and folklore and formed Udal League with view to
   having udal rights restored to Orkney and Shetland. Founded Viking
   Club 1892 and was Librarian and chairman of its Council 1902. The
   Club published its 'Saga Book' and 'Old Lore Miscellany' to which he
   contributed papers throughout his life such as the series regarding the
   mixed blood ties of the Norsemen entitled 'Orkney and Shetland Folk'.
      In 1899 carried out excavations at the Round Church and Bu in
   Orphir. Was awarded Civil List Pension by George V and Order of St
   Olav 1st Class by Norway and Order of the Falcon by Iceland.
                                            Saga Book Viking Society Vol III.

Johnston, Col. Henry Halcro, CB, CBE, DL, DSc, MD, CM, FRSE, FSL,
   RAMC - b.1856 Orkney d.1939 Kirkwall. Army doctor, botanist; s. of
   James Johnston of Coubister.
      Educ. Dollar Academy, Edinburgh Collegiate School, Edinburgh
   University. Joined Army Medical Department (later Royal Army

Medical Corps) 1881 and saw active service in Sudan, India (North West Frontier), South Africa (Boer War 1899-1902), Singapore, Gibraltar, being thrice mentioned in dispatches. Retired 1913 but recalled during World War I to become Administrator of all Military, General and Territorial Hospitals in Glasgow Area Scottish Command and later Assistant Director Medical Services Northern Command in York.

An enthusiastic student of plant-life he put together an outstanding collection of some 4,000 botanical specimens to be found in Orkney and Shetland which became property of Stromness Museum in which he was keenly interested being President of the Orkney Natural History Society for several years. After his death this herbarium was transferred to the Royal Botanic Gardens, Edinburgh. The transfer was supervised by another Orkney botanist *James Sinclair, one of Johnston's proteges, then on the Botanic Gardens staff just after World War II. Johnston's notes and observations on the herbarium, however, were retained in Orkney. He also wrote up the flora and fauna of Orkney, Shetland and Mauritius. Played rugby for Scotland against England and Ireland in 1877.   49, Orc 26/10/39, OH 24/10/39.

Johnston, Joshua - b.1719 Stromness d.1794 Stromness; s. of John Johnston, merchant, Stromness; m. Margaret Halcro of Coubister 1749. Indentured to *John Riddoch, Stewart Clerk of Orkney; qualified Edinburgh as Notary Public and Writer to the Signet. Practised as solicitor Stromness acting as the burgh's agent in the litigation against Kirkwall for freedom to carry on trade without interference from restrictions imposed by the Royal Burgh, the cause instigated by his father and brought to a successful conclusion by *Alexander Graham. At one time the family owned a third of Stromness and lands in various parts of Orkney which Joshua sold.   35(8).

Johnston, Robert Thomson (Spike) - b.1913 Buckie d.1987 Aberdeen. Newspaperman, cartoonist, novelist; s. of family owning *Banffshire Journal* where he learned his craft. Reporter on *Orkney Herald* for 6 years before World War II. Served in RAF in India rejoining the *Herald* for 7 years after the war as reporter, columnist, cartoonist then becoming sub-editor with Aberdeen *Press & Journal*. Service in India provided him with material for his first novel, 'Squadron Will Move', under pen-name R. A. Forsyth (RAF).

In Orkney best remembered for his Onlooker column in the *Orkney Herald* featuring his fictitious Orkney parish of Stenwick with its larger-than-life characters later collected in the 'Stenwick Annual' and 'Orcadian Nights', and his penetrating weekly cartoons satirising Orkney life in a kindly way drawn by 'Spike' the name by which he became known throughout the islands. A keen sportsman he played football and especially cricket as well as writing about them.   Orc 17/1/87.

Jomar - Kinsman of Earl *Rognvald II. Accompanied him and *Harald II on hunting expedition to Caithness 1158 when Rognvald was killed by *Thorbjorn Klerk. He wounded Thorbjorn in the attack on the Earl and killed him in the ensuing running fight.   3,35(7).

Jon Wing of the Uplands - Chieftain in Hoy early 12th century; bro. of Richard of Brecks in Stronsay; kinsman of *Sweyn Asleifsson with whom attacked and burned *Thorkel Flettir and 9 men in the house on Stronsay previously held by Sweyn's bro, *Valthjof but given to Thorkel by *Paul II after the murder of *Sweyn Breastrope by Sweyn Asleifsson at the Orphir Yuletide feast 1136.   3,35(7).

K

Ka, James - Chaplain of St Magnus Cathedral c1550. Accused of heresy. May have been the James Skea who was forced to escape to England because of his heretical views.   2.

Kaa, James - merchant Burgess of Kirkwall, m. Margaret Richan 1684.   4.

Kaa, John - merchant Burgess of Kirkwall, m. Agnes Louttit 1655.   4.

Kalf Arnisson - Norwegian chieftain of noble family. His niece, *Ingibjorg, dau. of his bro. *Finn, m. Earl *Thorfinn II. Norwegian King (St) *Olaf made him a 'great chief' but they fell out and Kalf went to England where King Knut promised him an earldom for support against Olaf. Returning to Norway he led the rebel nobles against Olaf culminating in battle of Stikkelstad 1030 where he may well have struck the actual blow that killed Olaf. After the battle went to Russia where he had a change of mind and heart about Olaf and returned to Norway in order to put Olaf's son Magnus on the throne.
    The friendship did not last and Kalf was again exiled coming to live with his niece and her husband Thorfinn II in Orkney along with his hird and 6 ships. But Earl *Rognvald I Brusisson with whom he had been associated in Russia in spite of their having been on opposite sides at Stikkelstad was in dispute with Thorfinn over his share of the Orkney Earldom. At first Kalf stood aloof from the dispute between the two Earls and hung back even at the sea-battle in the Pentland Firth 1046 but finally threw in his lot, and his ships, with Thorfinn. As

a result Rognvald was defeated after which Thorfinn made Kalf his 'viceroy' in the Western Isles.

He also went a-viking for a time and was chief of Edward the Confessor's bodyguard in England for a period. But on the promise by *Harald Hardrada, now King of Norway, to return his forfeited Norwegian estates to him he returned home to them taking an oath of allegiance to Harald. He was killed leading troops for Harald in an expedition against Sweyn of Denmark.   1,2,3,30,76.

Kalf Skurfia (Scurvy) - Danish viking who set himself up as lord of Orkney but was killed by *Torf-Einar when he became Earl c894.   1,2,3.

Kali Kolsson - see Rognvald II.

Kari Solmundarsson - Icelandic chieftain c976-990; member of Earl *Sigurd II's hird. Returning to Orkney from the Hebrides where he had been collecting tribute for Sigurd from Earl *Gilli he found fellow Icelanders *Helgi and Grim Njalsson under attack in the Minch by viking ships. He went to their assistance and together they routed the vikings.

He took the 2 bros. to Orkney where they, too, joined Sigurd's hird and not only warned him of an impending Scots attack but fought with him in the ensuing battle which he won.

Kari later went to Norway and again had to rescue the same 2 bros, this time from imprisonment and death after which he returned to Iceland and married their sister, Helga, dau. of Njal Thorgeirsson.

According to Njal's Saga, when his father-in-law, Njal, died in the burning of Bergthorsknoll, Kari escaped and vowed unrelenting vengeance on the Burners, the Sigfusson clan. While spending the winter in Fair Isle he paid a secret visit to Orkney and overheard one of Njal's killers, *Gunnar Lambasson, guest at a Yuletide feast hosted by Sigurd II, giving a very biassed account of the 'Burning'. Njal's Saga relates that, incensed by what he overheard, Kari burst into the hall beheading Gunnar with one sweep of his sword - the severed head rolling across the table in front of Sigurd and his guests, among them the Irish King Sygtrygg Silkbeard. He then escaped into the winter darkness of a northern night.

Some of the story must be treated with caution as he is known only through references in Njal's Saga which contains large elements of imaginative reconstruction rather than straight history.   38.

Karl Hundison, King of Scots - Probable nick-name of shadowy Celtic leader defeated by Earl *Thorfinn II in sea-battle off Deerness c1029 and again at Tarbatness c1030. Variously suggested by historians as an unrecorded King of Scotland, King Duncan, King Macbeth and several others but recently more plausibly identified as possibly Gillicomgain, a mormaer (petty king) of Moray, a family with which the Orkney Earls had long been at odds. Gillicomgain was bro. of Malcolm, King of Scots and cousin of Macbeth, King of Scots 1032-57.   2,76.

Katherine - wife of Earl *Magnus V who survived him as Dowager Countess of Orkney 1329.   1,2.

Keith, Sheriff David Barrogill, MC, MA, LLB - b.1892 Thurso d.1980 Thurso. Lawyer, artist. Educ. Miller Academy, Thurso, Edinburgh University, Edinburgh College of Art. Graduated MA 1911, LLB 1918 between which dates served in family law firm of solicitors in Thurso before being commissioned in Cameronians during World War I winning Military Cross at battle of the Somme 1916. Also served in Judge Advocate General's Department.
      Returning to family firm after the war was factor for a number of big estates in Caithness covering over 250,000 acres establishing himself as a leading expert on Scottish land law. During World War II served on Scapa Flow defences (OSDeF) again in Judge Advocate General's department spending 5 years in Orkney to which he returned 1946 as Sheriff Substitute for the next 22 years and in his spare time was prolific painter of the Orkney scene.   Orc 3/1/80.

Kemp, Major General Geoffrey MC, RA - b.1891. Served in field artillery, wounded and won Military Cross World War I. Instructor Gunnery, Army School of Artillery between the wars. As Brigadier posted Orkney September 1939 on outbreak of World War II to command and expand Orkney and Shetland Defence Force (OSDeF) mainly concerned with air and coast defence of Navy's Home Fleet Base in Scapa Flow. On assuming command had only 8 Heavy Anti Aircraft, 3 Light Anti Aircraft and 5 coast defence guns at his disposal with a few auxiliary troops, the total army garrison numbering not much over 1,000 men. By the time he left the command with the rank of Major General 1943 these figures had risen to 88 HAA, 36 LAA and 37 coast defence guns served by some 30,000 land-based troops making Scapa Flow one of the Allies most strongly defended naval anchorages. 26,95.

Kemp, Robert - b.1908 Longhope d.1967 Edinburgh. Dramatist, journalist, broadcaster; father was minister in Longhope. Educ. Robert Gordon College, Aberdeen and Aberdeen University. Joined editorial staff of *Manchester Guardian* and then BBC Scotland in which capacity he visited Orkney on several occasions to make programmes. Prolific playwright mainly on Scottish themes such as 'The Other Dear Charmer' and was widely acclaimed for his adaptation of Sir David Lindsay's 'Ane Satyre of the Thrie Estatis' 1640 for the Edinburgh Festival of 1948.   *Scotsman* Nov. 1867.

Kent, Tom - b.1863 Firth d.1936 Kirkwall - Photographer. Learned his craft while working in Chicago drug-store and returned to Orkney 1898 to become professional photographer with a shop on Broad Street, Kirkwall selling photographic materials, stationery and books. With an artist's eye for composition he became renowned for his land and seascapes of Orkney and his records of everyday life and people in the islands establishing a unique visual archive of Orkney in the early 20th century. *Shoal and Sheaf* p. 182.

Ketil Flatnose - Norwegian chieftain, who emigrated to north of Scotland 890 after *Harald Fairhair's unification of Norway and became ruler of the Hebrides. Father of *Aud the Deep-minded; grd father of *Thorstein the Red. *Grelod, wife of Earl *Thorfinn I Skullsplitter was his grt grt grd dau. 2,3,71,76.

Kinclaven, Lord - see Stewart, John, Master of Orkney.

King, David - one of Earl Patrick Stewart's Sheriffs Depute 1610. 2.

Kinnoull, Earls of - see Hay.

Kirkness, David - b.1854 Westray d.1936 Kirkwall. Maker of Orkney straw-backed chairs, joiner; after attending school in Westray served apprenticeship as joiner in Kirkwall; started on own account early 1880s developing his skill as master maker of Orkney straw-backed chairs and 'creepies'. In addition to the wooden framework he made the actual straw seats himself as they needed a special 'knack', but 'imported' the straw backs from skilled makers in Westray, Papay and Deerness. During his lifetime he made over 14,000 of them which were sent all over the world several being acquired by the Royal family. OH 7/10/36.

Kirkpatrick, Daniel - Coxswain of Longhope Lifeboat *TGB*. Winner of 3 Silver Medals for bravery and seamanship in rescue operations around Orkney. Lost along with his 7-man crew, including his 2 sons, Daniel and John, known as Ray and Jack, on 17 March 1969 when *TGB* capsized while going to the assistance of small cargo ship *Irene* which had lost power in the eastern Pentland Firth during extreme storm conditions. *Irene* ran ashore on the east side of South Ronaldsay without loss of life. Orc 20/3/69.

Kitchener, Field Marshal Earl Herbert - b.1850 Ireland d.1916 off Marwick Head, Orkney. Commissioned in Royal Engineers. Saw service in Middle East, Sudan (battle of Omdurman 1898), C-in-C South Africa 1900 (Boer War), C-in-C India, Secretary for War 1914. Having embarked in Scapa Flow was lost off Marwick Head 5 June

1916 when cruiser *Hampshire*, in which he was travelling with his staff to Russia, was sunk by German mine. The Kitchener memorial tower and plaque erected by local public subscription on Marwick Head 1926 was unveiled by General Lord Horne.   26,44,62.

Knightson, Capt. Thomas - Pirate from Pittenweem, Fife, in service of Earls *Robert and *Patrick Stewart 1583-93. Brought captured ships in to Kirkwall where their cargoes were seized by the Earls. Was Stewart for Patrick and Provost of Kirkwall 1619-21.   2.

Kol Kalisson - c1100. Lendirman of Agder, Norway. m. Gunnhild, sister of Earl (St) *Magnus; father of *Kali Kolsson Earl (St) *Rognvald II. Supervised design and building of St Magnus Cathedral 1137 in fulfilment of vow by his son Rognvald to erect such a minster, 'the finest in the north', should he be successful in asserting his legitimate claim to half the Orkney Earldom currently held by Earl *Paul II who rejected the claim. Kol negotiated on his son's behalf but with Paul's continued opposition they mounted two expeditions to Orkney adding force to persuasion in pursuit of their claim. The second attempt succeeded 1136 and work began on the Cathedral the following year 1137.   1,2,3,35(7).

Kolbein Hruga (Cubbie Roo) - Norwegian chieftain who settled in Orkney c1142; m. Herbjorg, grt grd dau. of Earl *Paul I; father of Kolbein the Elder, *Bishop Bjarni the Skald, Sumerledi, Aslak and Frida who m. *Sweyn Asleifsson's son, Andrew. Was foster-father to *Sweyn's son Olaf. Built castle in Wyre, his main seat. 'Most outstanding of men' (OS).

Hruga = heap in Old Norse so presumably a large man giving rise to folklore legend of the giant Cubbie Roo who was supposed to hurl boulders from island to island at his enemies; some of these missiles landing in the sea became holms or skerries.   1,2,3.

Kugi of Rapness - Chieftain warden of Westray. Submitted to Earl *Rognvald II on his 2nd and successful attempt to claim his share of Earldom 1136. 'A wise man and wealthy' (OS).   1,3,35(7).

L

Laing (Meason), Gilbert, b.1769 Kirkwall d.1832 Rome, of Rothiesholm - s. of *Robert Laing of Strynzie and Barbara Blaw; bro. of *Malcolm and *Samuel Laing; m. Mary Wemys, Fife 1811.

Edinburgh merchant 1791-1808; represented Kirkwall at annual Convention of Royal Burghs. Inherited fortune and property. including Wanlockhead Lead Mines in Dumfriesshire, Scotland's highest village, from his wealthy Orcadian patron Gilbert Meason of Moredon provided he assumed name of Meason 1808. Passed management of the mines to bro. Samuel 1810 and mortified £1,000 for upkeep of St Magnus Cathedral. Built and furnished castellated mansion at Lindertis. Founder member of Bannantyne Club 1823. Politically active Whig.

Collector of paintings including works by Breughel, Ruysdael and Italian masters publishing work on 'Landscape Architecture of the Great Painters' 1826 and 1828 based on years spent visiting galleries in Italy where he met *Sir Walter Scott in Naples in winter 1831-2.   4,90.

Laing, Malcolm - b.1762 Kirkwall d.1818 Kirkwall. Advocate, historian; eldest s. of *Robert Laing of Strynzie and Barbara Blaw; bro. of *Gilbert and *Samuel Laing. Educ. Kirkwall Grammar School, Edinburgh University.

Called to Scottish Bar 1785 but preferred academic career. Represented Kirkwall at General Assemblies of Church of Scotland 1789-1805; Convener of Orkney Commissioners of Supply (forerunner of County Council) 1805; MP for Orkney and Shetland 1807-12. Author of 'History of Scotland' 1802.

Built Papdale House near Kirkwall on land bought for him by his father, Robert, where he entertained an old acquaintance from his legal days, *Sir Walter Scott 1814. Introduced Merino-Cheviot sheep on his farm of Stove in Sanday.   4,44,90.

Laing, Robert - b.1722 d.1803, of Strynzie - A leading 18th century Orkney merchant; m. Barbara Blaw by whom had family of at least 16 including *Gilbert, *Malcolm and *Samuel. Four others died within a twelve-month period 1794-5 - 2 sons in Jamaica of yellow fever, 2 daughters of tuberculosis at home.

Dean of Guild 1783, Provost of Kirkwall 1788-92. Bought land at Papdale for son Malcolm 1783. Also bought North Isles estates of the *Fea family of Clestran including Stove in Sanday c1770.   4,20(11),70,90.

Laing, Samuel, b.1780 Kirkwall d.1868 Edinburgh, of Papdale - Norse
scholar, soldier, entrepreneur, agricultural improver, linguist, author,
translator of 'Heimskringla'; youngest s. of *Robert Laing of Strynzie
and Margaret Blaw; bro. of *Gilbert and *Malcolm; m. Agnes Kelly,
1809, Provost of Kirkwall 1820-34.

Educ. Kirkwall Grammar School and in an Edinburgh 'counting
house'. Went to Kiel to learn German and later from a London
counting house became secretary to a merchant in Holland and British
Consul in Rotterdam, rapidly learning Dutch. When hostilities with
Napoleonic France resumed 1803 after failure of the abortive Treaty of
Amiens Laing risked his life helping 3 British naval officers escape
from Holland. Then skating back to Rotterdam on the frozen canals
reached England himself on a neutral ship bringing with him valuable
intelligence regarding build-up of French-led invasion forces in Dutch
ports.

Commissioned in Royal Staff Corps served on construction of the
Royal Military Canal cut to isolate south coast beaches from interior in
event of invasion. After short spell in London, posted to Gibraltar then
Portugal. Took part in early battles of Peninsular War 1808 surviving
Sir John Moore's historic and hazardous retreat to Corunna and the
subsequent battle 1809.

Returned to UK, left the army, settled in Edinburgh and succeeded
bro. *Gilbert as manager of Wanlockhead Lead Mines. Represented
Kirkwall at annual Convention of Royal Burghs 1810-17. Merchant in
Edinburgh 1812 until, after heavy financial losses in post-war
depression after Waterloo, came back to Orkney and started Stronsay
herring fishery 1816. Settled at Papdale succeeding bro. *Malcolm in
estate 1818.

Played leading role in Orkney affairs both as agricultural improver
and as Provost of Kirkwall but collapse of the kelp trade and cost of his
many improvement schemes, including Kirkwall Grammar School
and Stronsay pier and fisheries, again ruined him financially. He still,
however, hoped to be MP for the constituency after the Reform Act
1832. Very popular in Orkney itself he did, in fact, top the poll 1833 but
the Shetland vote tipped the balance in favour of his opponent,
*George Traill of Rattar and Hobbister, the announcement of which
caused a riot in Kirkwall during which *John Traill Urquhart received
fatal injuries.

Forced by mounting debts to leave UK, his bankrupt estate was left
in the hands of trustees while he retired to Levanger near Trondheim
in Norway for 2 years, apparently a broken man. But with his talents,
resilient character and restless energy he soon learned Norwegian and
wrote 'Journal of a Residence in Norway, during the Years
1834,1835,1836'.

On the death of his wealthy son-in-law, Henry Baxter 1837, Laing's dau, was left a rich widow providing him with a comfortable home although much of his time was spent travelling round Europe and writing innumerable books. His great literary achievement, however, was yet to come with the translation of *Snorri Sturlusson's 'Heimskringla' the saga history of the kings of Norway in 1844. This first complete translation of Icelandic history and literature direct from the original language (Sir Walter Scott had previously produced an 'abstract' from a Latin version) into English caused quite a literary sensation and remains in print to this day.   44,90.

Laing, Samuel, b.1812 d.1897, of Crook - s. of *Samuel Laing of Papdale. Financier, fiscal adviser to Government, MP. Educ. St John's College, Cambridge graduating 1832; m. Mary, dau. of Capt. Cowan RN.

Chairman, London Brighton & South Coast Railway Co. and of Sydenham Crystal Palace Co. 1848-54. Secretary to the Treasury 1859-60 then went to India as Finance Minister. Compiled report for Government on fiscal situation in India and published account of his visit, 'Mission to India' 1864. MP for Northern Burghs (including Kirkwall) 1852-57, 1859-60, 1865-68; MP for Orkney and Shetland 1873-85.   4, *Who's Who of British MPs* Vol I 1976.

Laughton, Willie - see Skatehorn.

Law, Bishop James - d.1632 Glasgow; s. of a Fife laird. Appointed Bishop of Orkney 1605/6 charged with task of restoring order in the diocese which for two generations had been under malign control of the Stewart Earls, *Robert and his son, *Patrick who, when Law arrived on the scene was exercising despotic, even tyrannical, rule over the Earldom but was virtually bankrupt. Determined to oust Patrick from the Bishopric estate Law first obtained occupation of the Earl's Palace in Kirkwall as his official residence and then re-payment of some Bishopric rents.

In 1608 he informed James VI & I of the Orcadians' complaints regarding Patrick's oppressive rule in the islands. With *Sir John Arnot to whom Patrick, now imprisoned in the south, was deeply in debt, he was appointed Commissioner with powers of Sheriff to investigate Patrick's misdeeds. He also organised famine relief for the islands and was described, according to Craven, as 'Saviour of Orkney'.

When Patrick's illegitimate son *Robert led what amounted to a rebellion in Orkney on his imprisoned father's behalf 1614 Law, along with a force led by George Sinclair, Earl of Caithness, played a prominent part in its suppression. Robert was duly arrested, tried and hanged in Edinburgh 1614.

Law, essentially a political bishop, described as being 'a man of consummate ability, tact and resolution' was appointed Archbishop of

Glasgow in 1615 only days after the surrender of Kirkwall Castle. 'One
of the outstanding churchmen of the century.' - Professor G.
Donaldson.   1,2,4,12,13,21.

Leask, James Thomas Smith - b.1859 Stenness d.1939 Largs. s. of Robert
Leask, Coldomo, Stenness. Educ. Kirkwall Burgh (Grammar) School.
Glasgow solicitor. Secretary of Glasgow Orkney & Shetland
Benevolent Society for 40 years, President of Glasgow Orkney Literary
& Scientific Society. Drawing on his extensive knowlege of Orkney
folklore and legend he was able to produce the authentic and popular
'A Peculiar People and other Orkney Tales'. Orc 5/1/39, OH 11/1/39.

Leitch, Georgina Walter Scarth, DL - d.1975 Kirkwall. Provost of
Kirkwall Town Council. Born and brought up in Edinburgh but with
strong Orkney links; m. Robert Leitch, Kirkwall, 1937.
    Elected Kirkwall Town Council 1945 and with a break of only one
year served on it and Orkney County Council for 30 years becoming
Kirkwall's first woman Provost and incidentally its last Provost of all
when Town Councils disappeared in the re-organisation of local
government 1975. She was also the first woman to be appointed
Deputy Lieutenant of the County and was particularly interested in
health, education and social welfare especially care for the elderly
starting the first 'meals on wheels' for the housebound.   Orc 7/8/75.

Leith, Peter - b.1886 Appiehouse, Stenness d.1958 Appiehouse. Farmer,
antiquarian; authority on Orkney history and lore; regular contributor to
Proceedings of Orkney Antiquarian Society, *The Orcadian*, *The Scotsman*.
Interested in astronomy, photography; supplied 'Scottish National
Dictionary' with details of Orkney dialect words and how they were
used. Wrote Stenness chapter for 3rd Statistical Account.   Orc 10/7/58.

Leonard, James - Lived at Digro, Rousay during latter part of 19th
century. Crofter, stonemason, Free Kirk precentor, chairman of Rousay
crofters. His evidence to the Napier Crofter Commission 1883 was
hostile to the Rousay laird, *General Burroughs who evicted him from
Digro forcing him to leave the island. He was later employed as a
coalman in Oban.   9.

Leslie, Harald Robert, KT, CBE, MBE(Mil), TD, MA, LLB, QC, DL,
b.1905 d.1982 Edinburgh, Lord Birsay - Advocate; s. of Robert Leslie,
Master Mariner, Stromness; m. Robina (Rena) Margaret Marwick
MA, ChB, dau. of *Provost J. G. Marwick, Stromness; Educ. Earlston
Public School, Berwickshire, Glasgow High School, Glasgow
University.
    Called to Scottish Bar 1937; during World War II served in Royal

Scots and HQ 15 (Scots) Division, 8 Corps and 21 Army Group, awarded MBE and mentioned in dispatches; demobbed with rank of Lieut. Col. and resumed legal career; appointed Advocate Depute, Scottish Bar 1947-51; Sheriff Principal Roxburgh, Berwick and Selkirk 1956-61, being particularly proud of the fact that one of his predecessors on the Bench was Sir Walter Scott; Sheriff Principal Caithness, Sutherland, Orkney and Shetland 1961-65 Chairman Scottish Land Court 1965-79 assuming title of Lord Birsay (he owned Queenafiold overlooking Loch of Boardhouse); Knight of the Thistle 1973; Lord High Commissioner to the General Assembly of the Church of Scotland 1965 and 1966.

Chairman Scottish Committee of British Council, Executive Edinburgh Council of Social Service, Cttee on Gen. Medical Services to Highlands and Islands and many other organisations.

Keenly interested in all things Orcadian he spent as much time as he could in the islands. Stood as Labour candidate in 1956 General Election being defeated by *Jo Grimond.

Presided over, and took active part in the 1968 International Historical Conference held in Orkney marking the Quincentenary of the Impignoration whereby Orkney passed from Scandinavian control to the Scottish Crown.   Orc 2/12/82, 49(1981-90).

Lethaby, William Richard - b.1857 d.1931. Architect and designer. Leading figure in Arts and Crafts Movement of late 19th century. Founder Principal of Central School of Arts and Crafts, London 1894 and Professor of Design Royal College of Art closely connected with Morris Movement for Protection of Ancient Buildings.

Designed reconstruction and restoration of Melsetter House and estate buildings, S. Walls 1898, and Rysa Lodge, Hoy, 1904.   72.

Lex - see Costie, Chrissie.

Liddell, Rev. Francis - b.1750 d.1834 Edinburgh. Educ. Edinburgh University; ordained 1776; m. Helen Walls, his housekeeper 1804. Eccentric Minister of Orphir for which parish he compiled the First Statistical Account. Was in constant trouble with Synod and General Assembly on accusations of drunkenness and other irregularities which he vehemently denied but was eventually forced to 'reside anywhere out of the bounds of the Synod of Orkney'. Retired to Edinburgh where he died aged 84.   2,6, *Presbytery Minutes.*

Lifolf - Earl *Hakon's cook who, on his master's orders, became unwilling executioner of St *Magnus on Egilsay 1117 or possibly 1116.   1,3.

Ligonier, Frances - b.1742 d.1813; sister of Earl Ligonier; m. Col. Dr.

*Thomas Balfour of Elwick; mother of *William Balfour 4th of Trenaby and Balfour.
Described as supercilious, ironic with a sharp wit and fond of argument she loved literature especially poetry. Was outraged at her dau., *Mary's elopement and marriage to Rev. Brunton. 17, Orc 23/7/1987.

Lindsay, Alexander - 16th century Scottish seaman, pilot, navigator. Compiled c1540 'A Rutter of the Scottish Seas', a set of sailing instructions and information for mariners, including details of tides, anchorages, headlands and the coastline of Scotland in general from the Humber right round the north, including the Pentland Firth and Scapa Flow, to the Solway. It was almost certainly used by *James V and his fleet of 16 ships during the circumnavigation of Scotland with Cardinal Beaton 1540. Lindsay was in all probability on board the king's ship, *Salamander*, when the fleet dropped anchor in the Flow.
26, *Alexander Lindsay, A Rutter etc* by A. B. Taylor, Royal Maritime Museum.

Lindsay, Thomas, d.c1797, of Caldale - Introduced linen manufacture to Orkney at behest of his uncle, *Andrew Ross, factor of Earldom estate for *Sir Lawrence Dundas. Successful in developing the industry in Orkney during latter part of 18th century.   2.

Lindsay, William - d.1803. Notary Public; Provost of Kirkwall 1784-88; clerk to his uncle *Andrew Ross from whom, with bro. *Thomas, inherited estate of Sound in Shapinsay later selling it to *Thomas Balfour.   4,17.

Linklater, Eric - b.1899 Swansea, South Wales d.1974 Aberdeen. Novelist, playwright, journalist, essayist, poet. s. of Orkney-born Master Mariner Captain Robert Linklater, his mother being dau. of a Swedish sea captain and though born in South Wales always rightly regarded himself as an Orcadian; m. *Marjorie McIntyre, Edinburgh,
Educ. Cardiff, Aberdeen Grammar School and University where he studied medicine before switching to Eng. Lit. and later in life was elected its Rector. Served in army in both World Wars being wounded in France during WWI when infantryman in Black Watch. Commissioned into Royal Engineers in WWII serving on Scapa Flow defences where he started troops newspaper *The Orkney Blast* before moving to Ministry of Information and War Office in Public Relations writing numerous booklets, among them 'Northern Garrisons', 'Defence of Calais', '51st Division'.
Following graduation from Aberdeen after WWI entered journalism as assistant editor of *Times of India* Bombay 1925. Published first novel 'Whitemaa's Saga' 1929 with its mainly Orkney setting.

precursor of many more written throughout his life ('Poet's Pub', 'Private Angelo', 'Juan in China', 'Laxdale Hall', 'The Impregnable Women' etc). Visited USA on Commonwealth Fellowship resulting in his novel 'Juan in America'. Travelled extensively, USA, Far and Middle East, Scandinavia, Italy. Returned after WWII to Merkister, his home on shores of Harray Loch - he was a keen and skilled angler - but later lived at Nigg in Ross-shire. 16.

Linklater, Marjorie - b.1909 Edinburgh d.1997 Orkney; dau. of Ian MacIntyre WS, Edinburgh and Ida Van Der Gucht. Educ. Edinburgh, Dowie House, Berkshire and Royal Academy of Dramatic Art, London making 3 appearances on West End stage. Returning to Scotland m. *Eric Linklater 1933, making their home at Merkister, Harray. Moved with family to Easter Ross 1947 where she served on Ross and Cromarty County Council 1953-69, also on Highlands and Islands Development Board and Scottish Arts Council. Very active in the anti uranium mining campaign in Orkney and elsewhere and in the Stormy Bank Group protesting against nuclear developments at Dounreay. Joined Scottish National Party 1947. Founder chairwoman of Pier Arts Centre, Stromness and the St Magnus Festival in which she inaugurated the Johnsmas Foy. 16,Orc 3/7/97.

Ljot Thorfinnsson - Earl of Orkney for some period prior to 978; 3rd s. of *Thorfinn I Skullsplitter; succeeded his bros. *Arnfinn and *Havard Harvest-Happy as Earl; m. *Ragnhild, dau. of *Eric Bloodaxe 977. She had previously been married to both these bros. in turn before having them killed. He, however, survived the marriage and ruled Earldom successfully but later died from wounds received at battle of Skittenmire in Caithness c978 fighting the Scots and Caithness chieftain, *Skuli, another bro. who had ambitions to succeed to the Orkney Earldom but he was also killed in the battle. 1,2,3,35(7),76.

Login, Sir John Spencer - b.1809 Stromness d.1863, Felixstowe; s. of John Login, shipowner/agent and Margaret Spence, Stromness. Qualified in Medicine, Edinburgh. After brief spell as naval surgeon 1831 entered service of East India Company 1832 serving in Bengal Horse Artillery and was in charge of their medical services during the Afghan war. He was appointed to the C-in-C's staff in the Punjab 1840 and when the Punjab was annexed by Britain he became guardian of Rajah Duleep Singh with whom he maintained a life-long friendship. Knighted in 1854 he retired four years later returning to UK. Went back to India to organise work on the expanding railway system but had to come home again owing to ill health.

Login's Well on the main street in Stromness, which for many decades provided water for the Hudson's Bay Company ships making

their last call before crossing the Atlantic, was on his family's property.
OH 3/11/1863, *Sir John Login and Duleep Singh* - Lady Login 1890.

Low, Rev. George - b.1747 Edzell d.1795 Orkney. Naturalist, Minister of
Birsay; m. Helen Tyrie, dau. of *Rev. James Tyrie, 1774.
    Educ. St Andrews; licensed by Cairston Presbytery 1771; tutor to
family of George Graham, Stromness merchant. Ordained 1774 and
Minister of Birsay and Harray for 21 years. The study and recording in
detail of Orkney's fauna and flora and the islands' early history
became an all-absorbing interest for him. When the naturalist and
explorer, *Sir Joseph Banks, founder of Royal Botanic Gardens at Kew
in London, called in at Orkney when returning from Iceland 1772, Low
showed him and his party Orkney's wild-life and archaeological
treasures and, in fact, carried out some excavations on burial mounds
with them at Bay of Skaill.
    In 1774 at the request of Thomas Pennant, the most distinguished
traveller and writer on natural history subjects of his day who
financed the trip, Low made his celebrated 'Tour' of the South Isles of
Orkney and Shetland in order to supply him with information about
the Northern Isles. Four years later he completed his coverage of the
islands by visiting the North Isles and the Orkney Mainland. His book,
'Tour Thro' Orkney and Schetland' with its detailed descriptions of
what he saw and his comments was not published until 1874 - long
after his death. It is one of the Orkney classics. The second part of the
'Tour' on the North Isles of Orkney had to wait until 1920 when it was
first published in the 'Old Lore Miscellany' of the Viking Club.
    After the manuscript had been lost for some considerable time his
'Fauna Orcadensis' was found and published in Edinburgh 1813 but
the missing parts of his 'Flora Orcadensis' were not found for
publication until 1991 although much of his research for it was used
without acknowledgement after his death by Pennant and others,
including *George Barry for his 'History of Orkney'. Low's own
'History of Orkney' has never been published. Among many other
works he wrote a 'Treatise on the Microscope' and, in fact, made one
himself to help in his studies of plant-life. It is ironic that in later life he
became blind - perhaps through too much use of just such an
instrument in poor light.   8,18,47.

Lyell, Sir Leonard, b.1850 d.1926, of Kinnordy (later Lord Lyell) -
Professor of Natural Science at University College of Wales. Liberal
MP for Orkney and Shetland 1885-1900 the first MP for the
constituency to be elected under the extended franchise. Supporter of
legislation to protect interests of crofters.
    49,1916-28, *Sons and Daughters of Shetland* - Margaret Robertson.

M

MacClure, Ian, OBE, FRCSE - b.1898 d.1982 Ayrshire. Orkney's first resident Surgeon Superintendent. Flew with Royal Naval Air Service during World War I and was severely wounded, losing a leg. On demobilisation held surgical appointments in England, Scotland, Ireland before being appointed Surgeon Superintendent, Balfour Hospital, Kirkwall 1928, a position he held for 34 years until his retirement 1962. Renowned almost equally for his informality and colourful language as for his almost legendary surgical skills. There was no easy access to facilities further south by air ambulance in those days and in emergencies he frequently had to perform difficult, often life-saving, operations on the spot.

In spite of his 'wooden leg' he was a fine golfer and a good badminton player. He was also an accomplished musician playing bassoon in the Kirkwall Amateur Orchestra.   Orc 16/4/82.

MacGillivray, Evan, MBE - b.1908 Kirkwall d.1987 Kirkwall. Librarian. Educ. Kirkwall Burgh (Grammar) School; m. (1) Elizabeth Flora McGaw, district nurse (2) Ingegerd Lundgren, Swedish broadcaster and journalist. Worked in printing department and book shop of *Orkney Herald* and later in other book shops notably the world-famous Bumpus in London. Joined Navy in World War II serving in North Atlantic and Mediterranean patrol vessels, destroyers etc, commanding his own ship in D-Day landings off Normandy.

Appointed Orkney County Librarian after war building up the services by merging and modernising Kirkwall, Stromness and County Libraries based on old Kirkwall Free Library. Added reading rooms, reference, children's and gramophone record sections, school libraries and the Orkney Room containing practically every book written in, on or about Orkney and its history. He also established the Orkney Archive with the huge collection of documents from Skaill House charter chest and in 1962 by tact and diplomacy secured the Balfour papers from Balfour Castle which were in danger of destruction. To cover all Orkney he pioneered a Family Book Service for the outer isles readers supplying them free of charge with regular batches of books of their own choice while on the Mainland he introduced the Mobile Library van service.

He was also responsible for setting up the Tankerness House Museum and the Corrigall Farm Museum as well as organising a series of international conferences on matters of archaeological and historical interest connected with Orkney for which he was made

Knight of St Olaf by Norway. After his retirement he lived in
Stockholm.   Orc 13/7/87.

McGonagall, William Topaz - b.c1825 d.1902. Scottish versifier famous
for his unscanned doggerel and odd rhyme patterns often using
current events of his day such as 'The Tay Bridge Disaster' for subject
matter. Had some of his early education in South Ronaldsay where his
parents, who were pedlars, lived near St Margaret's Hope for several
years and where, with his elder bro. Thomas he attended the Parish
School. Publication of his 'Poetic Gems' 1890 earned him the
reputation of being 'the worst poet in the world' but he was, and still
is read with affection.   *Orkney View* No. 29 April/May 1990,
Oxford Companion to English Literature 1985.

Mackenzie, Alexander, of Ardloch - Highland chieftain who, just before
Culloden 1746, led limited invasion of Orkney by a small company of
Highlanders in an attempt to raise money and recruits for the Jacobite
cause. Landed South Walls and made demands on Melsetter estate of
the pro-Hanoverian Moodie family before crossing Scapa Flow to
occupy Kirkwall for several days. Sheriff Depute *Andrew Ross and
Provost *James Baikie, both anti-Jacobite, fled to Shetland.
Disappointed by the small amount of money forthcoming and by lack
of volunteers for their army they went on to Stromness where they
managed to extort rather more money from merchants there than in
Kirkwall but no more recruits. Returned to Caithness through South
Walls ransacking and looting Melsetter House on the way   11.

Mackenzie, Francis - b.1832 d.1895 London. Bro. of Osgood Mackenzie,
founder of Inverewe Gardens, Wester Ross. Francis farmed Stove in
Sanday 1856-1866. Remembered for his 'Highland Host' of 25 farm-
workers brought in to Sanday from Wester Ross, who were famed for
the speed at which they could build Galloway dykes, a stone-walling
technique unfamiliar to Orcadians. Introduced sowing and reaping
machines to Orkney and installed steam power to drive machinery at
Stove. Deeply religious, he was a Baptist, he preached to his 'Highland
Host' on Gaelic.   7.

Mackenzie, James - Kirkwall lawyer; s. of James Mackenzie, Town Clerk
of Kirkwall and Marion Traill of Tirlot. Indefatigable compiler and
author of 'The General Grievances and Oppressions of the Isles of
Orkney and Shetland' during his involvement in the Pundlar Process
(1733-59) as legal agent, man of business and factor for *Sir James
Steuart of Burray, in which he produced abstruse historical arguments
supporting claims by the Orkney lairds against the Earl of Morton for
reduction of their dues. His collection of transcribed documents (The

Mackenzie Manuscript) including Orkney's first Rental 1492 is preserved in the Orkney Archive. 2.

Mackenzie, Bishop Murdo - b.c1596 d.1688 Kirkwall. m. Mary Macaulay, Fortrose; their 2 sons Thomas and (Sir) Alexander became respectively, Minister of Sandwick, and Sheriff Orkney Bishopric; their 2nd dau. m. *George Balfour of Pharay.

Educ. Aberdeen. Chaplain to Lord Reay's Regiment in Germany under Gustav Adolphus of Sweden c1630-32; Minister of Contin, Ross-shire 1637; Dingwall Presbytery representative at Glasgow General Assembly 1638; Minister Inverness 1640 and Elgin 1645 when he was apparently a confirmed Presbyterian of 24 years standing and said to be zealous Covenanter. When episcopacy was re-established at the Restoration, however, he complied with new order reverting to his original Church. Appointed Bishop of Moray 1662, and Bishop of Orkney 1676 when aged close on 80.

Arrived in Orkney at Scapa 1677 when, according to legend, he was invited to drink the customary copious toast from the now-vanished St Magnus Cup which had to be taken in one draught to ensure a successful occupation of the diocese - it is said that he not only complied but asked for a refill - making doubly sure.

Resident in Orkney throughout his episcopate he made a point of visiting the outlying parishes in the islands and was involved in restoration of St Magnus Cathedral and its steeple damaged by lightning 1671 arranging dispatch of Great Bell to Rotterdam for recasting 1682. Showed great humanity towards Covenanters who survived wreck of *The Crown* on Scarvataing, Deerness 1679 after being sentenced to deportation to the North American colonies for their part in the battle of Bothwell Brig 1679.

A strict disciplinarian he was described as '. . . a most worthy Bishop and greatly beloved for his hospitality, peaceful disposition, piety, brotherliness and prudent government'. 4,21,69.

Mackenzie, Murdoch - b.1712 Orkney d.1797 Minehead, Somerset. Surveyor, cartographer, teacher; s. of *James Mackenzie and Marion Traill of Tirlot; grd s. of *Bishop Mackenzie. Headmaster Kirkwall Grammar School 1734. Published 'Proposals for surveying and charting of the Orkney Islands' 1743 and in 1749 submitted a paper to the Royal Society on 'The State of the Tides in Orkney'. The following year 1750 published 'Orcades, or a Geographical and Hydrographical Survey of the Orkney and Lewis Islands'. He was then employed by the Admiralty and surveyed the entire west coast of Scotland, Ireland and the west coast of England and Wales as far south as Pembrokeshire. The results were published as a 'Nautical Description of the west coast of Great Britain from the Bristol Channel to Cape

Wrath' and a 'Nautical Description of the coast of Ireland'. He
published 'A Chart of the Atlantic Ocean' 1760 and in 1771 was
succeeded as Admiralty Surveyor by his nephew *Murdoch
Mackenzie the younger. In 1774 elected Fellow of the Royal Society
and that same year produced 'A Treatise on Maritime Surveying'.
1,4,44, *Maps and Plans* 1988 - David Smith,
Memoirs of Hydrography Pt I, 1969 - L. S. Dawson.

Mackenzie, Commander Murdoch the younger RN - b. 1743 Kirkwall
d.1829 Minehead, Somerset - s. of Thomas Mackenzie, Kirkwall
merchant and Elizabeth Blaw; nephew of *Murdoch Mackenzie (1712-
97).
Midshipman aboard HMS *Dolphin* during circumnavigation of the
globe by Commodore John Byron 1764-66. Succeeded his uncle as
Admiralty Surveyor 1771. Surveyed coasts of Cornwall, Kent, South
Devon 1773-1779 when promoted Lieutenant and in 1780 surveyed
channel between Isle of Sheppey and mainland with his cousin and
assistant, *Graeme Spence, and the following year they surveyed the
Needles off the Isle of Wight. Although his eyesight was failing he
remained Admiralty's chief nautical surveyor until 1788. Made
Commander 1814. 44, *Memoirs of Hydrography* Pt I 1969 - J. S. Dawson.

McKenzie, Thomas, CBE - b.1891 d.1954. Salvage expert. Served
apprenticeship in ship-building before becoming diver with Clyde
Navigation Trust 1911-14 then with Admiralty 1914-1919. Joined Cox
& Danks at their ship-breaking yard in Kent and came north to Scapa
Flow after *Cox bought submerged hulks of scuttled German Fleet
1924 becoming joint Chief Salvage Officer for the company with
*Ernest McKeown. Involved in raising all the ships from destroyers to
battleships, first with Cox & Danks and then with Metal Industries Ltd
after they took over in 1933. During World War II became Chief
Admiralty Salvage Officer for North of Scotland, Orkney, Shetland
and Faroe with rank of Commodore. Principal Salvage Officer to
Allied Naval Commander Expeditionary Force (North Europe) 1945.
Director Metal Industries.   26,49,78, Orc 27/4/54.

McKeown, Ernest - Salvage expert. Former Royal Navy artificer who
became joint Chief Salvage Officer with *Thomas McKenzie for Cox &
Danks in raising scuttled German Fleet in Scapa Flow between the two
World Wars.   26,78.

Mackintosh, William Rodger - d.1918 Kirkwall. Journalist, author, editor
and proprietor of *The Orcadian*; m. Elizabeth, dau. of James Anderson,
owner and editor. Native of Ayrshire appointed editor of *The Orcadian*
1877 becoming proprietor 1895 and began modernising the printing

works 1902. A skilled shorthand-writer he covered public inquiries of the Napier Commission on crofting providing it with verbatim reports which he subsequently published in book-form entitled 'The Orkney Crofters' 1889. Author of 'Glimpses of Kirkwall in Olden Times' 1885 and 'Curious Incidents from the Ancient Records of Kirkwall' 1892 and 'Around the Orkney Peatfires', all of which have become local classics.

MacLellan, David, of Woodwick - Described as 'servitor to Mr *John Dick'. Depute Sheriff but by shrewd commercial enterprise including ship-owning and judicious moneylending he had by 1653 become principal landowner in Orkney with an annual rental of £1,700. In addition to the Woodwick estate he also owned Wyre which he sold to *Hugh Craigie 1659.   1,4.

MacLennan, William OBE - Last Orkney-based Chamberlain of the Orkney Earldom estate; b. Strathconon, Ross-shire where his father was a well known breeder of Cheviot sheep. After serving as Chamberlain for Lewis he was appointed Chamberlain of Orkney Earldom 1898 to 1930 when he retired and was not replaced, the estate having by then been almost entirely sold to sitting tenants 1921-23. Played an active part in local affairs being Honorary Sheriff, JP, Commissioner of Supply, County Councillor, Treasurer of Burgh of Kirkwall, Chairman of both Birsay and St Ola School Boards as well as being correspondent for the Board of Agriculture and Fisheries. Author of 'The Flockmaster's Companion'.

McNeill, Florence Marian - b.1885 St Mary's, Holm d.1973. Folklorist, author. Educated. Holm Public School, Edinburgh and Glasgow Universities.
     After 2 years of travel became Secretary to Association for Moral and Social Hygiene and during this period was active in the Suffragette Movement. After breakdown in health was tutor in Athens and freelance journalist in London. Returning to Scotland 1926 worked on Scottish National Dictionary. Best known for work on folklore - 'The Silver Bough' in 4 volumes,'The Scots Kitchen', 'The Scots Cellar' and 'Hallowe'en', drawing frequently on her childhood recollections of Orkney. She wrote one novel 'The Road Home'.   *Scottish National Biographical Dictionary.*

MacWilliam family - Descended from the marriage between *Malcolm III Canmore, King of Scots and *Ingibjorg, widow or perhaps dau. of Earl *Thorfinn II. It appears that this marriage was annulled since subsequent Kings of Scots were descended from Malcolm's second marriage to St Margaret. The MacWilliams continued to press their claims, and in the second half of the 12th century received the support of Earl *Harald II Maddadsson which brought him into disastrous conflict with King William the Lion. The MacWilliam line was extinguished in 1230 with the killing of a female infant, the last of the line.   2.

Maddad, Earl of Atholl - d.before 1136; m. Margaret dau. of Earl *Hakon Paulsson, half sister of Earl Paul II. Father of Earl *Harald II Maddadsson.   1,2,10,35(7).

Madeleine de Valois - First wife of *James V. Granted the revenues of the royal and earldom lands of Orkney and Shetland as part of her marriage portion, though died within months of coming to Scotland.

Maelbrigte Tusk - Celtic chieftain who as recorded in OS was defeated in battle c892 near Dingwall by Earl *Sigurd I who cut off his head and slung it from his saddle bow but Maelbrigte's protruding buck-tooth (Tusk) grazed Sigurd's thigh causing blood-poisoning from which he died.   1,2,3,10,35(7),76.

Magnus III Barelegs - b.c1074 d.1103. King of Norway c1074-1103; s. of Olaf III The Peaceful. Last of Norwegian kings bent on expansion of Norse influence and possessions in the west. Led expedition 1098 to Orkney, Western Isles, Ireland, North Wales. In Orkney took joint Earls *Paul I and *Erlend II prisoner sending them to Norway where they died c1098. Set up his own son *Sigurd (still a child) to rule Orkney with help of a Council. Sons of the 2 captured earls, *Hakon Paulsson and (St) *Magnus Erlendsson accompanied him to Western Isles, Ireland and Isle of Man but Magnus refused to fight for him at sea-battle off Anglesey in Menai Straits. On return voyage he established 'frontier' between Norse Hebridean islands and mainland Scotland. Killed in Ulster during 2nd expedition to west 1103.

Said to have acquired nickname 'Barelegs' when he adopted kilt instead of trousers.   1,2,3,30.

Magnus I Erlendsson (Saint Magnus) - Earl of Orkney c1105-1117; b.c1070 Orkney d.c1117 Egilsay; s. of Earl *Erlend II; grd s. of Earl *Thorfinn II; cousin of Earl *Hakon Paulsson; m. Ingirid 'of the most noble family in Scotland' 1106. According to the saga the marriage was never consummated.

As young man went a-viking in true Norse fashion. King *Magnus Barelegs stopping off in Orkney c1098 during his raiding expedition to the west took his father Earl *Erlend II and uncle, Earl *Paul I, prisoner sending them back to Norway where they died. In spite of this outrage against his family the future saint, along with his cousin Hakon, accompanied Magnus Barelegs on his continued foray as far as Wales. But at the sea-battle off Anglesey he refused to fight for the king. With the battle raging round him in the Menai Straits he remained on the open deck singing psalms and reading the Scriptures earning the disgust of the king and his followers. The Saga writer later regarded his behaviour as indicative of sanctity.

During the voyage north after the battle he jumped ship off the west coast and made for Scottish Court where he stayed for several years being granted Earldom of Caithness by King Edgar. When Magnus Barelegs died 1103 his son Sigurd, to whom he had given nominal 'kingship' of Orkney, sailed east from the isles to rule Norway jointly with his bro. Eystein. In the absence of Magnus from Orkney at the Scottish Court Hakon was left in control of the Earldom eventually being granted title of Earl by Norway. Magnus then successfully claimed and obtained his father's share of the Earldom and the cousins ruled their respective halves in 'good fellowship' for several years c1105-14 with only occasional friction but when Magnus spent 1114 in England at the Court of Henry I Hakon annexed all Orkney and Caithness during his absence.

On his return to Orkney tension between the cousins reached crisis point. Open conflict was only narrowly averted through intervention by mutual friends among the gødings but others fomented trouble. To settle matters a 'peace conference' was convened for Easter on Egilsay, the Earls and their followers to travel there with not more than 2 ships each, a condition with which Magnus complied arriving the night before the projected meeting. In the morning Hakon was seen approaching the island - but with 8 ships fully manned with armed men.

When these unequally matched parties confronted each other the leading men of both sides, exasperated by the continued acrimony engendered by a divided Earldom, demanded that one Earl should die. With the disparity between the forces present there was little doubt as to which Earl it would be. Magnus offered to accept banishment, imprisonment or even mutilation but all were refused and he was killed by an axe-blow on the head delivered by Hakon's cook, *Lifolf, a reluctant executioner.

Magnus was buried initially in Christ Church, Birsay, from where a number of miracle cures were reported resulting in his canonisation probably c1134 by *Bishop William who at first had refused to believe in them. His bones were taken to Kirkwall c1136 and placed above the altar in St Olaf's Church until the shrine in his Cathedral was ready to receive them. At the Reformation they were immured in a pillar south of the altar for safe keeping. Bones were found in this pillar 1919, a wound on the skull conforming with the account of his execution.   1,2,3,4,10,19,35(7),100.

Magnus II - Earl of Orkney c1239. Possibly s. of Gilbride, Earl of Angus by a grd dau. of Rognvald II and so 1st Orkney Earl of Angus line but ancestry obscure. May be descended from Earl *John through his dau. or by marriage of one of Earl *Harald II Maddadsson's daughters. 1,35(7).

Magnus III - Earl of Orkney 1256-73. Like other Earls both before and after him he held the Orkney earldom from Norway and Caithness from Scotland. And so, in the crisis of 1263 when King *Hakon IV Hakonsson of Norway decided to strengthen his waning influence and possessions in the islands and west of Scotland by force Magnus was in a difficult position holding Orkney from Hakon and Caithness from Alexander III. Nonetheless he sailed west from Bergen with Hakon's fleet but, possibly because of these divided Norse/Scots loyalties, left expedition in Orkney and so did not take part in battle of Largs 1263. Later obtained renewal of Orkney Earldom from King Magnus V Lagabøt, son of Hakon IV Hakonsson, and established close relationship with Norwegian Crown.   2,35(7).

Magnus IV - Earl of Orkney 1273-84; s. of *Magnus III. Visited Norway, where Orkney was held in high esteem, for official installation as Earl of Orkney at ceremony in Tønsberg 1276. Attended Scottish Parliament 1281 as Earl of Caithness.   1,35(7).

Magnus V - Earl of Orkney b.c1295 d.c1321; s. of Earl *John II; m. Katherine who later acquired land in Orkney as Dowager Countess in her own right. Succeeded his father while a minor under wardship of Weland de Stiklaw. Held Orkney Earldom from Norway and Caithness from Scotland. Sealed renewal of Treaty of Perth 1312 on behalf of kings of both countries. Also sealed Arbroath Declaration of Independence 1320. Was last of Angus line of Orkney Earls. 1,2,35(7).

Magnus Havardsson - s. of Sanday chieftain *Havard Gunnisson and kinsman of Orkney Earls. Commanded one of the 15 ships engaged in Earl *Rognvald II's Crusade 1151-3 and was with Rognvald and Earl *Harald II Maddadsson in Caithness when Rognvald was killed by *Thorbjorn Klerk. Urged Harald to avenge Rognvald's death right away and when he declined to do so Magnus led the counter-attack himself killing Thorbjorn. 'A man of high distinction'. (OS).   1,3.

Malcolm III - b.c1031 d.1093, 'Canmore', King of Scots 1058-93. m. (1) *Ingibjorg, either dau. or widow of Earl *Thorfinn II, the son of which marriage was Duncan II briefly King of Scotland d.1094 (2) (St) Margaret, sister of Anglo Saxon Edgar Atheling. The *MacWilliam descendants of the first marriage with their claims to the Scottish throne continued to cause trouble into the 13th century.   2.

Malise - Earl of Orkney 1336-65. 1st of the Strathearn line. Descendant on distaff side from Earl *Gilbert II; grd father of *Henry I 1st of Sinclair line of Orkney Earls.

Granted Orkney Earldom on extinction of Angus line with death of Earl *Magnus V. Claim to Earldom tenuous but upheld by Norway. Had relinquished Earldom of Strathearn to Edward Balliol of England 1344; m. Marjory, sister of William Earl of Ross.   2.

Malise Sperra - cousin of Earl *Henry I Sinclair based in Shetland where he may have been sysselman. Made unsuccessful claims to Orkney Earldom. Killed by Henry I 1389.   1,2.

Margaret - b.1283 Norway d.1290. 'Maid of Norway'. Queen of Scotland 1286-90. Grd dau. of Alexander III King of Scotland; only dau. of Erik II King of Norway and Margaret, dau. of Alexander III on whose death 1286 she became sole direct survivor of Scottish royal line. With view to unification of Scotland and England she was betrothed to infant Prince Edward (future Edward II of England) son of Edward I of England (Hammer of the Scots) 1289 but she died off Orkney, or perhaps in Orkney itself, during voyage from Norway to Scotland a year later. Her father Erik had wanted her to be handed over in what was still Norse territory.

The legend grew in Orkney that she had landed and died in St Margaret's Hope, South Ronaldsay which was then said to have been named after her but, in fact, she was never *Saint* Margaret and at the time of her death the legendary site of her landing would still have had its Norse name Rognvaldsvoe. The confusion arose because there was a chapel there dedicated to the real St Margaret, 2nd wife of King *Malcolm III Canmore or possibly St Margaret of Antioch.   1,2,10.

Margaret - Countess of Atholl; dau. of Earl *Hakon Paulsson; half sister of Earl *Paul II; m. *Maddad Earl of Atholl; mother of Earl *Harald II Maddadsson.

Plotted with *Sweyn Asleifsson and others to get half-share of Orkney Earldom for her son Harald. After Maddad's death she bore an illegitimate son to Sweyn's bro. *Gunni Olafsson and later eloped with Shetlander *Erlend Ungi. Her son Harald, disgusted by her behaviour, laid siege to the Broch of Mousa in Shetland where the couple had taken refuge 1153. Unable to take the broch by force, however, he relented and allowed them to marry on condition that Erlend would support him in future military operations.   1,2,3.

Margaret - dau. of Christian I of Denmark; m. James III of Scotland 1468. Unable to raise all of the 60,000 Rhenish florins required for her dowry Christian pledged his rights and lands in Orkney for 50,000 of them (the Impignoration). The following year having been able to raise only a further 2,000 florins he pledged Shetland for the remaining 8,000. The pledges were never redeemed and the islands came under control of Scottish Crown.   1,2,10,75.

Martin, Andrew - d.1615 hanged Edinburgh. Servant of Stewart Earls particularly *Patrick and his bro. *Henry but distrusted by their father, Earl *Robert. With Patrick's illegitimate son *Robert raising rebellion in Orkney 1614 on his imprisoned father's behalf Martin accompanied him when he occupied Palace at Birsay. He also drew up the Bond of Association for the rebels, those Orcadians still loyal to Patrick, but did not sign it himself having misgivings as to the viability of the rising. He was, however, still a member of the council of rebels after their attack on Kirkwall and the occupation of the Earl's Palace, Cathedral and Castle but with the collapse of the rebellion gave himself up to *George, Earl of Caithness who, with *Bishop Law, led the force sent north to quell the rising. Martin was sent to Edinburgh for trial and subsequent execution along with Robert and others involved.   12,13.

Marwick, Ernest Walker - b.1915 Fursan, Woodwick, Evie d.1977 Rendall. Folklorist, local historian, poet, broadcaster, author; s. of Evie farmer Thomas Marwick and Jamesina, dau. of Rev. Robert Walker. Brought up at The Mount and then Laga.
    Educ. Evie School until he was 10 after which largely self-taught. Worked on family farms then in Stevenson's bookshop, Kirkwall during World War II and the *Orkney Herald* 1955-60 as feature-writer and columnist before attending Newbattle Abbey College under *Edwin Muir; m. Janette nee Sandison of Sanday, former missionary nurse in Jordan, widow of Dr. Park, Kirkwall.
    Compiled and edited 'Anthology of Orkney Verse' 1949 and Walter Traill Dennison's 'Orkney Folklore and Traditions' 1961 and wrote 'Folklore of Orkney and Shetland' 1975. Contributed many papers to learned societies in both UK and Norway as well as freelance features to magazines and newspapers many of which are collected in 'An Orkney Anthology' edited by J. D. M. Robertson. His history of 19th century Orkney, 'Journey from Serfdom' which appeared in serial form in *The Orcadian* 1954 has, like his autobiography 'A Sufficient Place', still to be published in book form. Was specially interested in Orkney's connection with Hudson's Bay Company.
    A founder of first BBC local radio programme 'Town and Country' 1960 he was a regular presenter and interviewer on it and was a leading figure in the establishment of the Orkney Sound Archive. Had encyclopaedic knowledge of Orkney, its history and folklore and taught himself Norwegian to further his studies. In 1968 with *Laura Grimond and others formed Orkney Heritage Society with primary

aim of saving Papdale House, built and occupied by the *Laing family, from threatened demolition but which widened its interests, among them playing a prominent part in the movement which successfully opposed proposal to mine uranium in the West Mainland.

Made Freeman of Kirkwall 1976 and awarded Honorary MA Degree from Edinburgh University. Killed in motor accident 1977. 31,46.

Marwick, Dr. Hugh, OBE, MA, DLitt, LLD. - b.1881 Rousay d.1965 Kirkwall. Philologist, archaeologist, historian, teacher, administrator; s. of Hugh Marwick, ship's carpenter and crofter; m. Jane Barritt 1914.

Educ. Rousay Public School, Free Church Training College, Aberdeen, Edinburgh University, from where graduated MA with 1st Class Hons. in spite of being unable to attend final year owing to ill-health so studied at home. Had been pupil-teacher in Rousay in order to earn enough to attend Aberdeen Training College and again taught in Newbattle in order to afford putting himself through Edinburgh University.

Chief Teacher of English, Burnley Grammar School, Lancashire 1914-1916 when appointed Rector, Kirkwall Burgh (Grammar) School, a position he held for 15 years during which time he obtained his DLitt with a thesis on remnants of the old Norse language still extant in the local dialect and published as 'The Orkney Norn' 1929, one of Orkney's classics. From 1931 until retirement 1946 he was Orkney's Director of Education. He was made OBE 1938; Freeman of Kirkwall 1954. Received Knighthood of St Olaf from Norway and Honorary Doctorates from Aberdeen and Bergen Universities.

Made detailed study of Orkney place-names producing 'Orkney Farm Names', 'Place Names of Rousay', and of Birsay, 'Merchant Lairds of Long Ago', and wrote 'Orkney' in the County series. Contributed many papers to learned societies including Orkney Antiquarian Society, of which he was secretary for many years, and as President to its post-war successor, Orkney Record and Antiquarian Society and also to the Scottish Antiquarian Society.   Orc 27/5/1965, *Saga Book of Viking Society* Vol XVIII Part I 1966, 82.

Marwick, Sir James David, LLD, FRSE, DL, JP - b.1826 Leith d. 1908 Glasgow. Lawyer, local government officer; s. of William Marwick and Margaret Garrioch, Kirkwall; m. Jane Watt, Edinburgh. Educ. Kirkwall Grammar School, Edinburgh University. Solicitor, Edinburgh; served on Edinburgh Town Council and appointed Town Clerk, Edinburgh 1861; Town Clerk, Glasgow 1873-1903. Knighted 1888. Interested in photography and historical research especially into local government on which he produced a number of books.   35(1).

Marwick, James George - b.1876 Stromness d.1960 Stromness. Tailor, naturalist; m. Maggie Scarth, Twatt. Educ. Stromness Public School, served apprenticeship as tailor Glasgow, London to follow his father in the family business. Served on Stromness Town Council for total of 38 years 1913-1955 with 4 years out on army service in Orkney and Middle East during World War I. After the war 1919 took up his business career again and rejoined Town Council becoming Provost 1931. For over 50 years he was Stromness correspondent for *The Orcadian* for much of which time he also contributed the weekly 'Nature Notes'. Author of 'The Adventures of *John Renton' published 1936.   Orc 13/10/60.

Mary - b.1542 Linlithgow d.1587 Fotheringhay; Queen of Scots 1542-1567. Dau. of *James V and *Mary of Guise; half-sister of James V's illegitimate son *Robert Stewart who became Earl of Orkney. Created her 3rd husband, James *Hepburn, Earl of Bothwell, 'Duke' of Orkney - a hollow title. After Mary's defeat and capture at Langside 1568 he fled north to his 'Dukedom' where he hoped to find refuge and support from *Gilbert Balfour but instead was denied access to either Kirkwall or Noltland Castle.

A half-length portrait of Mary known as the 'Orkney Portrait' and attributed to Farini was in the possession of the Traills of Westness and Woodwick until 1833 when it was sold to the Duke of Sutherland.   1,2,75,96,99.

Mary of Guise - Second wife of *James V and mother of Queen *Mary. Granted the revenues of the royal and earldom lands of Orkney and Shetland as part of her marriage portion. When she received this on her husband's death she commissioned the production of the first assessment of the cash value of those revenues. She was probably responsible for the appointment of *M. Bonot as governor of Orkney.   13.

Masterton, Col. James - b.1715 d.1777; s. of Edinburgh merchant; Aide de Camp to Duke of Cumberland 1745; man of business in the south for Sir Lawrence Dundas after he acquired Orkney earldom estate 1766. MP for Stirlingshire. Managed the 8 or 9 MPs seats controlled by Dundas.
2,17, *History of the House of Commons 1754-1790* Vol III (1964).

Maxwell, Bishop Robert - b.c1490 d.1541; s. of Sir John Maxwell of Pollock. Provost of Collegiate Church of Dumbarton. Appointed Bishop of Orkney c1524 succeeding *Bishop Reid before which had been involved in legal and parliamentary affairs in Edinburgh. Probably made first visit to Orkney on his consecration c1526.

Member of Scottish Parliament and a Lord of the Articles 1535. 'Nobly entertained the King (*James V) at his own charge' and Cardinal Beaton in Kirkwall 1540 during their cruise round Scotland.

Had 3 bells cast in Edinburgh Castle which he donated to St Magnus Cathedral 1528.   1,2,4,21.

Maxwell, Dr. William FRSE - b.1873 Leith d.1957 Edinburgh. Master Printer. Of Orcadian parentage, closely related to Bailie Albert Maxwell, merchant, Kirkwall and a frequent visitor to Orkney. Rose from comparatively humble beginnings to become managing director of famous Edinburgh printing firm R. & R. Clarke which produced books for George Bernard Shaw with whom Maxwell became a friend and collaborator. Was also closely associated with Thomas Hardy, Rudyard Kipling, the Sitwells, Hugh Walpole and Charles Morgan in the printing of their books. President British Federation of Master Printers 1929.   *Times* 14/10/57, *Scotsman* 12/10/57, OH 22/10/57.

Meason, Gilbert - see Laing, Gilbert.

Menzies, Sir David - b.c1377 d.1449 - of Weem. Inherited lands in Atholl and Breadalbane c1411; m. Marjory Sinclair, dau. of Earl *Henry II Sinclair who made him sole tutor to his young son the future Earl *William and, prior to c1420, appointed him governor and administrator of Orkney, when Bishop *Thomas Tulloch was entrusted with 'all Royal rights' in Orkney by Norwegian/Danish Crown (Erik III). Two years later 1422 the Bishop was given a grant of the castle and fortress of Kirkwall and a second grant of the islands by Erik, this time as a definite fief. And in 1424 Menzies obtained '. . . the earldom and country of Orkney as much as there justly belongs to the Crown and Kingdom of Norway to manage, administer and preserve it' and this was confirmed by the Bishop. Menzies was thus closely associated with Bishop Tulloch in governing the islands and seems to have retained much of the control in his own hands.

His harsh regime, however, resulted in a 'Complaint to the Queen of Norway (and Denmark) by the People of Orkney' that same year, 1424. This alleged 'tyranny, oppression, assault, false imprisonment, exorbitant fines, commandeering of ships and confiscation of their cargoes, flouting of laws and denial of the right of appeal to the King of Denmark'. It demanded that Orkney be ruled by 'the rightful earl' ie William but again in 1424 both Menzies and William were together at Durham to greet James I returning to Scotland from captivity in England on payment of ransom. Menzies was made hostage in England pending payment of the ransom and was again detained at Durham but soon released to return to Scotland.

Relations between Menzies and William were not good William having taken over rule of Orkney while Menzies was hostage.

In spite of his reputation as a harsh and oppressive ruler in Orkney he was said to be a pious man giving much of his own land to the

Church and indeed became a monk in Melrose never returning to the islands. 2,20(6), *The 15th century Genealogy of the Earls of Orkney . . . etc*
Barbara Crawford in *Mediaeval Scandinavia* 10/1976.

Middlemore, Thomas - b.1842 Edgbaston d.1923 Melsetter, Orkney; Educ. Edgbaston, Paris, London University, BA; retired to Orkney from the Midlands 1898 having made a considerable fortune in the Birmingham-based family leather business a great part of his success having come from mass-producing bicycle saddles. Lived at Westness, Rousay before buying the Melsetter estate and most of Hoy 1898 employing the distinguished architect *William Lethaby to rebuild the Moodie family mansion. County Councillor for Walls and Chairman Walls District Committee 1898-1922. Closely involved in the up-grading of roads in Hoy and Walls and in improved methods of agriculture.   Orc 24/5/23.

Millais, John Guile, FZS - b.1865 d.1931. Explorer, naturalist, soldier, wildfowler, artist, author. Eldest s. of Sir John Everett Millais RA the distinguished Pre-Raphaelite painter.
   Educ. Marlborough and Trinity College, Cambridge. Paid 22 visits to Orkney mostly while serving in Seaforth Highlanders stationed at Fort George. Spent part of 8 winters in the islands based on Stromness in order to complete his collection of wildfowl and sea-birds. First naturalist to recognise Orkney Vole as a distinct species 1904. On leaving the Army travelled widely recording impressions and observations in both print and paint from Newfoundland, Iceland, South and East Africa including the White Nile. Author of 'Wildlife of Scotland' reprint published 1974.   47.

Miller, Hugh - b.1802 Cromarty d.1856. Stone mason, geologist, theologian, journalist, poet; s. of seaman. Journeyman mason 1822; editor of 'The Witness' which after Disruption 1843 became mouthpiece of Free Church of Scotland. Became interested in the fish fossils found near Stromness which led to his writing 'In the Footprints of the Master' subtitled 'The Asterolopis of Stromness' providing a background from which Charles Darwin developed his theory of evolution.   47.

Miller, Professor Ronald MA PhD FRSE FRSGS - b.1910 Stromness d.1990 Stromness. Geographer; s. of Councillor John Robert Miller, lightkeeper, Stromness and Georgina Park; m. Constance Phillips SRN SCM. Educ. North Queensferry, Stromness Academy, Edinburgh University where he became first geographer to take Honours in a Scottish University.
   Research Fellowship Marine Laboratory Scottish Home Dept.

Aberdeen 1931-33; PhD 1933; Asst. Lecturer Manchester University 1933-6 where developed interest in Regional Geography and Climatology going to Nigeria as Education Officer 1935-45 to widen his knowledge of these subjects. Served in Royal West African Frontier Force during World War II.

Lecturer Edinburgh University 1947-53 during which period was Visiting Professor, Universities of Montpellier, Oslo, Bergen, Simon Fraser College, Canada. Appointed Professor of Geography Glasgow University 1953-76. President Royal Scottish Geographical Society 1974-7.

On retirement served as a Stromness member on Orkney Islands Council 1978-82. Author of 'Orkney' 1976, 'Hoy and Eday', 'Africa' and numerous papers and articles including contributions to *Scottish Geographical Magazine*. Edited Orkney volume of Third Statistical Account of Scotland 1985.   Orc 23/8/90.

Millie, Bessie - Reputed witch in Stromness who 'sold favourable winds' to sailors who paid her sixpence before leaving port.

She was visited by *Sir Walter Scott 1814 who used her as model for Norna of the Fitful Head in his novel 'The Pirate' based on life of *Gow the Pirate who she claimed to have known. If so she would have been close on 100 years old in 1814 when described by Scott as having a typical witch's profile - hook-nose and pointed chin almost meeting.   *The Pirate* - Walter Scott.

Monteith, Patrick, 1564-1597, of the Fair Isle, (formerly of Saltcoats) - Follower and servant of Earl *Robert Stewart being Sheriff Depute, Chamberlain of Shetland and Captain of Kirkwall Castle during Earl's absence 1570. Held lands from Earl in Egilsay, Wyre and St Ola. Was one of party which took over St Magnus Cathedral 1568 during dispute with Bishop's men. Later quarrelled with Earl *Patrick Stewart over money matters, repayment of loans and alleged debts.   12,13.

Monteith, Robert, 1st of Egilsay - nephew of *Patrick Monteith of Fair Isle. m. (1) Katherine Boswell of Kinghorn (2) Katherine Nisbet. Held or acquired lands and property in Westray, St Ola, Kirkwall, Fair Isle but particularly in Egilsay of which he was first of family to use designation 'of Egilsay'.

From 1591 onwards was in dispute with Earl *Patrick Stewart who held him responsible for his uncle's alleged debts to the earldom while Chamberlain. This he denied but was warded for debt and on release declared outlaw and forced to flee the islands. Patrick duly plundered his properties to the tune of £29,000 Monteith suing him in the courts for redress. Some degree of accommodation was reached between them 1599 and Monteith was confirmed in his ownership of properties in Egilsay, Wyre and St Ola but the Earl disputed this possession and invaded the Egilsay and St Ola lands stripping them to the value of £10,000. Further legal actions ensued for the next 8 years the courts finally rejecting Earl *Patrick's claims awarding him only £500.

Monteith was in Edinburgh 1614 when Patrick's illegitimate son *Robert raised a rebellion in Orkney on behalf of his father then imprisoned in Dumbarton Castle. Monteith offered to put down the rebellion provided the Privy Council supplied him with 60 men and a ship. The offer was accepted but it was superseded by another from the Sinclair Earl of Caithness who had a few scores to settle in Orkney after his family's defeat at Summerdale 1529.

After Earl Patrick's execution in Edinburgh 1615 Monteith was confirmed in possession of his Orkney lands and for many years acted as agent for *John Stewart, Master of Orkney, later Lord Kinclaven and Earl of Carrick.

Monteith was a speculator and money-lender and also author of 'Description of Orkney' 1632 followed by 'Description of Shetland' both of which were used by Sir Robert Sibbald in his 'Topography of Scotland'.   4,12,13.

Monteith, Robert, 2nd of Egilsay - s. of *Robert Monteith 1st of Egilsay; 3 daughters one of whom, Marjorie, m. William Douglas of Spynie who, after her death 1674 inherited estate so becoming 1st Douglas of Egilsay.   4.

Montgomery, Field Marshal Viscount Bernard Law (Monty) b.1887 d.1976 of Alamein - Commander 8th Army in Western Desert 1943 and C-in-C Ground Forces for Allied campaign in Normandy and Western Europe 1944. Paid morale-boosting visit to troops in Orkney before D-Day 1944.   26,49.

Montrose, Marquis of - see Graham.

Moodie, Captain Benjamin, b.1723 Aikerness, Evie d.1769. 8th of Melsetter - 3rd s. of *Capt. James Moodie snr RN and 2nd wife *Christiana Crawford, widow of William Bellenden of Stenness; m. Henrietta Sinclair of Olrig, Caithness c1755. Succeeded to Melsetter estate 1744 it having been administered by his mother, often in disagreement with him, since his father's murder 1725.

Strongly anti-Jacobite, his house at Melsetter was looted by a party of rebel Highlanders under *Mackenzie of Ardloch 1746, while he was in Edinburgh. He was then given the rank of Captain and sent to Orkney with a detachment of 40 soldiers to arrest any Jacobite lairds he could find particularly *Sir James Steuart of Burray whose men had murdered his father, and to burn their houses and confiscate their estates. He succeeded in capturing Steuart but never located the North Isles lairds who went into hiding although he did burn their houses. Went to London 1746 to claim compensation for damage caused to Melsetter by *Mackenzie of Ardloch's Highlanders before Culloden. Close associate of *Andrew Ross, Sheriff Depute and factor for Earl of Morton. 11,41.

Moodie, Captain James snr RN, b.c1645 d.1725, 7th of Melsetter. m. (1) Jane Douglas, probably dau. of Earl of Morton (2) *Christiana Crawford, widow of William Bellenden of Stenness; father of Capt. *Benjamin Moodie jnr.

Joined Navy c1661 and saw active service at sea for over 50 years including operations in the Channel, a convoy to Turkey, a convoy across the Atlantic, and fighting on the coasts of Spain - winning distinction and royal thanks for his relief of Denia 1707. His last period of sea-service was 1715-17 when he commanded a ship of the line in the Baltic after which, disappointed at not being given Flag rank, he retired to Orkney on half pay and married for 2nd time.

Tried unsuccessfully to enter Parliament 1712 and in 1714 took over administration of his Melsetter estate, which while he was at sea, had been in charge of his nephew, *Capt. James Moodie, who not only laid claims to it but had been unscrupulously milking it to his own advantage during his uncle's absence. He was dismissed forthwith and in 1720 Capt. James Moodie snr. was confirmed in his right of possession by Court of Session.

Of a naturally pugnacious, aggressive nature and anti-Jacobite in sympathies he quarrelled bitterly with *Sir James Steuart of Burray and also challenged *Robert Honyman of Graemsay, Sheriff Depute and Steward of Orkney over his management of local affairs and politics. Honyman, who had certain claims on the Melsetter estate, however, was accompanying him to a meeting of the Justices in St Magnus Cathedral in October 1725 when they were ambushed by members of the Steuart of Burray faction on Broad Street, Kirkwall, and Moodie was shot by one of them, *Oliver Irving, and died from his wounds. 11,41.

Moodie, Captain James jnr, 6th of Melsetter - nephew of *Capt. James Moodie snr RN; Lieutenant in Scots Guards 1690s taking part in the Netherlands campaigns; acted as factor of Melsetter estate for his uncle during his absences on active service in the Navy. Like uncle was of aggressive nature but with more charm than integrity, administering the estate to which, incidently, he laid claim, to his own advantage. Was at first anti-Mortonian with some Jacobite leanings but switched allegiance after the Hanoverian succession. MP for Orkney and Shetland and Secretary to Commissioners of Army

Accounts 1717-22. Deputy Lord Lieutenant of Orkney 1716-22 and
had tack of some of Bishopric estate. Close associate of *William
Bellenden of Stenness. Used troop of Highlanders to prevent Customs
officers from seizing one of his cargoes of smuggled goods 1719 and
by 1721 what little popularity he may once have enjoyed was in
decline. In 1722 fought, almost literally, to retain his seat in the
Parliamentary election once again bringing in a party of Highlanders
in an unsuccessful attempt to influence the result. Lost the seat to
*Col. George Douglas, who became 13th Earl of Morton.
     Subsequently served in the Spanish army in Italy commanding a
garrison at Venice with rank of Colonel. Sought support from secretary
of exiled Young Pretender about becoming a lay-brother but was
advised the cloister was not for him.   11,41.

Moodie, Captain William George, DSC - b.1879 Leith d.1961 Edinburgh.
s. of George Moodie, himself a seaman, and Catherine McLeod who
died when he was an infant. He was brought up and went to school in
Skelwick, Westray where he had family connections; m. (1) Jemima
Ann Hewison (2) Eva Nisbet. Aged 16 went to sea in Orkney-owned
schooner *Mary Traill*, his first command being topsail schooner *Galatea*
of Kirkwall. After spell in fishery cruisers returned to sail and in 1914
was skipper of Finstown-owned *Sunbeam* when sunk by German
submarine off Wick.
     With his crew volunteered for Royal Navy in Q-Ships, those
innocent-looking merchantmen which lured U-boats within range and
then revealed their true purpose with previously concealed guns.
Capt. Moodie in command of one of these, HMS *Ready* avenged his
sinking off Wick by sending a U-boat to the bottom in the Bay of Biscay
for which he was awarded the DSC.
     In 1920 he took command of 341-ton SS *Amelia* on her regular
weekly cargo-run between Leith and Kirkwall and remained with her
for over 30 years apart from a short spell during World War II when he
was on pilot-service in the Forth.   Orc 2/11/61, 26.

Mooney, Rev. Harald, MA - b.1906 Kirkwall d.1989 Kirkwall - Minister of
Deerness Parish Church and then joint parishes of Deerness and St
Andrews for 55 years 1929-84; s. of *John Mooney. Educated Kirkwall
Grammar School, Edinburgh University. Inherited his father's interest
in Orkney history and wrote the official story of St Magnus Cathedral
as well as contributing papers to 'Orkney Miscellany' on Deerness
Church history and the 'Wreck of the *Crown* and the Covenanters in
Orkney'.   Orc 7/9/89.

Mooney, John - b.1862 d.1950. Kirkwall businessman (Director R. Garden
Ltd). Town Councillor. One of Orkney's leading historians in 20th

century. Founder member of Orkney Antiquarian Society to which he contributed numerous papers. Books include 'Eynhallow', 'St Magnus Earl of Orkney', 'Cathedral and Royal Burgh of Kirkwall', 'Kirkwall Charters and the Danish Treaty'.   OH 10/10/50, Orc 12/10/50.

Morton, Earls of - see Douglas.

Mountbatten, Admiral of the Fleet Lord Louis, b.1900 d.1979, Earl Mountbatten of Burma - Served as midshipman in *Beatty's flagship HMS *Queen Elizabeth* in Scapa Flow during World War I and again in the Flow in World War II was Captain (D) commanding 5th Destroyer Flotilla in HMS *Kelly* taking part in Norwegian campaign 1940. Subsequently Supreme Commander South East Asia Command (SEAC) and Viceroy of India.   26,49,83,95.

Muir, Edwin - b.1887 Deerness d.1959 Cambridge. Poet, author, essayist, literary critic, translator. Brought up on family farm in Wyre and another near Kirkwall where attended Burgh (Grammar) School until family moved to Glasgow 1901; m. Willa Anderson 1919.

With his wife translated over 40 books mainly from the German, including 'The Castle', 'The Trial', 'America' by Kafka, and Brod's 'The Sleep Walkers'. His extensive poetry output includes 'One Foot in Eden', 'The Labyrinth', 'The Narrow Place' as well as a number of volumes of 'Collected Poems'. Among his prose works are 'The Story and the Fable' later extended into 'An Autobiography' and 'Scottish Journey' an account of a tour through Scotland in the mid 1930s, 'The Estate of Poetry' and a study of 'John Knox: Portrait of a Calvinist'.

After World War II appointed Director British Council in Prague until Communist take-over of Czechoslovakia after which he occupied similar post in Rome before becoming Warden, Newbattle Abbey Further Education College near Edinburgh and later Visiting Professor of Poetry at Harvard University, USA.

33, *In a Distant Isle, the Orcadian Background to Edwin Muir* - George Marshall, Edinburgh 1987.

Munch, P. A. - b.1810 d.1863. Norwegian historian specialising in saga and medieval periods. Visited Orkney 1849 and met local antiquarians including *George Petrie with whom he corresponded on Orkney's place in Norse history.   *Laerde Brev fraa og til PA Munch* (Learned correspondent of P. A. Munch) - Trygve Knudsen og Per Sveaas Andersen.

N

Napier, Francis, Lord Napier of Napier and Ettrick - Chairman of the Napier Commission on Crofting which heard evidence in Orkney 1883 the findings of which led ultimately to the Crofters Act 1886 giving crofters security of tenure and a right to judicially determined rents.   44.

Neill, Dr. Patrick - b.1776 d.1851. Field botanist; Secretary of Natural History Society of Edinburgh. Visited Orkney early 19th century when in the course of one summer he added 156 new species to the list of Orkney flora raising it to a total of 467 native species. His 'Tour of Orkney and Shetland' appeared in *Scots Magazine* 1804-5 and in book form 1806. His family were descendants of the *Traills of Elsness.   44,47.

Nicol, Oliverson - Odaller of Gairsay. Deprived of his odal rights by *Magnus Halcro c1540 he emigrated to Norway. Some 40 years later he returned to Orkney optimistically assuming he would get justice under the new regime of the Stewart earls and was successful in getting decreet against Halcro. Earl *Robert Stewart, however, having dispossessed Halcro, claimed the lands for himself giving them to an alleged former mistress, Isobel Brown. Oliverson took the case to Privy Council in Edinburgh 1587 who decided in his favour under the 'old Orkney laws' re-instating him to his odal rights in Gairsay.   2,12.

Ninian, Saint - Believed to have visited Orkney and to have established Christianity in the islands c500, a belief perhaps based on occurrence of place-names eg Rinansay (North Ronaldsay) and frequent Ninian - dedications in the islands. Ninian cult in Orkney and Shetland thought to be of late medieval origin.   84.

Nisbet, Bailie Harry - d.1770 North Ronaldsay. Keeper of Earldom Girnel in succession to his father *John. m. Anna Traill, dau. of *George Traill of Holland 1751.

   Gave evidence in Pundlar Process 1733-59 where it was stated that he 'had always weighed justly' and from 1734 had been using the more accurate beam and scale system of weights in place of what were described during the Process as 'these wicked instruments', the ancient Orkney pundlar and bismar.   4.

Nisbet, John - d.1707. Keeper of Earldom Girnel. m. Margaret Traill, dau. of James Traill of Westove, widow of Thomas Louttit of Lyking 1704. Elected to Kirkwall Town Council 1698, Dean of Guild 1703.

Said to have been first Girnelman to dispense with pundlar and bismar system of weights in favour of standard nationally recognised system. 4.

Nisbet, Nicol - Gardener to Earl *Patrick Stewart in Birsay presumably at the Palace. May have come to Orkney with Earl *Robert Stewart. First record of name in Orkney. 4,13.

Nisbet, Rev. William - Minister of Firth and Stenness; ordained 1747. Accused of adultery with a Mrs Agnew, sister of his bro's wife. for whom he had provided shelter in his manse when she came to Orkney after separating from her husband in the south. When the minister married Elizabeth Ritch, his near relative in 1764 Mrs Agnew found other accommodation nearby but within days of the wedding he visited her there and did not return to the manse for four nights. The outraged Presbytery and Synod censured him but he refused to accept their ruling so the case was referred to the General Assembly. In the meantime, however, he had been convicted on a charge of adultery, then an indictable offence, by a civil Circuit Court in Inverness and sentenced to two months in prison on a diet restricted solely to bread and water before being deported for life to the North American plantations. 4,6.

Nordal, Sigurd - Editor of Orkneyinga Saga, Copenhagen 1913-1915.

Nory, John - Royal chaplain in Denmark sent to Orkney 1461 by *Christian I as envoy summoning Earl *William to attend Danish Court to clarify position in view of possible demands by Scotland for transfer of Orkney to Scottish Crown. In the Earl's absence from Orkney at the time, one of his bailies, *Thomas of Kyrkness, replied on his behalf that his master was in Scotland fighting the Earl of Ross. 2,100.

Novell, Bishop Ralph - Elected by 'men of Orkney', almost certainly supporters of (St) *Magnus, between 1109 and 1114. May have come to Orkney with Magnus on his return 1114 from sojourn in Court of Henry I in England although Craven suggests that he may never have been in Orkney at all. At the time Orkney not only had 2 earls, Magnus and Hakon, but also 2 bishops. *Bishop William the Old, probably a Scandinavian consecration, supported Hakon while Bishop Ralph Novell consecrated in York and supporter of Magnus had the blessing of Rome both before and after the martyrdom, the Vatican referring to Bishop William as the 'intruder'. 2,21,100.

Ochiltree, Lord - see Sinclair, Sir James, of Killeith.

Oddi the Little - Skald with Earl *Rognvald II on his Crusade to Holy Land 1151. Composed verses at Narbonne.   1,2,3.

O'Dell, Professor Andrew Charles, MSc, FRSR - Geographer. b.1909 Transvaal, South Africa d.1966 Aberdeen. Educ. Westminster City School, Kings College, London.
    Demonstrator, Geography Dept. London School of Economics 1930-33; Lecturer, Birbeck College 1931; Naval Intelligence Division 1941-43; Dept of Health, Scotland 1943-45; Lecturer and Head of Dept of Geography, Aberdeen University 1945; Reader in Geography, Aberdeen 1949; Professor of Geography, Aberdeen University 1951.
    Travelled extensively in Highlands and Islands of Scotland including Orkney and led Aberdeen University archaeological expeditions to Shetland 1955-59 during which the St Ninian Isle Treasure hoard was discovered.
    Publications include Orkney section of the Report of the Land Utilisation Survey of Britain 1939, 'The Historical Geography of Shetland Isles', 1939, 'The Scandinavian World' 1956, 'Highlands and Islands of Scotland' 1962.   49(1960-69).

Ofeig - Earl *Hakon's standard bearer at killing of St Magnus on Egilsay 1117 but refused Hakon's order to carry out the execution himself. 1,3.

Ogmund - c1130. Father of Ragnhild, *Sweyn Asleifsson's first wife, mother of his oldest son *Olaf.   1,3.

Ogmund Crowdance - Fighting captain in King Magnus Hakonsson's fleet sent from Norway to Orkney 1264 'to guard the land' against threat of attack by Scots.   1,2.

Olaf II Haraldsson, b.c995 d.1030. King of Norway 1015-30. St Olaf - Converted to Christianity during long stay in the west and on return to Norway completed the work of national conversion started by *Olaf Trygvasson. Claimed Orkney Earldom as his own but divided it into three parts granting one third each to Earl *Thorfinn II and Earl *Brusi who were to hold them as vassals while retaining one third for himself. Earl *Rognvald I Brusisson was at Olaf's Court in Norway and fought alongside him at Stikkelstad 1030 where Olaf was killed.   1,2,3,30,76,102.

Olaf Hrolfsson - Gøding of Gairsay during rule of Earl *Paul II; m. Asleif. Father of *Sweyn Asleifsson, *Valthjof, *Gunni. With his ship as part of Paul's fleet took part in battle of Tankerness 1135 when *Olvir Rosta was defeated. After battle given charge of Duncansby, Caithness where Olvir killed him in revenge 1136 while his sons, Sweyn and Gunni, were away on fishing trip in Pentland Firth.   1,3,35(7).

Olaf Jarlsmagr - possibly s.-in-law of Earl *Harald II. Leader in movement to remove *Sverre from Norwegian throne and replace him by Sigurd, still a boy, son of King Magnus Erlingsson. Brought Sigurd to Orkney 1193 where welcomed by Harald II Maddadsson who gave him a ship and allowed him to be proclaimed King of Norway.
    Olaf and Sigurd were with the Orkney and Shetland force known as the Island Beardies which invaded Norway 1193 with some success at first but suffered utter defeat a year later at sea battle of Florvåg near Bergen when surprised by Sverre's fleet in 1194. Both Olaf and Sigurd were killed.   1,2.

Olaf Trygvasson - b.c964 d.999. King of Norway 995-999, grt grd s. of *Harald Fairhair. Succeeded to throne while on viking expedition to west during which he was converted to Christianity. He then attempted to impose his new-found religion on Orkney, Norway and Iceland with only limited success. While coming through the Pentland Firth on his way east to claim the Norwegian throne in 995 he surprised Earl *Sigurd II at anchor in Osmondwall (now Kirk Hope) in South Walls. With a superior force and imbued with proselytising zeal for his new religion he offered the Orkney Earl and his followers a choice between conversion to Christianity or death. Sigurd pragmatically chose conversion. His son Hundi was taken hostage to Norway where he died and Sigurd reverted to the old religion.   1,2,3,30,76,100.

Oliverson, Nicol - see Nicol Oliverson.

Olvir Rosta (The Unruly) - Sutherland chieftain; s. of Thorljot of Rackwick; grd s. of *Frakokk. '. . . the tallest of men and of very great strength, quarrelsome and a great manslayer' (OS).
    Had no real hereditary claim to Orkney Earldom but when *Kol's envoys having failed to persuade Earl *Paul II to accede to Earl (St) *Rognvald II's rightful claim to a share of the Earldom they offered a half share to Olvir and his grd mother, *Frakokk if they would actively support Rognvald's claim. They agreed and in 1135 mounted an attack on Orkney by sea planned to coincide with a simultaneous attack from Shetland by Rognvald which did not materialise owing to adverse weather. Olvir was soundly defeated and dispersed by Paul's outnumbered ships at battle of Tankerness 1136 where *Olaf Hrolfsson

of Gairsay, father of *Sweyn Asleifsson, and *Sweyn Breastrope distinguished themselves. Olvir took his revenge later that year with a surprise attack on Olaf, then living at Duncansby, Caithness, burning his house over him and killing him.

A few years later c1139 Sweyn Asleifsson in turn took revenge for his father's murder by a surprise attack on Olvir who was living with his grandmother Frakokk near Helmsdale in Sutherland. Olvir escaped to the Hebrides but Frakokk was burned to death in their house.   1,3.

Oman, Professor John Wood, DD - b.1860 Biggings, Stenness d.1939 Cambridge. Theologian; s. of farmer and former seaman. Educ. privately, Edinburgh University (1st Class Hons. Philosophy), Theological College of United Presbyterian Church of Scotland, Edinburgh, Universities of Erlangen, Heidelberg, and Neuchatel.

After entering Ministry and serving in Scotland for a short while called as Minister of English Presbyterian Church in Alnwick, Northumberland 1889. Became recognised 'as one of the most learned and original minds at work in theology' of his day. Appointed Professor of Systematic Theology, Westminster College, Cambridge, the Presbyterian Church of England College 1907 becoming Principal 1922 a post he held until retirement 1936. Honorary degrees of Doctor of Divinity conferred by Oxford and Edinburgh. Author of many theological publications including 'Vision and Authority' 1902.   44.

Omond snr, James - b.1833. Schoolmaster. Kirbister, Stromness. Father of *James Omond. Suffered ill-health and was bedridden in latter part of his life when he took up fiddle-making as a hobby and became so skilled that he produced over 200 eagerly sought-after instruments.
                                                                                           31.

Omond, James - b. Kirbister, Stromness d.1927 Kirbister, Orphir. Educationalist, naturalist, gardener, musician, sportsman with rod and gun; son of *James Omond snr.

Educ. Stromness Academy, Edinburgh Teachers Training College; schoolmaster Westray, Rendall, Orphir. Prominent in development of Further Education particularly with evening classes for farmers. Author of 'Orkney 80 Years Ago' 1911.

P

Paplay, Magnus - Commissary Clerk of Orkney 1567-95. Owned lands of Weyland near Kirkwall c1583 and claimed he had been granted a pension by Earl *Robert Stewart. After Robert's death, however, his son Earl *Patrick disputed Paplay's rights to either, banished him from Orkney and looted Weyland.   13.

Paplay, Thomas - s. of *Magnus Paplay; servant of *John Stewart, Master of Orkney, bro. and heir to Earl *Patrick. Paplay was accused c1595 of conspiring to murder Patrick which he admitted under torture implicating others including Master's 2 bros. and *Alison Balfour who was charged with abetting the conspirators by witchcraft, tried, condemned and executed.   2,4,13.

Paterson, Rev. Dr. Robert, DD - b.1795 Belmont, Lanarkshire d.1870 Kirkwall after 50 years in the Ministry. Educ. local school, Glasgow and St Andrews Universities. Ordained 1820. A Seceder and evangelist, nicknamed 'Pope of Orkney' by those who opposed him but 'Bishop of the Isles' by his many followers, he 'planted' most of the Secession congregations in the county attracting a great following. In Kirkwall the East or Secession Kirk, built 1797, enlarged 1805, was replaced 1847-49 by the Paterson Kirk named after him and now again called the East Kirk, was capable of holding 1400 people. Appointed by Synod to visit Canada 1846. Deeply involved in the mid-19th century North Isles evangelical revivalist movement and played active part in provision of education in Orkney.   4,34,91.

Paul I Thorfinnsson - Earl of Orkney c1065-1099. s. of Earl *Thorfinn II; bro. of Earl *Erlend II with whom he ruled jointly; father of Earl *Hakon; uncle of *St Magnus; m. dau. of Earl Hakon Ivarsson of Norway.
    With bro. Erlend accompanied *Harald Hardrada, King of Norway on expedition from Orkney to east coast of England culminating in battle of Stamford Bridge 1066 against the English under King Harold II Godwinson. Both escaped the general slaughter in the Norse defeat although Hardrada was killed. Returning to Orkney they continued to rule the Earldom jointly and in harmony for several years until their respective sons Hakon and Magnus fell out whereupon the fathers divided the Earldom into 2 parts, Paul's half being Birsay and the West Mainland. When King *Magnus Barelegs captured Orkney during his 1098 raiding expedition from Norway to the west he sent the 2 bros.

back to Norway as prisoners where they died that same year, Paul in
Bergen.   1,2,3,30,35(7),76,102.

Paul II Hakonsson The Silent - Earl of Orkney c1123-1136. s. of Earl
*Hakon; bro. of Earl *Harald I; uncle of Earl *Harald II Maddadsson.
Followed father's example of keeping Orkney under tight control and,
at first, in opposing development of growing St *Magnus cult.
Rejected claim by Earl (St) *Rognvald II to a share of Orkney who then
offered half the Earldom to *Olvir Rosta and *Frakokk in return for
help in overthrowing Paul.
    They accepted and attacked Orkney only to be routed by Paul's
fleet at battle of Tankerness 1135. Paul immediately made a pre-
emptive sea-borne strike in Shetland frustrating Rognvald's first
attempt to gain his Orkney heritage by force. The following year 1136,
Paul was in Westness, Rousay, when Rognvald made his second and
successful attempt again from Shetland having put the Fair Isle
warning beacon out of action by guile before occupying the North
Isles. Paul, taken unawares in more ways than one, was otter hunting
near Scabra Head in Rousay when *Sweyn Asleifsson in a
simultaneous surprise attack appeared from the west in a merchant
ship, kidnapped the Earl and took him to captivity in Atholl where
Paul's sister Margaret was married to Earl *Maddad. Paul was never
heard of again.   1,2,3,35(7).

Paynter, Andrew (Pictoris) - b.c1420. Bishop of Orkney 1478-c1502 and
tacksman of Crown and Earldom lands 1478-c1489 succeeding *Bishop
William Tulloch. Father of illegitimate son *Henry Phankouth,
Archdeacon of Shetland. Of German origin came to Scotland via
Denmark with Margaret, dau. of Christian I when she married James
III 1468 to whom he acted as physician and possibly astrologer and
magician. Probably played important part in drafting and grant of
Charter to Kirkwall by James III 1486. Received Charter of Regality for
bishopric lands 1490 the diocese having been transferred from See of
Nidaros in Norway to St Andrews in Scotland following the
Impignoration 1468. Active in Scottish Parliament 1489-91.   1,2,21,92.

Peace, T. Smith - b.1845 Kirkwall d.1934 Kirkwall. Architect, wood
merchant, yachtsman; s. of W. B. Peace, Shapinsay, founder of W. B.
Peace & Sons, woodmerchants, Kirkwall; bro. of *William Peace,
printer and publisher, founder of *Orkney Herald*, with whom he
worked for a time before moving south to become draughtsman and
architect.
    Was engaged in building of GPO Edinburgh taking evening classes
in draughtsmanship and design. Other tasks included extensions to
Roslyn Chapel and Doune Castle.

Returning to Orkney entered family firm concentrating on the architectural side of the business where, among many other buildings in Kirkwall he designed the Burgh School, (now Orkney Islands Council offices), Drill Hall, Junction Road, (now a furniture shop and offices), Masonic Hall, Town Hall, County Buildings (Sheriff Court), Victoria Street Hall (Baptist Church), Kirkwall Hotel, Garden Memorial (Balfour) Hospital and many other buildings and private houses throughout the County.

A keen and accomplished yachtsman he also designed and built boats including his own yacht, *Njala*. OH 12/4/34.

Peace, Col. T. Smith - b.1849 Shapinsay d.1930 Kirkwall. Auctioneer. After serving apprenticeship as bookseller with William Peace, proprietor and editor of *Orkney Herald*, spent some years in Edinburgh and Dublin before returning to Orkney 1875 to set up as auctioneer in a business which developed into Kirkwall Auction Mart under family control until it was acquired by a farmers' co-operative after World War II.

He was also County Assessor until 1923 after which he held the post jointly with his nephew, David B. Peace. Was Hon. Sheriff Substitute, JP, Kirkwall Town Councillor.

An enthusiastic Volunteer and later, Territorial Army officer, he joined Orkney Royal Garrison Artillery 1862 being commissioned 1887 after his return to Orkney rising to Colonel commanding Orkney force 1905 before retiring 1912 by which time the Volunteers had become part of the Territorial Army. He was awarded the Victoria Decoration for his Volunteer service. OH 25/5/30.

Peace, William - b.c1834 d.1878 Kirkwall. Publisher and proprietor of *Orkney Herald*; s. of W. B. Peace, woodmerchant, Kirkwall; *bro of T. Smith Peace, architect; m. (1) Margaret Bain, Cleat (2) Mary Low, Arbroath.

Founded and managed *Orkney Herald* 1860 which held strong Radical Liberal views both in politics and church matters. He acquired the firm for himself 1870. For a time published *The Northman*, a mid-week halfpenny broadsheet supplement to the 'Herald' as well as Peace's Orkney & Shetland Almanac and County Directory. Published a number of books on Orkney subjects including *Low's 'Tour' which was in process of publication when he died. OH 4/12/1878.

Peterkin, Alexander - b.1780 Macduff d.1846 Edinburgh. Sheriff Substitute for Orkney and Shetland 1814-23. Educated Edinburgh University after which combined his legal career with journalism and some soldiering. Started his professional career in Peterhead 1811. While in Orkney he compiled and published 'Rentals of Orkney Earldom' 1820, 'Notes on Orkney' 1822.

A staunch Whig and a nuisance to the established authorities in Scotland he was dismissed as Sheriff Substitute for his part in campaign to get Parliamentary vote for Shetlanders. Active in publication of *Orkney and Zetland Chronicle* 1824-25 which he used after his dismissal in order to continue his campaign for enfranchisement of Shetland. Associated with newspapers in Perth and Belfast and became editor of the *Kelso Chronicle* 1833-35. Involved in establishment of Secession Kirk in Orkney and wrote extensively on Kirk matters generally and church law in particular. Was friend and associate of *Sir Walter Scott and other literary figures of his day.   4,44, *Alexander Peterkin* - David Groves in *Scott Newsletter* No.19,1991.

Petrie snr, David - b.1752 d.1830. Clerk to Sheriff *Patrick Graeme and his factor of the Graemeshall estate 1782-1827.   43,56,70.

Petrie jnr, David - b.1788 Holm d.1869 Holm; s. of *David Petrie snr; succeeded father as factor of Graemeshall estate 1827-61. Also farmed Graemeshall and several other farms on the estate as tenant. A progressive farmer rather than an efficient factor. Played active part in surveys and valuations for the division of commonties in various parts of Orkney. Introduced first Shorthorn bull into Orkney which he used for crossing with his herd of Highland cattle.   14(2),43,70,79,98.

Petrie, George - b.1818 d.1875. Sheriff Clerk of Orkney. Antiquary, amateur archaeologist, local historian. On Kirkwall Town Council 1852. Was first to excavate Skara Brae and was instrumental in preservation of Skaill Viking Hoard of silver artefacts 1858, now in Royal National Museum of Scotland, Edinburgh. Excavated Norse sites in Westray Links 1847 and Lingro broch site, St Ola 1870. Collaborated with *James Farrer in excavation of Maeshowe 1861. Contributed papers to various learned societies including Scottish Society of Antiquaries.   4,31, *The Scottish Antiquarian Tradition* ed A. S. Bell 1981.

Phankouth, Henry - Archdeacon of Shetland 1501-29. Illegitimate s. of *Bishop Andrew Pictoris and next to him in the hierarchy of Orkney diocese after being legitimised by Rome on becoming priest. Based in Orkney where he had 2 houses in Kirkwall one at the Brig the other nearer the Cathedral. Also owned estates in Shetland apart from his official residence there.   92.

Phin of Finstown, David - b. Limerick, Ireland 1772. Soldier who joined army as drummer in the 66th Regiment of Foot (Royal Berkshire Regiment) and then 92nd of Foot (Gordon Highlanders) seeing service during Napoleonic Wars in Gibraltar, Egypt, the Baltic and the

Peninsula after which due to ill-health was posted to 9th Veterans Battalion and stationed in Orkney; m. Margaret Whyte of Kirkwall; taught for time in a private school in Harray 1819. Went into partnership 1821 with John Miller, local landowner who also operated the Mill of Firth, and who financed building of an inn in part of Firth that became known as The Toddy Hole. Phin ran the inn for 4 years until he fell out with Miller and was evicted with his family, having to leave Orkney. The inn, now the Pomona, is still in business and The Toddy Hole developed into Finstown, named after him.

Phin of Finstown - R. Fereday.

Ployen, Christian - Governor and Commandant, Faroe early 19th century. Visited Orkney 1839 en route to Denmark. Published 'Reminiscences' describing the voyage and the islands 1840.

Pollexfen, James Riddoch, b.1811 d.1878, of Cairston - Landowner, agriculturist; s. of Thomas Pollexfen, Comptroller of Customs at Kirkwall and Margaret Hutton. His Cairston estate stretched from Brig o' Waithe to outskirts of Stromness and he also owned 450 acres at Weyland near Kirkwall 1873.

The Cairston estate had been developed by his father, an enthusiastic land-improver ahead of his time, who in early part of the 19th century introduced improved varieties of ryegrass and green-top yellow turnips into Orkney .

His son James spent large sums for those days (£4,000) in drainage, farm buildings and machinery including a meal mill.   70,79.

Prien, Gunther - Lieut. Cmdr. in German Navy during World War II. Commanded U-boat (*U47*) which penetrated inadequate eastern defences of Scapa Flow naval base on night 13/14 October 1939 to torpedo and sink battleship *Royal Oak* at anchor with the loss of 833 lives. *U47* escaped back to Germany where Prien and his crew were feted and honoured by Hitler. Prien and *U47* were later lost off Iceland when sunk by depth charges from HMS *Wolverine*.   26.

Pringle, Robert Oliphant - Editor of *Irish Farming Gazette*. Reported 'On the Agriculture of the Islands of Orkney' published in the Transactions of the Highland and Agricultural Society of Scotland 1873.

Pytheas of Marseilles - Greek voyager of doubtful veracity who claimed to have circumnavigated British Isles including Orkney c325 BC. Unreliable account of voyage survives only in writings of Diodoras Siculus, Greek historian of 1st Century BC.   2.

R

Rae, Dr. John - b.1813 Clestrain, Orphir d.1893 London. Arctic explorer. Father was factor for Honyman estate and later agent for Hudson's Bay Company whose ships called regularly at Stromness for men and supplies on outward voyage to Bay. Educ, privately, Edinburgh University. Qualified as surgeon 1833.

Appointed surgeon at Hudson's Bay Company's Moose factory 1834. Chief Factor Fort Simpson 1849. Over period of some 30 years explored, surveyed, documented and mapped vast areas of Northern Canada especially its coastline discovering that the almost mythical North West Passage between the Atlantic and Pacific Oceans through the Arctic was indeed passable. Took part in number of expeditions, commanding several, searching for remains of the missing *Franklin expedition of 1845. Found evidence of its fate 1854 and suggested that members of the expedition could have resorted to cannibalism, such allegations making him *persona non grata* with the Royal Navy. Made trans-Greenland survey 1864 for Atlantic Telegraph Company. Occupied Berstane House, near Kirkwall 1867-8 after which lived and worked in London on Arctic and Canadian affairs.   23,44.

Ragnar Lodbrok (Hairy Breeks) - Legendary but actually real person mentioned in 12th century runes carved in Maeshowe though not necessarily a Danish king as sometimes suggested. Also features in poems attributed to Orkney poets including Earl *Rognvald II. Said to have fought 2 campaigns in Orkney and later to have ravaged the islands. Difficult, if not impossible, to date but belongs to a period before founding of the earldom as described in Orkneyinga Saga in which he is not mentioned.

2,30, *Scandinavian Kings in the British Isles* - Alfred F. Smythe.

Ragnhild - dau. of King *Erik Bloodaxe and *Gunnhild; m. Earls (1) *Arnfinn (2) *Havard Harvest-Happy (3) *Ljot, all sons of Earl *Thorfinn I Skullsplitter. According to Orkneyinga Saga she arranged for the first two to be killed, Arnfinn by *Einar Klining and Havard by *Einar Buttered-Bread promising both killers in turn the Earldom and herself as rewards but reneged when Orkney chieftains demanded that her husband, the Earl, should be a son of Thorfinn I, and so she married Ljot who survived and became 'a mighty chief'. No more is heard of her except that she was apparently still alive in 995 when she was reputedly denounced as evil by *Olaf Trygvasson when he forcibly 'Christianised' Orkney or at least its Earl.   1,2,3,22,30,35(7),76,100.

Ragnhild Ogmundsdatter - 1st wife of *Sweyn Asleifsson, mother of his oldest son, Olaf. 1,3.

Ralph I - Bishop of Orkney 1070-1100. 21,100.

Ralph II - see Novell.

Reid, Bishop Robert - b.c1495 Clackmannanshire d.1558 Dieppe, France. Father killed at Flodden 1513. Educ. St Andrews, MA 1515, and possibly Paris.

Commendator of Kinloss and Beauly; Bishop of Orkney 1541-1558; re-organised Orkney Chapter 1545; President College of Justice (Court of Session) 1549. Rebuilt Bishop's Palace, in Kirkwall adding the Moosie Too'er; re-constructed St Olaf's Church, carried out restoration work and extension of St Magnus Cathedral, especially on the west front; re-organised Kirkwall Grammar School and Sang School and encouraged education generally leaving legacy of 8,000 marks to establish a college in Edinburgh once widely believed to have been used for foundation of Edinburgh University although recent research has indicated that only a very small amount of this sum was actually used for such a purpose.

Close associate and counsellor of *James V performing a number of State duties including embassies to the Court of Henry VIII in England 1533, France 1535-6 to negotiate royal marriage between James V and *Madeleine, dau. of Francis V of France and possibly also to Rome. One of Commissioners appointed 1551 to arrange peace between England and Scotland and in 1554 one of Commission to standardise weights and measures. In 1558 was one of Commission sent to France to arrange and attend the marriage of *Mary Queen of Scots and the Dauphin. He died, possibly from poisoning, in Dieppe while on his way back to Scotland from this mission. Described by Professor Gordon Donaldson as 'One of the most outstanding churchmen and statesmen of the century'. 1,2,4,10,21.

Reid, Samuel, b.1825 Kirkwall d.1912 Kirkwall, of Braebuster, Deerness - Merchant, shipowner; s. of John Reid, shoemaker, Kirkwall; m. (1) Margaret Mackay of Warsetter (2) Jane Borwick. Started Kirkwall business 1846. Chairman Orkney Steam Navigation Co, Kirkwall Gas Co. Served on Kirkwall Town Council, Provost 1876-87. Chairman, Parish Council, Commissioners of Supply (forerunner of Orkney County Council), Orkney Harbour Commissioners, County Council, School Boards of Kirkwall and St Ola and also St Andrews and Deerness, Hon Sheriff Substitute, JP. Performed opening ceremony of new Kirkwall Town Hall 1887. Orc 31/8/12, OH 28/8/12.

Rendall, Robert - b.1898 Glasgow d.1967 Kirkwall. Poet, essayist, historian, archaeologist, (he discovered the existence of the Broch of Gurness while painting, for he was also an artist) naturalist, conchologist, theologian. Of Westray parentage his father being in the Merchant Navy. Family returned from Glasgow to Orkney 1905. Educ. Kirkwall Burgh (Grammar) School until 13 years of age then self-educated for the rest of his life.

Entered family drapery business in Kirkwall c1911. Joined Royal Navy 1916 serving in Scapa Flow during World War I. Went into semi-retirement from business 1946 and devoted himself, not only to his cultural and scientific interests but also to trout fishing and crofting. A dedicated lay preacher and member of the Plymouth Brethren, wrote several theological studies.

Published 'Country Sonnets' 1946, 'Orkney Variants' 1951, 'Shore Poems' 1957 and 'The Hidden Land' 1966. In 1956 produced 'Mollusca Orcadensia' and in 1960 'The Orkney Shore'. Greatly influenced by Classical and Norse writers and by the Georgian poets. Contributed features, essays and papers to a wide range of periodicals, newspapers and learned societies and in particular to the Journal of Conchology where his papers were very highly regarded. His collection of shells and seaweeds is preserved in the Stromness Museum.

Overcoming his profound deafness he was one of Orkney's most outstanding scholars - a modern Renaissance man.   5,24,45.

Renton, John - b.1848 Stromness d.1878 Solomon Islands. Seaman; eldest s. of James Renton, tailor, Stromness. Went to sea as a boy and after several world-wide voyages decided to forsake sail for steam but while in San Francisco 1868 was drugged and shanghaied on to a sailing vessel bound for McKean's Island. From there with 4 others he deserted and spent 5 weeks drifting in an open boat in the Pacific enduring thirst, hunger and tropical storms before sighting land, Malayta, in the Solomon Islands. Captured by natives but befriended by son of a chief and for next 7 years lived as a member of the tribe learning their language and crafts. On being rescued by an Australian ship returned to Stromness but later went back to the South Pacific as a Queensland Government agent recruiting islanders for labour in Australia. On an expedition to the Solomons he was murdered by natives.   *The Adventures of John Renton* - J. G. Marwick.

Reuter, Rear Admiral Ludwig von - b.1863 d.1943. Admiral command-ing surrendered German High Seas Fleet interned in Scapa Flow after Armistice 1918. Gave order to scuttle all 74 ships Midsummer Day 1919 after which became prisoner-of-war. Former cruiser captain.   26,61,63,95.

Richan, Captain William, RN. b.1741 d.1829, Kirkwall, of Rapness - Entered Royal Navy 1758; Lieutenant 1781. Built imposing town house in Kirkwall which became first Balfour Hospital (now West End Hotel). Served in Navy during war with Revolutionary France also using his ship HMS *Norfolk* for running contraband cargoes. When eventually caught by the Customs, who found even the ship's guns were loaded with tea and tobacco. Was not employed by RN again. Retired to Orkney on half pay and made a fortune out of kelp from the shores of his estates of Rapness, Westray, and Braebuster, Deerness. Even so the extravagant life-style of both himself and his wife, Esther, a cousin, resulted in crippling debts. He was made bankrupt and his properties were taken over by a Trust.

For a wager on one occasion his wife was said to have made a sandwich with a £50 note as filling and then to have eaten it for breakfast.

The London Morning Post 1/6/1829 wrote of him: 'During a period of service in all climates, exceeding half a century, (he) was never known once to have recourse to the punishment of flogging . . . Twice during the late war he manned ships under his command with volunteers'. 4.

Riddoch, James - b.1747 d.1818 - s. of *John Riddoch with whom he was joint Sheriff Clerk from 1764; m. Janet Young. Collector of Stamp Duties 1788; responsible for issue of liquor licences and became involved in the *Eunson smuggling case. Provost of Kirkwall 1814-1818. 4,17.

Riddoch, John - d.c1790. Provost of Kirkwall 1764-84. At various times Sheriff Clerk from 1732, Stewart (Sheriff) Substitute, Comptroller of Customs, sometimes described as 'a career official'; m. Mary Young of Castleyards 1734.

Supporter of Earl of Morton and then *Sir Lawrence Dundas after he bought the Earldom estate 1766. Anti-Jacobite and closely associated with Morton's factor *Andrew Ross; involved in Pundlar Process 1733-59.

As Sheriff Clerk 1736 was one of deputation meeting *Christiana Crawford of Melsetter, regarding ownership of Melsetter estate disputed by *Sir James Steuart of Burray.

During Stronsay kelp riots 1742 was wounded when, as Sheriff Substitute, he was trying to arrest ringleaders. While Provost strongly supported successful candidature of *Charles Fox as MP for Northern Burghs 1784.

In addition to official duties also engaged in money-lending enabling him to buy the Cairston estate near Stromness and style himself as Riddoch 'of Cairston'. 11,17,25.

Robert I b.1274 d.1329. King of Scotland 1306-1329. Robert the Bruce - According to a persuasive but unreliable legend he took refuge in Orkney from his enemies during the winter 1306/7 as guest of the Laird of Halcro. This was at the time when Scottish history and popular legend has him studying the perseverance of spiders in a cave on the island of Rathlin off the Irish coast. There is also a story, equally unreliable, that Halcro took a contingent of Orcadians to fight for him at Bannockburn 1314. Norse Orkney did, in fact, have pro-Bruce Norwegian connections but there is considerable doubt as to whether the legendary spiders were really Orcadian rather than a Rathlin species.   2,35(2).

Robertson, Duncan John, OBE - b.1860 Kirkwall d.1941 Kirkwall. Lawyer, County Clerk, poet, essayist; s. of Sheriff James Robertson 1846-75. Educ. Edinburgh Academy and University.

Became partner in Kirkwall law firm Macrae & Robertson. Clerk to Commissioners of Supply which became Orkney County Council, a position he held for 51 years as well as being County Treasurer. Was also Clerk to the Harbours Commissioners and Trustees of the Balfour Hospital. Factor of several of the big Orkney estates and Dean of the Faculty of the Orkney Bar. Vice Consul for Norway, Sweden and Denmark. Agent of Commercial Bank of Scotland.

One of his great interests was natural history especially watching birds. He owned the island of Eynhallow lying between Evie and Rousay which became Orkney's first bird sanctuary and from where he recorded the results of his observations in 'Notes from an Orkney Bird Sanctuary'. His collected verse appeared in book form 'Waith and Wrack' and he also contributed poems and essays on Orkney to a variety of publications including the first 'Orkney Book'.   5, Orc 5/6/41, OH 4/6/41.

Robertson, Lieutenant William Sinclair - d.1813; a Peninsular war veteran; m. Mary Baikie, dau. of Robert Baikie of Tankerness 1807. Lieutenant in 59th Foot, 92nd Foot 1808, and then 95th Foot, Rifle Brigade the same year and surviving the disastrous Walcheren campaign 1809 became Adjutant of this elite Brigade at the height of the Peninsular War from 1811 until he died of fever at Naso d'Aver in Portugal 1813.   14(4), Royal Green Jackets Museum, Winchester.

Roger - Bishop of Orkney 1100-1108. Consecrated by Archbishop of York.
                                                              21,100.

Rognvald I Brusisson - b.c1011 d.1046 Papa Stronsay. Earl of Orkney 1037-1046. s. of Earl *Brusi; grd s. of Earl *Sigurd II; nephew of Earl *Thorfinn II The Mighty.

Hostage and foster son of *King (St) Olaf at Norwegian Court 1021-1030 when fought alongside Olaf at battle of Stikkelstad. After the battle, in which Olaf was killed, he escaped east to Russia with Olaf's bro. *Harald (later Hardrada) where he won fame and high office under Jaroslav of Novgorod.

Then threw in his lot with group of nobles in Norway who succeeded in putting (St) Olaf's son Magnus I The Good on the Norwegian throne 1035 in place of King Knut (Canute) of England and Denmark who had occupied it since battle of Stikkelstad. Magnus, his one-time foster bro. granted him title of Earl of Orkney with its fiefs, ie, both his father Brusi's third and his own royal trithing along with 3 fully equipped warships to sail west and claim his heritage from his uncle Thorfinn II who had meantime taken control of all Orkney. Thorfinn agreed to accept Rognvald's claim to two-thirds of Orkney in return for support in maintaining his own share of the Earldom 1037.

They ruled amicably together for several years joining forces for summer raiding cruises along Scottish coasts until *Kalf Arnisson, kinsman of Thorfinn's wife, *Ingibjorg, banished from Norway by King Magnus I, descended on Orkney with a large following and almost literally ate and drank Thorfinn out of house and home whereupon he demanded return of the royal trithing from Rognvald who refused and sought help from Magnus in Norway. With a joint force collected from Norway, Orkney itself and Shetland he returned to the isles to contest Thorfinn's demand. The 2 fleets met in the Pentland Firth off South Walls 1046, and Rognvald's 30 ships were heavily defeated by Thorfinn's 60-strong fleet reinforced towards the end of the battle by Kalf's ships. Rognvald retired to Norway where at his own request Magnus gave him a single ship and straightway in the depths of that same winter he returned to Orkney catching Thorfinn off guard, burning his house over him. Thorfinn, however, escaped to Caithness from where he, in turn, came back to Orkney taking Rognvald by surprise while collecting malt for Yule-tide ale on Papa Stronsay and burned his house over him. Rognvald, too, escaped by a spectacular leap through the flames but was hunted down and killed by *Thorkell Fostri.

First recorded mention of Kirkwall by name occurs in Orkneyinga Saga where it is stated that Rognvald Brusisson was living there in 1046 the year of his death.   1,2,3,4,22,30,35(7),76.

Rognvald II Kali Kolsson (St Rognvald) - b.c1103 Agder, Norway d.1158, Caithness. Earl of Orkney 1136-1158. s. of *Kol Kalisson, lendirman of Agder, and Gunnhild, dau. of *Erlend II; nephew of *St Magnus.

Spent early years in England where met and became friendly with *Harald Gilli, claimant to the Norwegian throne. Granted Orkney and

Shetland 1129 by *Sigurd the Crusader, King of Norway and adopted
name of Rognvald after Earl *Rognvald I Brusisson.

Sigurd, who succeeded his father on the Norwegian Throne, died
the year after granting Earldom to Rognvald 1130 who did not
however, take it up until it was ratified 1134 by his old friend, Harald
Gilli, now King of Norway. Envoys were sent to Orkney 1134 to
establish his claim to a half share of Earldom which *Paul II, already in
possession, immediately rejected. Envoys went on to Scotland to enlist
support through Orkney family connections particularly with *Harald
II Maddadsson who had claims to at least a share of the Earldom but
also with *Olvir Rosta descended from *Frakokk of evil reputation,
who had none, but on being offered a half share agreed to give
Rognvald active support in his bid for the Earldom.

A two-pronged attack on Orkney was planned for summer 1135 by
Rognvald from Shetland, Olvir from Scotland. But in the event both
fleets were delayed by bad weather and with advance warning Paul
was ready for them defeating Olvir in sea battle off Tankerness before
sailing north to scatter Rognvald's ships storm-stayed in Shetland.
Rognvald, however, was not to be diverted and having gained support
of *Bishop William by vowing, if successful, to build 'a minster the
finest in the north' made a second and successful attempt, again from
Shetland, the following year 1136. With the backing of his father, *Kol,
having put the warning beacon on Fair Isle out of action by guile, he
landed in Westray while simultaneously *Sweyn Asleifsson, removed
the main opposition by kidnapping Paul in Rousay, giving Rognvald
the unopposed opportunity to take control of the entire Earldom and
in 1137 to fulfil the conditions of his vow by laying the foundations of
St Magnus Cathedral under the direction of his father.

Accompanied by *Bishop William he made his celebrated Crusade
to the Holy Land 1151 with 15 longships sacking at least one castle on
the way besides taking a number of vessels and their cargoes before
wintering at at a place thought to be Narbonne to enjoy the favours of
the unidentified 'fair Ermingerd'. Sometimes looking more like a
viking cruise than a pilgrimage they went on to the Holy Land where
Rognvald bathed in the Jordan and visited Jerusalem before leaving
his ships at Constantinople to travel back to Norway overland by way
of Rome 1153.

Returning to Orkney he became involved in the 'Three Earls'
dispute between *Harald II Maddadsson, *Erlend III and himself all
vying for control of the Earldom with the maverick *Sweyn Asleifsson
siding with one or other of them at different times. Rognvald
eventually gained control and held the Earldom until 1158 when he
was ambushed and killed by an exiled old enemy, *Thorbjorn Klerk
while on a hunting expedition with Harald II in Caithness.

Canonised in 1192, a most improbable Saint, his bones were

eventually enshrined in his Kirkwall Cathedral dedicated to the memory of his uncle St Magnus until for safety, presumably at the Reformation, they were hidden in the pillar to the north of the altar opposite those of his uncle whose resting place is in the pillar opposite on the south side.

There is some doubt about his canonisation - Gordon Donaldson, the late Historiographer Royal, pointed out that his right to be called Saint Rognvald was shaky to say the least, and there seems to be no official record of his canonisation. The saga speaks of his relics being 'translated', as those of Magnus had been, by the bishop of Orkney with the approval of the Pope, and his blood was said to have stayed miraculously fresh where it was spilt.

Poet, composing skaldic verse throughout his life especially during the Crusade, troubadour, pilgrim, sportsman, craftsman, and fighting man he was one of Orkney's most colourful and accomplished Earls.

'A properer man both in body and mind than any other man of his time' (OS). 1,2,3,22,30,35(7).

Rognvald Eysteinsson, d.c894, Earl of Møre, Norway. Counsellor and friend of *King Harald Fairhair who, according to the Orkneyinga Saga, granted him the Earldom of Orkney and Shetland in compensation for the loss of his son, Ivar, killed while accompanying Harald on his expedition west. Rognvald in turn passed the Earldom on to his bro. *Sigurd I, who had been one of Harald's forecastlemen, and after Sigurd's death to his own son *Hallad and finally to his illegitimate son *Torf-Einar. Yet another son was Hrolf the Ganger who won Normandy and one of whose direct descendants was William the Conqueror.

In a less biased version of the Orkney Earldom's foundation *Historia Norvegiae* describes how 'certain pirates of the family of the most vigorous Prince Ronald (sic), set out with a great fleet . . . and stripped these races of their ancient settlements'. 1,2,3,30,35(7),76,100.

Ross, Andrew - d.1775, Orkney. At various times Chamberlain of Earldom, Stewart and Sheriff Depute for Orkney 1742, factor for Earl of Morton, tacksman of Bishopric estate 1742-70. Deeply involved in Pundlar Process 1733-59 on Morton's behalf. Strongly anti-Jacobite, especially after being forced to escape to Shetland with Kirkwall *Provost Baikie when *Mackenzie's Highlanders invaded Orkney 1746. After Culloden collaborated with *Benjamin Moodie of Melsetter in punitive operations against the pro-Stuart Orkney lairds particularly *Sir James Steuart of Burray.

Described as 'the most advanced agriculturist in the islands' of his time and 'the most capable man in Kirkwall', he encouraged new farming methods including the growing of flax to supply the linen industry which he introduced to Orkney through the agency of his 2 nephews, the *Lindsay bros.

Held to be responsible for the un-roofing of the Earl's Palace to provide slates for Kirkwall's new Tolbooth then under construction on Broad Street in front of the Cathedral.

In 1768 acquired the Shapinsay estate of Sound. Was said to have been the model for Triptolemus Yellowley in Scott's novel 'The Pirate'.   2,4,11,17.

Ross, Sinclair - b.1890 Caithness d.1959 Kirkwall. Postmaster, writer on Orkney shipping. Educ. Miller Academy, Thurso; m. Margaret Groundwater, Towerhill, St Ola.

Entered Post Office service Thurso as telegraph boy; transferred to Kirkwall 1911. Served in RE Signals in East Africa World War I. Deputy Postmaster, Kirkwall World War II; Head Postmaster 1947-50. Served on Kirkwall Town Council and Orkney County Council. As young man played football for Orkney in inter-county against Shetland.

Developed deep interest in Orkney sailing ships of the past publishing 2 books on the subject, 'Sail Ships of Orkney' 1954 and 'Orkney's Wrecked Ships' 1957, also wrote features for Orkney and Caithness press.   Orc 13/8/59, OH 11/8/59.

S

St Findan - see Findan.

St Magnus - see Magnus Erlendsson.

St Ninian - see Ninian.

St Olaf - see Olaf II Haraldsson, King of Norway.

St Rognvald - see Rognvald II Kolsson.

St Tredwell - see Tredwell.

Sangster, John - Factor of Burray and South Ronaldsay estates for Earl of *Galloway who inherited them from *Sir James Steuart 1746. Continued as factor for *Sir Lawrence Dundas after he acquired the estates in 1768. Carried out extensive agricultural improvements, in particular, enclosing fields and sowing them with Dutch white clover and rye grass for a herd of 60-70 cattle. Tenant of Bu of Burray until 1778.   2,17, Low's *Tour*.

Sangster, Commander Robert - b.1771 d.after 1845, s. of *John Sangster. Joined Royal Navy 1793; Lieutenant in HMS *Queen* 1800; at sea until illness put him ashore in charge of Suffolk coast signal station 1811-13; 1st Lieutenant in 74-gun HMS *Scarborough*, flagship in North Sea 1814; following peace was on half-pay; given rank of retired Commander 1830.

Helped found Edinburgh and Leith Orkney and Zetland Society 1834 and was its Vice President 1834.

Scarth, Professor George W. - b.1881 Sandwick, Orkney d.1951 Montreal, Canada. Botanist. Educ. Kirkwall and schools in England, Edinburgh University.

Appointed Lecturer, McGill University, Montreal 1920; Professor of Botany, 1929. Member of Royal Society of Canada and Hon. Life Member American Society of Plant Physiologists.

An early ecologist wrote 'Ecology of Orkney Vegetation in relation to different classes of soil' 1911 and many research papers on botany and ecology including chapter on plants in first 'Orkney Book' 1909.
                                    47, Orc 27/9/51, *Proc. Royal Socy Canada* 1952.

Scarth, Colonel Henry William - b.1899 Kirkwall d.1972 Skaill, Sandwick; s. of Pillans Scarth and Madalena Harrison; grd s. of *Robert Scarth 1st of Binscarth; m. (1) Mary Robertson, dau. of *Duncan J. Robertson (2) Kathleen Edgar of Newtown St Boswells, Roxburghshire.

Educ. St Pauls School, London, Edinburgh University. Lieutenant Scots Guards 1919 seeing service in France and Northern Russia against the Bolsheviks after Revolution being awarded Order of St Anne and Order of St Stanislaus.

Solicitor with legal firm, Macrae & Robertson, Kirkwall 1923-29; Deputy County Clerk, Orkney County Council 1929-35; County Clerk, Roxburghshire 1935-40; Orkney Regional Deputy Commissioner for Civil Defence 1940-1944; with Allied Control Commission, Austria 1944-52. Hon. Sheriff Substitute. Orkney County Councillor 1956 becoming Convener 1959-67. Appointed Lord Lieutenant for Orkney 1967. Hon. Colonel Lovat Scouts, Highland Artillery TA and 51st Highland Volunteers.   67.

Scarth, Robert, b.c1795 d.1879, 1st of Binscarth - 2nd s. of Bailie James Scarth, merchant, Kirkwall; m. (1) Jessie Sinclair (2) Agnes Cathie (3) Jemima Stevenson. Factor for *Laing family and *Traill of Woodwick

1852-73 and for *General Burroughs (Rousay, Wyre) 1855-73; tenant of Trumland Farm, Rousay but lived in Papdale House, Kirkwall and later Binscarth, Firth which he built. Agent Union Bank, Kirkwall 1855. Inspector of Poor, Rousay 1845.

A leading exponent of agricultural improvement in Orkney, abolishing runrig when factor for Traills in North Ronaldsay 1831, squaring farms and building better houses and steadings which were then let on longer leases. When administering the Westove estate in Sanday he was responsible for reorganisation and modernisation of farming in Burness. While in Sanday he also drafted the Cross and Burness chapter of the Second Statistical Account for Rev. William Grant.

Planned Quandale clearances in Rousay. Had reputation of being hard, competent and knowledgeable. Described in *Orkney Herald* 17/8/1870 as '. . . a hard, a very hard, man not to be driven from his purpose either by threats or by soft answer . . . always keeping his promise though very chary of making one.'   9,25,70,79.

Scollay, Edward, b.pre-1577 d.1626, of Strynie - Received grant of Strynie, Stronsay from Earl *Robert Stewart 1587; a Sheriff Depute in Orkney and Shetland for Earl *Patrick Stewart 1605-10. Denounced as rebel and 'put to the horn', ie outlawed, 1610 for continuing oppressive rule in Orkney even after Patrick's incarceration in the south charged with treason and various other misdeeds but was member of assize in Edinburgh 1614 which tried and condemned Patrick's son *Robert for his abortive attempt to reinstate his imprisoned father in the Orkney Earldom.   2,13,14.

Scott, Sir Walter - b.1771 Edinburgh d.1832 Abbotsford, Roxburghshire. Distinguished Scottish novelist, historian, antiquary, lawyer. Visited Orkney and Shetland 1814 as guest of Northern Lights Commissioners on their annual cruise of inspection of lighthouses. Called on *Malcolm Laing at Papdale House, an acquaintance from days when both were lawyers in Edinburgh. His novel 'The Pirate' was the product of this visit although he had a poor opinion of Kirkwall and worse of Stromness.   4,37.

Scott-Moncrieff, Ann - b.1914 Kirkwall d.1943 Orkney - Author, poet, journalist. Dau. of Major John Shearer, Kirkwall. Educ. Kirkwall Grammar School. Spent a year 1931 on editorial staff of *The Orcadian* before going to London; m. Scottish writer George Scott-Moncrieff 1934. Author of children's books 'Aboard the Bulger' and 'Auntie Robbo' and a volume of short stories 'The White Drake and Other Tales'. Her very promising literary career was cut short when she was drowned in the Swannay Loch.   OH 17/3/43.

Shearer, Professor Ernest - b.1875 Orkney d.1945 Edinburgh. Agriculturist. Brought up on Orkney farm. Educ. Edinburgh University 1898-1904 graduating MA Hons in Economic Science and BSc Agric. m. Jane Tait, sister of *Professor John Tait.

Appointed Imperial Agriculturalist to Indian Agricultural Service 1904; Assistant Inspector General of Agriculture, India 1909; Principal, Giza Higher College of Agriculture with Egyptian Government including direction of a number of special farm schools 1911 and from 1919-1924 Chief Technical Officer in Egyptian Ministry of Agriculture. Appointed Principal of East of Scotland College of Agriculture 1924 and Professor of Agriculture, Edinburgh University from 1926 until he retired from both posts 1943.   OH 18/9/45.

Shearer, John, MA BSc - b.1898 Kirkwall d.1974 Kirkwall. Director of Education. s. of Robert Shearer, Kirkwall; m. Christina Pottinger, Stromness.

Educ. Kirkwall Burgh (Grammar) School 1903-15, Edinburgh University 1915-17 when enlisted in infantry and saw active service in Northern Russia after the Revolution. Returned Edinburgh University after war graduating MA and BSc (Hons) 1922. Taught maths and science Kirkwall Grammar School until 1927 when became Principal Teacher of Science, Stromness Academy. During World War II served in Orkney (Fortress) Company, RE on Scapa Flow defences later becoming full-time administrative officer for Orkney Home Guard. Returned to Stromness Academy after war until appointed Orkney Director of Education 1946 in which post he had to cope with the raising of the school-leaving age to 15 and was responsible for extensive programme of new school building, modernisation and extension of existing schools, the hostel service in Kirkwall for isles pupils, coping with growing demand for Further Education courses, expansion of library and museum services and building of community centres throughout county. After retiring as Director he became Chairman of the Orkney Education Committee and was responsible for the preservation of the old Grammar School threatened with demolition but which became headquarters of Orkney Islands Council. Edited New Orkney Book 1951.   Orc 17/10/74.

Shearer, Peter - b.1854 Stronsay d.1933 Kirkwall. Tailor. After learning his trade in Orkney and Edinburgh started business in Kirkwall 1883 but also established strong London connection making suits, often of Orkney tweed, for the well-to-do, visiting the capital every year.

When this trade vanished at the outbreak of World War I he turned his attention to tailoring uniforms for officers of the Grand Fleet lying in Scapa Flow and in particular he invented and made the 'British Warm', a rather less formal garment than the regulation naval or army greatcoat. It was first worn by Admiral *Colville, Admiral Commanding Orkney and Shetland but being approved for all ranks by the Admiralty and War Office it became widely worn by both services, a contingent of the Lincolnshire Regiment bound for France being the first unit to be officially equipped with it. His customers from the Fleet included Prince Albert, later King George VI, and *Admiral Lord Jellicoe, C-in-C Grand Fleet.

Served on Kirkwall Town Council, being Dean of Guild, Parish Council, Kirkwall and St Ola School Board.   Orc 15/6/33, OH June 1933.

Shirreff, John - Reporter to Board of Agriculture. Exponent of agricultural reform. Carried out survey in Orkney 1814 and submitted comprehensive report entitled 'General View of the Agriculture of the Orkney Islands', with Observations on the Means of their Improvement' in which he discussed in detail rentals, leases, feu-duties, abolition of runrig system of farming, cropping, livestock etc.

Sigtryg Silkbeard - King of Dublin. Guest of Earl *Sigurd II at Yuletide feast in Orkney and fought alongside him at battle of Clontarf 1014 against Brian Boru, King of Munster, fleeing the field after Sigurd was killed.   2,10,38,76.

Sigurd I The Mighty - First Earl of Orkney c874-893; bro. of Earl *Rognvald of Møre who passed on to him the Orkney Earldom after receiving it from King *Harald Fairhair of Norway as compensation for the loss of his son, Ivar, killed in battle while supporting the king. He thus became the 1st Earl of Orkney.

According to Orkneyinga Saga, as ally of *Thorstein the Red, Sigurd raided down to the Moray Firth defeating Celtic chief *Maelbrigte Tusk by guile probably near Dingwall. But riding north after the battle with Maelbrigte's head slung from his saddle-bow the chieftain's protruding buck tooth, the Tusk, grazed his leg and he died from the resulting blood poisoning.   1,2,3,10,22,35(7),76,100.

Sigurd II Hlodversson The Stout - Earl of Orkney c991-1014. s. of *Hlodver and *Eithne (Edna), dau. of Irish King Kjarval; grd s. of Earl *Thorfinn I Skullsplitter; father of Earls *Einar II, *Brusi, *Sumerledi by unidentified 1st wife and Earl *Thorfinn II by 2nd wife dau. of King Malcolm II.

According to Njal's Saga he controlled 'Ross and Moray, Sutherland and the Dales', perhaps an exaggerated claim, and in OS he is described as '. . . a mighty chief with wide dominions'. Held Caithness against the Scots and, in alliance with his kinsman, Gilli, a Caithness chieftain, raided each summer in the Hebrides, Scotland, Isle of Man and Ireland. Fought pitched battle at Skitten Mire near

Wick c995 defeating Scots Earl Finnlaech although said to be outnumbered 7 to 1. Victory ascribed in Orkneyinga Saga to the magic raven banner stitched by his mother. It was claimed that whoever carried it into battle would be killed but that the force behind him would prevail. Three standard-bearers died with it at Skitten Mire, it is claimed, but Sigurd was victorious. After the battle Sigurd returned their odal rights to the Orkneymen who had fought for him - rights taken from them by *Torf-Einar in return for his paying the fine imposed on the islands by *Harald Fairhair.

Sigurd was forcibly 'converted' to Christianity 995 by *King Olaf Trygvasson of Norway who having surprised him anchored in Osmondwall (Kirk Hope) gave him and his followers the choice of death or conversion. Pragmatically he chose 'conversion' but after his son, Hundi, taken hostage by Olaf, died Sigurd reverted to the old religion and was killed at battle of Clontarf outside Dublin 1014 wrapped in his mother's curse-laden raven banner which his standard-bearers this time had refused to carry.   1,2,3,10,22,35(7),38,50,76,100.

Sigurd Magnusson The Crusader - b.1090 d.1130. King of Norway 1103-1130. Youngest s. of *Magnus Barelegs who, while on raiding expedition to Orkney and the Western Isles 1098, left him, aged 8, with an advisory council to be nominal 'king' of Orkney. On death of father 5 years later he returned to Norway and ruled jointly with bros. Eystein (1103-23) and Olaf (1103-1115). Went on Crusade to Holy Land with 60 ships 1107-1111 the first Scandinavian monarch to do so. In 1129 granted share of Orkney Earldom to *Rognvald II.   1,2,3,30.

Sigurd Slembi Djaka (Sham deacon) - c1130 Norwegian chieftain; s. of a priest and claimed royal descent. Held in high favour by Earl *Harald I but not with his bro, Earl *Paul II. The Earls, who could not agree, had divided the Earldom between them but were still so opposed to one another that a civil war seemed more than likely. Sigurd sided with Harald and fearing that *Thorkell Fosterer, close friend of Paul, might exert undue influence with him in possible war with Harald, was involved in his murder. Paul was outraged and although some sort of peace was patched up between the bros, Harald paying compensation for Thorkell's killing, Paul banished Sigurd from Orkney when he went to the Scottish Court before going on a pilgrimage to the Holy Land.   3.

Sigurd of Westness - Gøding responsible for defence of Rousay. Held Westness from his kinsman by marriage and close friend Earl *Paul II; m. Ingibjorg, grd dau. of Earl *Paul I. Fought his ship with Paul II at battle of Tankerness 1135 and next year was host to Paul at Westness 1136 when Rognvald II made a 2nd and successful attempt to claim his share of Earldom. Simultaneously Paul was kidnapped by *Sweyn Asleifsson while hunting near Westness and taken south into Atholl and oblivion.   1,2,3,35(7).

Simpson, Dr. W. Douglas, CBE MA DLitt LLD - b.1896 Aberdeen d.1968 Aberdeen. Archaeologist, historian, librarian. Educ. Aberdeen Grammar School and University (1st Class Hons History). After being Lecturer in British History at Aberdeen became the University's Librarian, a position he held until his retirement.

An expert on Scottish castles he was particularly interested in Cubbie Roo's Castle on Wyre and Noltland Castle in Westray and also in the Bishop's Palace and St Magnus Cathedral lecturing on them during the annual University Weeks organised in Orkney by Aberdeen University in the 1950's always drawing packed audiences for he was an inspiring lecturer. Among his many national appointments was Chairman of the Ancient Monuments Board which, of course, had a great interest in Orkney's archaeological remains.

49, Orc 17/10/68, *Aberdeen University Review* Vol XLIII.

Simpson, Professor Sutherland, BSc, MB, ChB, MD, DSc - Physiologist; b.1863 Flotta d.1926 Ithaca, NY, USA.

Educ. Flotta Public School, Kirkwall Burgh (Grammar) School, Heriot Watt College, Edinburgh University. As young man wanted to go to sea but when unable to find a ship at Leith became laboratory assistant and technician at Edinburgh University earning enough to put himself through University studying at night classes and serving as crewman on his father's herring smack out of Flotta during vacations.

Appointed Professor of Physiology, Cornell University, USA, 1908. Fellow of Royal Society of Edinburgh; Member of British Association and British Medical Association. Author of extensive range of research papers including many on the nervous system, body temperature and secretory glands.   Orc 26/5/27, OH 10/3/26.

Sinclair, Agatha - dau. of *Sir William Sinclair of Warsetter; legitimacy confirmed 1547.   2.

Sinclair, David - c1380-1400; bro. of Earl Henry I Sinclair; grd s. of Earl Malise.   2.

Sinclair, Sir David, d.pre-1524, of Sumburgh - illegitimate s. of Earl *William Sinclair; uncle of John, Earl of Caithness killed at battle of Summerdale 1529; father of *Magnus Sinclair, summarily executed after Summerdale. Was, at various periods, in the service of both the King of Scotland and of Denmark. Foud in Shetland, Chamberlain of

Ross and Keeper of Redcastle and Dingwall Castles and one-time Governor of Bergen Castle in Norway. Very wealthy owning estates in Shetland and Orkney.   2, *Sir David Sinclair, Foud of Shetland* - Barbara Crawford in *Scandinavian Shetland* ed. John Baldwin 1978.

Sinclair, Edward, b.c1508 d.c1608, of Eday - Granted feu of Eday by *Bishop Bothwell but when 'decrepit', (said to be 100 years old) surrendered it to his son *William who later, he claimed, tried to strangle him whereupon he sought protection from Earl *Patrick Stewart.   2,13.

Sinclair, Edward, d.1560, of Strom, Shetland - Illegitimate s. of *Sir William Sinclair of Warsetter; bro. of also illegitimate *James Sinclair of Brecks of Summerdale fame, by same mother; nephew of *Lord Henry Sinclair.

Fought at Summerdale 1529 together with bro. James of Brecks with whom he had seized and occupied Kirkwall Castle the year before. Both legitimised 1535. Appointed Sheriff Depute and became *de facto* ruler of Orkney under various Superiors from c1545. Led Orkney force at battle of Papdale 1557 defeating troops from English warships commanded by *Vice Admiral Sir John Clere who was drowned trying to regain his ship.   2,93.

Sinclair, George, b.c1566 d.1643, Earl of Caithness - Grd s. of *John, Earl of Caithness killed at Summerdale 1529. Strong antipathy towards Earl *Patrick Stewart challenging him to a duel in 1597 with both having to appear before Privy Council 1599 to find surety for their good behaviour. Disliked and distrusted Orcadians generally.

Appointed King's Lieutenant by Privy Council 1614 and, with *Bishop Law, led force of 2 ships, troops and artillery to put down the rebellion instigated by the imprisoned Earl *Patrick Stewart but led in person by *Robert Stewart, his illegitimate son. Following suppression of the rebellion took leaders, including Robert, prisoner and ordered destruction of the Castle.

Had supported his kinsman *William Sinclair of Eday, when Patrick deprived him of his West Mainland lands and tried to intervene when Patrick did the same in Eday but Patrick's warships lying in wait frustrated his efforts at support.   1,2,13.

Sinclair, Henry I, Earl of Orkney 1379-c1400 - grd. s. of Earl *Malise; m. Janet Haliburton. Of Roslin branch of Sinclair family; became Earl of Orkney following interregnum of several years when there was no ruling Earl, there being at least 2 other claimants to the title and lands, *Alexander de Ard and *Erngisl Suneson, both, like himself, descended from daughters of Malise.

Henry had support of *Bishop William and eventually received feudal grant of Earldom from Hakon VI of Norway promising to defend the islands and provide military support to Norway if required but on the other hand being forbidden to erect permanent fortifications in Orkney, a clause in the agreement he promptly ignored by building the immensely strong Kirkwall Castle.

In expedition to Shetland killed a possible rival claimant to Orkney Earldom, *Malise Sperra. A dubious and unconfirmed legend has it he was involved with *Zeno in exploration of Faroe, Iceland and possibly North America. Killed in Orkney c1400 probably while repelling intrusion by an English force sent to protect its returning fishing fleet. 2,22.

Sinclair, Henry II, Earl of Orkney c1400-1420 - s. of *Henry I; father of Earl *William Sinclair; m. *Egidia Douglas, grd dau. of Robert II of Scotland.

No record of his having visited either Orkney or Norway, involvement in royal and public affairs having kept him in mainland Britain. Captured by English at battle of Homildon Hill 1402 and again 1405 off Flamborough Head when escorting the youthful James I of Scotland to France. Was also in service of Duke of Burgundy for a time.

In 1419 appointed brother-in-law, *David Menzies of Weem, married to his sister, Lady Margaret Sinclair, to be his Commissioner and representative in Orkney.   2,10,22.

Sinclair, Henry, d.1513 Flodden, Lord Henry - Tacksman of Orkney 1489-1513. s. of *William Sinclair of Newburgh; grd s. of Earl *William Sinclair; bro. of *Sir William Sinclair of Warsetter; nephew of William Sinclair, Earl of Caithness; father of *Lord William Sinclair, captured at Summerdale; m. Margaret Hepburn, who held the tack after his death until 1540.

First came to Orkney 1480 to manage lands which had been acquired by his grandfather but which, due to the runrig system of farming, were inextricably mixed up with those of the earldom and bishopric.

In 1484 obtained sub-tack of rest of Orkney including custody of Kirkwall Castle and right to administer justice. Inherited Ravenscraig near his burgh of Dysart from his father 1487 and 2 years later recognised as Lord Sinclair 'Chief of that blood' and given tack of Orkney and Shetland in his own name.

A shrewd businessman, soldier, courtier and fond of books he reorganised land-holdings in Orkney, compiling the 1492 and 1500 Rentals, and eased Orkney's transition from Norse to Scottish rule.

Captain of James IV's flagship, *Great Michael* 1512 and Master of the Royal Machines and Artillery the following year. Killed at Flodden 1513.   1,2,10,22,97,101.

Sinclair, Henry, d.1563, of Strom (later of Brough) - s. of *Edward Sinclair of Strom; m. Catherine Kennedy. Aiding intrigues by *Bellenden of Achinoull he headed Catholic opposition in Orkney to *Bishop Adam Bothwell but lacked father's quality of political leadership. The bone of contention between him and the Bishop concerned questionable disposal of bishopric lands as much as religion. 12.

Sinclair, Sir James, b.pre-1500 d.1536 Tankerness, of Brecks (later of Sanday) - Illegitimate s. of *Sir James Sinclair of Warsetter (mother probably of Cara family, South Ronaldsay); bro. of *Edward Sinclair of Strom (same mother); m. Barbara Stewart whose bro. married Margaret Tudor, mother of James V.
    A man of action. With bro. Edward captured Kirkwall Castle in surprise night attack 1528 ejecting distant cousin Lord *William Sinclair, Justice and Governor of Orkney, forcing him to take refuge in Caithness. The 2 bros. then, with a force of Orkneymen and some Shetlanders, defied the Scottish Crown at battle of Summerdale 1529 defeating the invading army commissioned by James V and led by *John, Earl of Caithness, who was killed and *Lord William Sinclair, who was captured for the 2nd time and sent packing out of the islands.
    From then on he ruled Orkney himself. Legitimised 1535, knighted and granted doubtful feudal tenure of Sanday and Stronsay by James V who now ignored previous animosity. Believed to have committed suicide at the Gloup of Linksness, Tankerness 1536. 1,2,10,20(15).

Sinclair, James, BSc - b.1914 Bu, Hoy d.1968 Kirkwall. Botanist. Educ. Hoy Public School, Stromness Academy, Edinburgh University, Moray House Teachers Training College.
    Taught in Kirkwall Grammar School and Stronsay PS 1938-41. RAF Radar Operator, India 1941-46. Returned UK to Herbarium of Edinburgh Royal Botanic Gardens 1946. Curator Herbarium Singapore Botanic Gardens 1948-65 when retired due to ill-health.
    At very early age encouraged to develop his youthful interest in plants by Orkney botanist *Col. Henry Halcro Johnston. Later while teaching in Stronsay studied and wrote about the island's marine algae and again during service in the Far East became deeply interested and, in spare time, studied plants of areas in which he was stationed resulting in his Singapore appointment where he made a complete collection of the local plants. On expeditions to most of the Malay Peninsula, Sumatra, Sarawak and the Philippines collecting specimens and writing on their plant-life he developed a particular interest in the custard apple and nutmeg families. Contributed chapter on 'Our Orkney Flora' in the 'New Orkney Book' and many other publications. Orc 22/2/68.

Sinclair, John, d.1529 Summerdale, Earl of Caithness - Grd s. of Earl
*William Sinclair; cousin of *Lord Henry Sinclair and *Sir William
Sinclair of Warsetter.

Given royal mandate with *Lord William Sinclair to invade Orkney
and re-capture Kirkwall Castle from which Lord William, as Governor
and Justice of Orkney, had been ejected, and to punish those
responsible, *James Sinclair of Brecks and his bro. *Edward Sinclair of
Strom. Leading the Caithness force which crossed Scapa Flow landing
on the Orphir shore the Earl was killed at the ensuing battle of
Summerdale 1529 and Lord William taken prisoner.   1,2.

Sinclair, Sir John, b.1754 d.1815, of Ulbster. 'Agricultural Sir John'.
Agriculturist. Educ. Edinburgh, Glasgow, Oxford Universities; called
to English Bar; MP in various parliaments for Caithness, Lostwithiel
and Petersfield between 1780 and 1811. Stood for Northern Burghs
(Kirkwall) 1784 and for Orkney 1796 but failed in both attempts.

Landowner, politician, propagandist for agricultural improvement
who practised what he preached on his own extensive Caithness
estates which he inherited 1770 residing in Thurso Castle. Initiated and
involved in establishment of Board of Agriculture 1793 and Society for
Improvement of British Wool.

Self-appointed economic adviser to Prime Minister William Pitt
who, with his close associate, Henry Dundas, occasionally accepted
some of his ideas but more often ignored them.

A man of exceptional energy and ability keenly interested in
scientific matters, he was author of 160 books and 376 pamphlets. He
also raised 2 battalions of Fencibles in Caithness 1794 and 1795.

One of his greatest achievements was the compilation, preparation
and publication of the First, now known as the 'Old' Statistical
Account of Scotland for which between 1791 and 1800 he persuaded
almost every Minister of the Church of Scotland to write an account of
his own parish based on a questionnaire to provide overall conformity.
This invaluable work appeared in 21 volumes of which the relevant
chapters were extracted, edited and published under the title 'The
Orkney Parishes' by *J. Storer Clouston.   2,44.

Sinclair, Magnus, of Sumburgh - s. of *Sir David Sinclair. Fought on
Caithness side at Summerdale 1529 and was executed without trial
after the battle.   2.

Sinclair, Margaret - dau. of *James Sinclair of Brecks; m. *Magnus Halcro
of Brough.   2.

Sinclair, Lady Margaret - widow of *Lord Henry Sinclair who, after his
death at Flodden 1415, was granted his tack of Orkney which as she

was an absentee tackswoman was managed by *Sir William Sinclair of Warsetter. In 1528 she gave custody of Kirkwall Castle and right to administer justice to her son *Lord William with unhappy results as far as he was concerned. 1,2.

Sinclair, Marjorie - mother of *Robert Stewart, illegitimate s. of Earl *Patrick Stewart. Possibly of the Tuquoy or Sandwick Sinclairs. 2,13.

Sinclair, Oliver, of Pitcairns - s. of Oliver Sinclair of Roslin grd. s. of *William Sinclair, Earl of Orkney. Favourite of *James V from mid-1530s. Appears to have used his position to secure the rehabilitation of *James and *Edward Sinclair, the victors of Summerdale. Accompanied the king on his circumnavigation of Scotland, visiting Orkney, and the following year became tacksman and sheriff of Orkney and constable of Kirkwall Castle. He was appointed commander of the king's forces on the campaign that ended in humiliation at the Battle of Solway Moss and his career was stopped in its tracks. The king died shortly thereafter and Sinclair's interests in Orkney passed to *Mary of Guise as her jointure; she pursued Sinclair for arrears of duty during the 1540s. He returned to Orkney in 1560 and received a grant from *Bishop Adam Bothwell, his stepson, of the bishopric lands in Eday. He married *Katherine Bellenden, sister of Sir Thomas Bellenden of Auchnoull. Through his family connections with Sinclair, Bellenden, Bothwell and Stewart, he provides an important link in the chain between the two earldom dynasties of Sinclair and Stewart. 12,13.

Sinclair, Thomas - 'Warden' of Orkney 1435; s. of *David Sinclair; nephew of Earl *Henry I; grt grd s. of Earl *Malise, appointed by King Erik III of Denmark to manage his royal estates in Orkney while Earl *Henry II was an absentee and whose Earldom estates were managed by *David Menzies, a system of dual control which inevitably led to trouble and even violence between them largely fomented by Menzies. On one occasion he was forced to seek sanctuary from Menzies in St Magnus Cathedral. Was probably a member of King Erik's Hird. 1,2.

Sinclair, Sir William, of Roslin - m. *Isabella, dau. of Earl *Malise; father of Earl Henry I. 2.

Sinclair, William, Lord Sinclair - s. of Lord *Henry Sinclair and Lady *Margaret Sinclair who, after Lord Henry's death, gave him custody of Kirkwall Castle as Governor with power to administer justice. He enjoyed these appointments until 1528 when his relatives, the bros. *James Sinclair of Brecks and *Edward of Strom, captured him in a night raid on the castle and ejected him from Orkney. Taking refuge in

Caithness he sought and received active support for an attempt to regain his Orkney status from another distant relative, *John Sinclair, Earl of Caithness, which culminated in the battle of Summerdale 1529 where the Earl was killed and Lord William himself was taken prisoner and ejected from Orkney for the second time within a year by the same two Sinclair bros. who led the Orkneymen to victory in the battle.   1,2,10,12.

Sinclair, William, b.1408 d.1471, Earl of Orkney 1434-71 - s. of Earl *Henry II Sinclair and *Egidia Douglas, grd dau. of Robert II of Scotland. His aunt, Marjory, sister of Earl Henry II was married to *David Menzies of Weem, William's guardian during his minority and governor and manager of Orkney for his absentee father, Henry II. William himself also married a royal Douglas taking Elizabeth, grd dau. of Robert III, as his first wife. She had claims to extensive estates in Scotland to add to his own Sinclair properties in Dysart, Roslin and Caithness; m. (2) Marjorie Sutherland, dau. of Alex. Sutherland of Dunbeath 1456.

On coming of age he visited Orkney 1422 before going to Denmark to establish his right to the Orkney Earldom. Menzies proved unhelpful and William was not officially installed as Earl until 1434 when he was granted Earldom by Erik III on feudal terms. In meantime he decided to act on his own behalf and in spite of their differences he and Menzies visited James I being held prisoner in Durham by the English. When Menzies in turn was hostage in the Tower of London William established control in Orkney but found himself in conflict with *Bishop Thomas Tulloch who had been appointed by Erik III to look after the Danish royal interests and estates in Orkney. William under terms of his installation as Earl of Orkney was summoned to the Danish Court to explain his differences with the Bishop but never complied, an indication that he considered himself primarily as a Scottish nobleman owing allegiance to the Scottish Crown from which he held his mainland titles and estates rather than as vassal of the Danish king though holding Orkney Earldom from Denmark. Appointed Admiral of Scotland during reign of James I he accompanied the king's daughter, Margaret, to France on occasion of her marriage to the Dauphin and in 1449 was Steward at the wedding of James II to Mary of Guelders. Was Chancellor of Scotland 1453-56 and created Earl of Caithness 1455.

His final summons to the Danish Court came in 1461 and again he ignored it on grounds of having more important things to do in Scotland and Bishop *William Tulloch was appointed Danish Councillor of State with powers of sysselman.

With the possibility of Orkney being ceded to Scotland now becoming a probability William continued to distance himself from Denmark and unsuccessfully tried to delay negotiations for the marriage of *James III and *Margaret, dau. of Christian I of Denmark. When the marriage did, in fact, take place 1468 with Orkney being pawned by Christian in part payment of his daughter's dowry William resigned the Orkney Earldom to James III 1470 in return for properties in Scotland and other concessions including a pension and retention of the Caithness Earldom. Last Earl of Orkney to hold the Earldom from Norway and/or Denmark.   1,2,10,22,42,93.

Sinclair, William, of Eday - s. of *Edward Sinclair who, in his old age, handed over his feudal rights to him. Edward, the father, then complained to Earl *Patrick Stewart that he was being ill-treated by his son whereupon Patrick ejected William from his estates in the West Mainland and laid siege to his property in Eday. William appealed to his kinsman, *George Sinclair, Earl of Caithness, for help and with close on 100 Highlanders from the north of Scotland tried to regain Eday but was repelled by Patrick's warships lying in wait for him. 2.

Sinclair, Sir William, d.1735, of Warsetter - Bro. of Lord *Henry Sinclair during whose frequent absences from Orkney, he managed affairs in the islands. Holding lands in Sanday, Stronsay, Westray, St Andrews, the Warsetter Sinclairs became the ruling family in Orkney. Father of illegitimate sons *James Sinclair of Brecks and *Edward Sinclair of Strom and legitimate son Magnus.

Continued to manage Orkney affairs after Lord Henry's death when the tack passed to his widow, *Lady Margaret, an absentee tackswoman who drew the revenue but played little or no active part in management of the estate.   2,10,22.

Sinclair, William, of Newburgh, 'William the Waster' - Only s. of Earl *William by 1st marriage to Elizabeth Douglas; father of Lord *Henry Sinclair and *Sir William Sinclair of Warsetter. Of doubtful mental competence. In 1467 was said to have taken *Bishop William Tulloch prisoner forcing him to take certain oaths possibly in an attempt to force the Bishop to renounce the authority he had received from Denmark to manage Christian I's affairs in Orkney. Although virtually disinherited he contested the issue and finally obtained Ravenscraig and its lands near Dysart.   2.

Skatehorn - b.c1840 Kirkwall d.1913 County Home, Kirkwall. Real name William Laughton; s. of pedlars who came to Orkney from Aberdeen-shire. A popular drop-out and vagrant; early in his 'career' decided regular work did not suit him so opted for a vagrant life-style sleeping rough under a dyke in summer and in some friendly farmer's barn in winter. Among his accomplishments were boxing, fencing, swimming, which he learned during service in the Naval Coast Volunteers and he was also credited with being an expert dancer. Usually depicted on postcard portraits by *Tom Kent wheeling a penny-farthing bike wearing ragged cast-off clothes with holes stuffed with straw. A well-liked kenspeckle character.   31, *Shoal and Sheaf* - ed D. Tinch.

Skea, Bessie - see Grieve, Mrs Jemima Bessie.

Skea, James - see Ka, James.

Skuli Thorfinnsson - s. of Earl *Thorfinn I Skullsplitter; younger bro. of Earls *Arnfinn, *Havard, *Hlodver, *Ljot. Became chieftain in Caithness with title of Earl but he also claimed Orkney Earldom and with Scots support invaded the islands but was repelled by Ljot who pursued him to Caithness and in the ensuing battle of the Dales c978 defeated and killed him.   1,2,3,35(7).

Smith, Charles, b.c1749 Stenness d.1824 Leith, of Tormiston - Portrait painter. 2nd s. of William Smith, Bailie of Stenness and Charlotte Whitefoord, grd dau. of Sir Alan Whitefoord Bt, of Ayrshire. Studied art and painting at Royal Academy, London under Sir Joshua Reynolds the leading portrait painter of his day. Painted portraits in West Indies for some time before going to India 1783 where became Court Painter to the Great Mogul Shah Allum. Returning to London embarked on undistinguished literary career writing several books and poems and one play which failed at Covent Garden.   20(13).

Smythe, Patrick, d.1655, of Braco - Came to Orkney from Perthshire c1615 in household of his guardian *Bishop Graham who granted him extensive bishopric lands in Holm including Meall; m. (1) Katherine, eldest dau. of Bishop Graham 1618 (2) Margaret Stewart, widow of Hugh Halcro (3) Isabella Anderson - there were 14 children by 1st marriage and 11 by 2nd and 3rd.

A shrewd businessman he was closely associated with his father-in-law, in granting of bishopric lands to friends and family.

Drowned in Stronsay Firth 1655 and succeeded in Holm estate by his 4th son also Patrick who sold it to his uncle, Patrick Graham, 2nd son of Bishop Graham, who moved from Greenwall, Holm to Meall renaming it Grahamshall and so becoming 1st Graham of Grahamshall subsequently termed Graemeshall.   2,57.

Snaekol Gunnisson - s. of Gunni (probably grd s. of *Sweyn Asleifsson) and Ragnhild, grd dau. of Earl *Rognvald II; nephew of *Harald Ungi. Through descent from Rognvald II claimed family estates in Orkney and possibly the Earldom itself. Found an ally in his cousin *Hanef

Ungi, sysselman for the Norwegian Crown in Orkney. Both were involved in killing of Earl *John Haraldsson 1230 during a drunken brawl in Thurso and, pursued by John's followers, fled to Orkney taking refuge in Cubbie Roo's Castle on Wyre. The pursuers were unable to take the castle by force and a truce was arranged to allow both sides to lay their respective cases before the Norwegian Court. Hanef, having influence at the Court, managed to evade possible retribution and disappeared as did Snaekol. John's party of gødings returning west empty-handed were all lost when their vessel known as the 'Gødings' ship' foundered 1232. 1,2.

Snorre Sturlusson - b.1179 Iceland d.1241 Iceland. Historian, lawyer, saga writer, poet. Elected Supreme Judge of Iceland, Speaker of the Althing 1215; Chamberlain at Norwegian Court 1219. Author of 'Heimskringla, Saga of the Norse Kings' with frequent references to Orkney, and the Prose Edda. Meddled politically in Norwegian affairs incurring anger of *Hakon IV at whose instigation he was killed. 3,30,76,102.

Somerledi - Earl of Orkney c1014-1018. Eldest s. of Earl *Sigurd II by his 1st wife; bro. of Earls *Brusi, *Einar II; half bro. of Earl *Thorfinn II; uncle of Earl (St) *Rognvald II. After death of his father at Clontarf 1014 succeeded to the Earldom to rule jointly with his bros. Brusi and Einar II but died shortly afterwards. 1,2,3.

Spence, Graeme - Hydrographer. Descended from *Bishop Mackenzie. Was assistant to his cousin *Commander Murdoch Mackenzie and succeeded him as Maritime Surveyor to Admiralty 1788.

Described as 'late Maritime Surveyor' in 1812 he submitted to the Admiralty his 'Proposals for Establishing a Temporary Rendezvous for Line of Battle Ships in a National Roadstead called Scapa Flow formed by the South Isles of Orkney' emphasising its suitability as a naval base to such an extent that it became rather more than a 'Temporary Rendezvous' for the Royal Navy in two World Wars. 14(4),26.

Spence, Magnus FEIS - b.c1853 Birsay d.1919 Craigiefield, St Ola. Botanist, geologist, meteorologist, antiquarian. Schoolmaster Stenness and Deerness late 19th early 20th century. Epitome of traditional Scots dominie with wide scientific interests. Author of 'Flora Orcadensis' 1914, which also contains sections on climate, geology and natural selection. Contributed section on meteorology to first 'Orkney Book' 1909. Carried out investigations into origin and purpose of Ring of Brogar. During World War I supplied the Navy in Scapa Flow with daily meteorological reports from his weather station in Deerness. His herbarium is preserved in the Stromness Museum. 47, Orc 28/8/19.

Spence, William - b.1846 Eday d.1926 Australia; Labour and trade union leader. Family emigrated Victoria, Australia 1852 where he worked as shepherd before moving to the goldfields holding Mineral Rights when only 14 and following the goldrushes to Ballarat where he organised the Miners' Union 1874 leading 600 members into the Amalgamated Miners Association of Victoria 1878. As a result became exceedingly unpopular with the mine owners. In 1882 became general secretary of the Association which expanded to cover Tasmania, Queensland and New Zealand. With the federation of coal, gold, silver, and copper miners it became the Amalgamated Miners of Australia with a membership of 25,000 by 1884. Turning his attention to the industrial organisation of workers in the 'outback', especially the sheep-shearers, he became Foundation President of the Amalgamated Shearers Union of Australia 1886. Sat for Labor 1898 in New South Wales Legislative Assembly pressing for the Federation of Australian States which was achieved 1901 with the formation of the Commonwealth of Australia of which he was Postmaster General 1914-15. During his career he was also a militiaman in the Ballarat Rifle Rangers. JP, borough councillor, Sunday School Superintendent and Methodist lay preacher. *The Shearers* - Orkney Room, Orkney Library.

Spike - see Johnston, R. T.

Steuart, Alexander - Younger bro. of *Sir James Steuart of Burray. Involved and present with his brother and servants when they shot and killed *Capt. James Moodie snr RN of Melsetter on Broad Street, Kirkwall 1725. It was revenge killing for humiliation suffered by Steuart after he had been intercepted and thrashed while poaching game on Moodie's Melsetter lands. After the murder he escaped into exile becoming successful merchant in Amsterdam maintaining trading links with Orkney although never returning to the islands. 11.

Steuart, Anne, Lady Steuart - dau. of David Carmichael of Balmedie, Aberdeenshire; wife of *Sir James Steuart and as outspoken and as fervent a Jacobite and Episcopalian as he was, wearing, and ordering her servants to wear, the White Cockade, emblem of the Jacobites.
     After her husband was taken to London for trial charged with treason she was herself taken prisoner by *Benjamin Moodie and sent south on board HMS *Eltham* where her fellow prisoner was Flora MacDonald who had helped the Young Pretender escape capture after Culloden.   11.

Steuart, Sir James Bt, b.1694 Burray d.1746 London, 3rd of Burray - s. of Sir Archibald Steuart Bt; cousin of his heir *Lord Garlies (later Earl of Galloway); m. *Anne Carmichael of Balmedie.

Succeeded father as laird of Burray 1707. Domineering, arrogant, staunch Jacobite and Episcopalian, leader of Orkney lairds of similar persuasion. Brought up while minor by pro-Hanoverian Earl of Morton's family, who held the Earldom, and was at first friendly towards them but became more closely associated with his fervently Jacobite cousin, Lord Garlies. Quarrelled with Morton partly over presentation of a Presbyterian minister to Burray charge while a long-running Steuart feud with Moodies of Melsetter intensified over a similar difference of opinion regarding the Presbyterian minister of Walls and Flotta.

Both feuds simmered for several years, that with Moodies culminating in Kirkwall murder of *Captain James Moodie snr of Melsetter 1725 by the Steuart faction. Present when fatal shot was fired, the Burray laird and bro. *Alexander escaped capture, fled Orkney and went to ground for several years before Sir James himself obtained a royal pardon, ironically through good offices of the Earl of Morton. Restored to his Burray estate developed kelp industry and became a Burgess of Kirkwall. He was one of the most advanced of Orkney's early agricultural improvers - the inventory of the Bu after his death lists waggons, carts, improved ploughs, and a turnip drill plough in use at a time when it was generally said that such things were not to be found elsewhere in Scotland.

Steuart animosity towards the Mortons continued, however, even to the extent of Sir James pursuing and physically assaulting the Earl and his party at Graemeshall 1739. Morton returning from South Ronaldsay, had landed on and crossed Steuart's Burray lands without his permission. Sir James claimed that this, with associated contentious matters regarding one of his servantmen, was an infringement of his proprietorial rights in Burray.

He also alleged that over the years the Mortons, as Superiors of the Earldom, and their factors had covertly manipulated the old and admittedly corrupt Orkney system of weights and measures in order to increase dues payable to the Earldom by the local lairds. The lairds naturally supported him in the ensuing legal action, known as the Pundlar Process, which dragged on for 26 years 1733-59 through the Court of Session ending in victory for the Earl of Morton and financial ruin for many of the lairds.

Although not physically 'out' in the '45 he gave enthusiastic support to the Jacobite cause in words if not deeds intriguing with fellow supporters across the Pentland Firth and with officers of a Spanish ship carrying arms and funds for the rebel cause. After Culloden 1746 he refused to go into hiding staying on in Burray where he was captured by party of soldiers under Captain *Benjamin Moodie of Melsetter, son of Captain *James Moodie murdered by the Steuarts in 1725. Was paraded through Kirkwall before being lodged in

Tolbooth and then marched to Stromness for embarkation en route to jail in London where died of fever, probably typhus, while awaiting trial. 11,20(12).

Stewart, Adam - illegitimate son of James V, buried in St Magnus Cathedral beneath a stone slab with the Scottish royal arms.

Stewart, Adam - illegitimate s. of *John, Earl of Carrick. Held lands in Eday after father's death. 12.

Stewart, Alexander, b.1694 d.1773, 6th Earl of Galloway - An extreme Jacobite. Styled Lord Garlies until he succeeded to Galloway Earldom 1746 the same year in which he inherited the Burray and South Ronaldsay estates of his kinsman *Sir James Steuart who had died in Southwark Jail, London, awaiting trial for his part in the '45. Attended meeting in Burray 1747 of lairds opposed to Earl of Morton and continued litigation in the Pundlar Process (1733-59) initiated by Sir James. Sold South Isles estates to Sir Lawrence Dundas 1768. 2,11,83.

Stewart, Archibald, 4th of Brugh - One of the Jacobite North Isles lairds who, having written a letter supporting the Young Pretender, which was intercepted by Duke of Cumberland, were branded as rebels and went into hiding after the '45, sometimes being forced to take refuge in the Gentlemen's Ha' sea-caves in Westray to avoid capture by Government troops led by *Benjamin Moodie who nonetheless burned down his mansion of Cleat in Westray.

The Stewarts of Brugh could claim royal descent through Edward Stewart, illegitimate son of Earl *Robert Stewart, himself illegitimate son of *James V of Scotland; Archibald was thus grt grt grt grd son of *James V. 4,11.

Stewart, Barbara - widow of *Sir James Sinclair of Brecks after whose death was granted Bishopric lands in Burray by *Bishop Bothwell. She was decended from Robert II, King of Scots, and her bro. Henry, Lord Methven, was the 3rd husband of Margaret Tudor, dau. of Henry VII of England and mother of *James V. 2,13.

Stewart, Bernard - Strong-arm bodyguard, Master Stabler and Farmer to Earl *Patrick Stewart; later Keeper of Palace of Birsay under *Finlayson having switched allegiance from Patrick after his arrest and detention in the south but entertained Patrick's son *Robert at Birsay 1612 when he came north the first time to collect rents etc. on his father's behalf. After a few days, however, Robert ejected his host from the Palace keeping his wife prisoner as hostage. Bernard retreated to Kirkwall.

When Robert mounted his real rebellion 2 years later one of his first targets was Bernard's house in Kirkwall. This attack was beaten off but a second attempt some days later succeeded when the rebels occupied the strategic points in the town. Bernard was captured and sent south where he gave the authorities information about rebels.   13.

Stewart, Charles WS, NP - b.1675 Edinburgh d.1731 Kirkwall. Cousin of William Stewart MP of Weyland. Commissary and Stewart Clerk of Orkney 1698; Burgess of Wick 1702; Admiral Substitute of Orkney 1712; Commissary Clerk of Orkney 1725.

Present on Broad Street, Kirkwall 1725 when *Captain James Moodie snr of Melsetter was shot and killed by Steuarts of Burray. Said to have held Sir James Steuart back during the affray.   35(8).

Stewart, Edward - illegitimate s. of Earl *Robert Stewart by Marjorie Sandilands of Wick who received grant of land at Weyland near Kirkwall. Became 1st Stewart of Brugh, founder of that family line.   12.

Stewart, Lieut. George, RN - b.1766 d.1791. s. of Alexander Stewart of Massater.

Serving on board Captain Bligh's HMS *Bounty* in Pacific 1789 when crew mutinied and set Bligh and 18 crewmen adrift in open boat. Mutineers kept Stewart on board until they reached Tahiti where he was put ashore while they made for Pitcairn Island. Another naval vessel, HMS *Pandora*, called at Tahiti 1791 when Stewart swam out to her and was immediately put under arrest. *Pandora* was wrecked on way back to UK and Stewart was among those lost. Married Peggy, dau. of local chief, by whom he had a daughter. Peggy died when he was arrested.   35(6).

Stewart, James, d.1802, 5th of Brugh - s. of *Archibald Stewart and Isabel, heiress of William Balfour of Pharay. Leading merchant laird in Orkney during latter half of 18th century. Bought Fair Isle 1766 at roup in Edinburgh for £850 and held extensive Orkney estates especially in Westray where he lived at Cleat. Shipowner trading to British, European and occasionally North American ports.   17,48.

Stewart, James of Graemsay - illegitimate s. of Earl *Robert Stewart, probably his favourite son but after father's death fell foul of his half bro. Earl *Patrick who imprisoned him and pulled down his house during dispute over repayment of debt owed by Earl. Was also in dispute over some of his servants imprisoned by Patrick for helping *Monteith of Gairsay avoid Earl's edict banning travel out of Orkney. Appointed Justice of Peace 1611 but again unable to perform duties adequately owing to Patrick's interference.   12,13.

Stewart, Sir James, of Killeith (later Lord Ochiltree) - Became principal
tacksman, Sheriff and Chamberlain taking over management of
Earldom estate from *Bishop Law 1613. An absentee tacksman, his
rents were collected by his hated resident Deputy and bro-in-law,
*John Finlayson. Tack terminated 1622 when he escaped abroad to
avoid creditors. Accused of tampering with Orkney weights and
measures to his own advantage when collecting Earldom dues.   13.

Stewart, John, b.c1568, Master of Orkney, later Lord Kinclaven and Earl
of Carrick - 3rd s. of Earl *Robert Stewart and Jean Kennedy; bro. of
Earl *Patrick and, after death of their older bro. Henry, became heir
presumptive to Earldom.

   Acquitted on charge of plotting murder of bro. Patrick 1596 when
it was alleged he had consulted a reputed witch, *Alison Balfour, to
bring about his bro's death. Shortly after acquittal was involved in
Shetland killing of *Henry Colville, Parson of Orphir who had been
involved in extracting confession from her under torture.

   In dispute with Patrick over financial and landholding matters
after their mother's death but later, using his influence at Court,
interceded on his bro's behalf when Patrick was charged with
disobeying Privy Council orders to appear before them to answer
allegations of tyrannical misrule in Orkney and even treason.

   Accompanied James VI when he went to London 1603 to succeed
Elizabeth I on English throne and continued to enjoy royal favour
although an arrogant and often troublesome courtier. Created Earl of
Carrick in Eday by Charles I but his hopes of gaining Orkney Earldom
were not realised although he obtained £3,600 pension from the
Earldom revenue 1621.   2,13.

Stewart, Patrick (Black Patie), b.c1565 d.1615 Edinburgh. Earl of Orkney,
Lord of Shetland 1593-1615 - 2nd s. of *Earl Robert Stewart and Jean
Kennedy, sister of Earl of Cassilis; m. Margaret Livingston, dau. of
Lord Livingston, widow of *Sir Lewis Bellenden 1596; father of
illegitimate son *Robert and possibly two unnamed daughters all by
unknown mothers.

   Notorious for despotic, tyrannical rule over both Orkney and
Shetland with reputation for arrogance, rapacity, extravagance and
double-dealing but credited with a degree of personal charm and
definite artistic taste especially in architecture having commissioned
several fine buildings including Earl's Palace, Kirkwall and Scalloway
Castle, Shetland, both built by forced labour.

   Received charter of Orkney Earldom, Shetland and bishopric lands
1600 but held the islanders in contempt feuding with many of leading
island families and even his own bros. legitimate and otherwise.
Deeply in debt by 1606 but ignored summons to appear before Privy

Council to answer complaints regarding his oppressive rule in the islands and even a charge of treason subsequently dropped 1607.

Successfully opposed over acquisition of bishopric rents and occupancy of Earl's Palace by Bishop *James Law, on his appointment to diocese 1607. In following year Law, confidant of James VI & I, complained to the king on islanders' behalf over Patrick's oppressive rule. He was duly commanded by the King to appear before Privy Council who ordered his detention in Edinburgh Castle to answer complaints alleging, among others, acquisition of goods and property by extortion, restriction of islanders' movement by closure of the ferries, making laws to his own benefit by allowing him powers of banishment and even the death penalty.

Hopelessly insolvent and with many implacable enemies in both Orkney and Shetland he was indicted on 7 charges of treason on grounds of usurping royal authority 1610 after which kept in close confinement in Edinburgh Castle. He denied charges pleading justification for his actions on the islands' Country Laws which Privy Council abolished 1610.

He appointed his illegitimate son *Robert as his deputy in Orkney with instructions to regain his 'houses' there and to collect rents preparatory to his hoped-for restoration to the Earldom. He was duly declared a rebel and incarcerated in Dumbarton Castle. Robert's attempt to comply with his father's orders resulted in what did amount to a rebellion against royal authority which was put down by an expedition led by *George Sinclair, Earl of Caithness and Bishop Law. Found guilty of treason after trial, Patrick was beheaded 1615. There is a story, probably apocryphal, that his execution was delayed for several days to give him time to learn the Lord's Prayer.

1,2,4,10,12,13,22,75,101.

Stewart, Robert, b.c1533 d.1593. Earl of Orkney, Lord of Shetland - Illegitimate s. of *James V of Scotland and Euphemia, dau. of Lord Elphinstone; half-bro. of *Mary Queen of Scots and James Stewart, Earl of Moray; m. Jean Kennedy, dau. of Earl of Cassillis; father of Earl *Patrick.

Overbearing, unscrupulously greedy for land by whatever means, notorious for harsh, oppressive rule in Orkney and Shetland though not quite to same degree as his son Patrick who succeeded him. Appointed Commendator of Holyrood 1538 while still an infant. Scholar at St Andrews 1540. Accompanied half-sister Mary to France 1548. Returned to Scotland 1551 and with one brief visit to France in mid 50s was probably at Scottish Court until 1557. Met and welcomed Queen Mary, at Leith on her return from France 1561 and remained at her Court. Received Orkney and Shetland from her in grant of doubtful legality 1564/5 and appointed Sheriff but not given title of Earl. Present in Holyrood when her Italian secretary and fellow

Catholic, David Rizzio, was assassinated 1566 but was not apparently involved in murder plot led by her husband, Lord Darnley, although he did play an ambivalent part later in the Kirk o' Field killing of Darnley himself 1567.

Replaced as Sheriff of Orkney 1566 by *Gilbert Balfour, and all his Orkney 'rights' were swept away when Mary m. *Earl of Bothwell creating him 'Duke' of Orkney 1567. After defeat of Mary's party and Bothwell's flight to Scandinavia via Orkney and Shetland Robert made his first actual appearance in Orkney itself apparently to establish himself in power 1567.

Inducing Balfour to surrender Sheriffship he also gained occupancy of Kirkwall Castle but not control of St Magnus Cathedral, the tower of which could be used as a threatening vantage point overlooking the Castle. His followers, however, seized it, too, the following year killing 2 Bishop's men in the process further discrediting his actions in Orkney and with Regent Morton refusing to accept his payment of feus the legality of his claims to the Earldom became even more suspect. He solved the problem to some extent by exchanging his own holding of the Abbey of Holyrood for the remains of the Orkney Bishopric lands thus giving him a legal status in the islands.

For the next few years consolidating his hold on Orkney made himself Provost of Kirkwall and with Gilbert Balfour in exile took over Noltland Castle and with it the Westray rents. During this period, too, began building Palace at Birsay.

But he had acquired many enemies both in and out of Orkney, some of them with considerable influence, who in 1575 submitted to the Privy Council the 'Complaint of the Inhabitants of Orkney and Zetland' setting out a catalogue of his alleged oppressive and illegal actions. As a result he was warded in Edinburgh Castle while the complaints were investigated. Little of whatever evidence was taken in Orkney during these investigations is extant though more exists from Shetland. With Regent Morton's power on the wane during his wardship Robert was able to gain favour with his nephew, the youthful James VI and although allowed to return to Orkney 1578 spent much time in the south becoming Privy Councillor 1580 and in 1581 achieved ambition being created Earl of Orkney, Lord of Shetland and Knight of Birsay along with confirmation of his doubtful 1564/5 feu and also powers of judiciary and admiralty which the 'Complaint' had accused him of usurping.

Confirmation of his Bishopric rights 1585 gave him absolute and legal control in the islands. As a result he became even more overbearing and tyrannical with increasing instances of using his judiciary powers to acquire land by extortion. Falling out of favour with James VI who was investigating land-grabbing propensities of

Sheriffs in general and Orkney's Sheriff in particular 1597 Robert saw the red light and began returning some of the lands he had acquired by coercion to their rightful owners, the so-called 'Gentlemen Odallers' but that same year 1587 he was described in official documents as the 'lait erle of Orkney' having apparently been deposed.

An old enemy *Patrick Bellenden was commissioned to 'fetch' Robert to Edinburgh but on arrival in Orkney with three armed ships he was opposed by Robert in person leading a force of still-loyal Orcadians. Bellenden was unable to collect rents and skat as instructed and retired empty-handed leaving Robert in Orkney where he remained much subdued until he died 1593.   1,2,4,10,12,22,75,101.

Stewart, Robert - b.c1592 d.1615 Edinburgh - illegitimate s. of Earl *Patrick Stewart by Marjorie Sinclair of either Westray or Sandwick.

Sent as his deputy to Orkney 1612 by dispossessed father Patrick, then warded in Edinburgh, to collect rents and skats, hold courts as Sheriff and to recover castles and palaces - all contrary to Privy Council orders. But on arrival of *Bishop Law in Orkney armed with royal authority, Robert surrendered the Castle and other fortified places much to his father's disgust. In 1614 Patrick, now a prisoner in Dumbarton Castle, sent Robert back to Orkney on a second mission with similar objectives. He succeeded in seizing first the Palace in Birsay and then the Castle, St Magnus Cathedral and Earl's Palace in Kirkwall but after betrayal by some of his followers was finally forced to surrender to a force, which included artillery, acting with royal authority and led by *George Sinclair, Earl of Caithness, and Bishop Law. Robert was taken prisoner to Edinburgh, tried and hanged 1615.   1,2,4,13,22,75,101.

Stevenson, Robert Louis - b.1850 Edinburgh d.1894 Samoa. Author of 'Treasure Island', 'Kidnapped', 'Master of Ballantrae' and many other novels. s. of Thomas Stevenson; grd. s. of *Robert Stevenson.

Came to Orkney 1869 with his father, who followed in the family tradition of building lighthouses, visiting St Magnus Cathedral and the Palaces in Kirkwall.   Orc Jan/Feb 1967.

Stevenson, Robert - b.1772 Glasgow d.1850 Edinburgh. Grd father of *R. L. Stevenson. Assisted his father-in-law, Edinburgh lamp-maker. Thomas Smith, in designing and building first North Ronaldsay lighthouse tower 1789 and then succeeded him as Chief Engineer for Northern Lighthouse Board for 47 years from 1796 during which time planned and built 27 lighthouses round Scottish coast - including two in Orkney - Start Point and Pentland Skerries. Installed first flashing light in Scotland at Start Point, Sanday 1806.

Strange, Sir Robert, RA - b.1721 Kirkwall d.1792 London. Artist and
engraver. s. of David Strange, Burgh Treasurer, Kirkwall; grd s. of
Malcolm Scollay of Hunton, Stronsay; m. Isabella Lumisden, sister of
Young Pretender's secretary who is said to have saved him from arrest
by Hanoverian army in Inverness after Culloden by concealing him in
her voluminous skirts.

Educ. Kirkwall and destined for legal career but had hankering to
serve in Royal Navy. He was so seasick on his one voyage in a warship,
however, that he decided to stay ashore and having always been keen
on drawing apprenticed himself to leading Edinburgh artist and
engraver, Richard Cooper.

A staunch Jacobite he was 'out' in the '45 serving in the Prince's
Lifeguards at Culloden. His portrait of the Prince is the only one
known to have been drawn from life in Scotland during the '45 and he
also produced designs for proposed Jacobite bank notes.

Escaped to Continent after Culloden and was honoured for his
engravings by Academies in France and Italy and on returning to
London received similar honours being made an RA and, in spite of
his former Jacobite activities, was knighted by George III for whom he
had produced engravings.   51.

Strathearn Earls of Orkney - see Malise.

Sutherland, Forby - Flotta-born seaman. Sailed in Capt. Cook's ship
Endeavour on his first antipodean voyage 1768-71 when after
discovering New Zealand they reached Australia where Sutherland
died May 1770 and was buried on what was renamed Sutherland
Point, the first known Briton to be buried in Australian soil.   81.

Sutherland, Captain James (later Lord Duffus) - b.1747 Skelbo,
Sutherland d.1827 London; became Lord Duffus 1826. Factor for
Orkney Earldom estate 1795-99 farming Bu of Burray himself after
*Thomas Balfour had moved to Shapinsay where he introduced
improvements on his estate of Sound along modern lines.

A sharp businessman, but harsh, domineering and unscrupulous;
Sutherland believed strongly in traditional methods of farming
viewing 'improvements' and innovations generally, especially those
being introduced by Balfour in Shapinsay with deep contempt openly
treating them with derision. He built up a herd of Highland cattle at
the Bu.

While serving in the 26th of Foot had caused scandal when he ran
off with General's wife 1771. Allegedly fathered large number of
illegitimate children during his time as factor in Orkney and certainly
named 10 of these daughters in his will, 2 of them marrying Ministers
and one the Sheriff Clerk.   2,17,70,79,98, *Orkney View* No. 35, 1991.

Sutherland, Marjorie - dau. of Alexander Sutherland of Dunbeath kinswoman of Earl of Ross; 2nd wife of *William Sinclair, Earl of Orkney c1456; grd mother of *John Sinclair, Earl of Caithness killed at Summerdale. 2.

Sverre Sigurdsson (The Imposter), b.c1150 d.1202. King of Norway 1184-1202 - Brought up in Faroe; claimed to be illegitimate son of King Sigurd Haraldsson of Norway (The Mouth d.1155). Grd father of *Hakon IV. Visited Orkney 1168.
Emerged from comparative obscurity 1179 to pursue claim to Norwegian throne eventually defeating Magnus V 1184 to seize Crown and became one of Norway's greatest monarchs.
Defeated attempted invasion of Norway by fleet from Orkney and Shetland (Island Beardies) at battle of Florvåg near Bergen 1194. Afterwards accepted Earl *Harald II Maddadsson's submission imposing severe terms including sequestration of Island Beardie estates to Norwegian Crown, half of all fines to go to Norwegian Crown, a royal sysselman to be appointed to collect revenue and administer the forfeited Orkney estates, Shetland to be detached from Earldom and administered directly by Norway. The Earldom itself was restored to Harald on his giving oath of fealty to Sverre who thus tightened his grip on the islands the Earls losing some of their independence. 1,2,3,30,35(7).

Swanson, Captain George Bain MBE - b.1870 Longhope d.1945 Stromness. Master of 231-ton RMS *St Ola I* for 31 of her 59 years on the trans-Pentland Firth mail run, and master of the Firth and its dangerous tides as well. Described as 'a true viking' he joined the *Ola* 1906 after qualifying 'deep sea' commanding her in both World Wars becoming an almost legendary man of the sea, known to thousands of travellers, renowned for his seamanship, in this most testing of seaways. 26,95, OH 16/10/45, Orc 11/10/45.

Sweyn Asleifsson, b.pre-1135 d.1171 Dublin, of Gairsay - 2nd s. of *Olaf Hrolfsson of Gairsay and *Asleif; bro. of *Valthjof and *Gunni Olafsson; m. Ingirid, widow of Isle of Man chieftain.
One of Saga's most charismatic personalities, the 'Ultimate Viking' of *Eric Linklater's biography. Aggressive, ruthless, often devious, a brilliant tactician especially in sea fighting, master of the surprise attack. Had great personal charm and capacity for friendship, even towards former enemies, but not always reliable in his loyalties. Closely involved with the Earls, monarchs and chieftains of his time.
After *Olvir Rosta murdered his father 1135 Sweyn was at Earl *Paul II's Yule feast in Orphir where after exchange of insults he killed

the Earl's favourite and forecastleman, *Sweyn Breastrope. As a result, outlawed by Paul, he took refuge in Tiree with *Holdbodi.

Next year 1136 surprised and kidnapped Paul in Rousay taking him to oblivion in Atholl while Earl *Rognvald II took control of the Earldom. Sweyn reappeared, came to terms with Rognvald and regained his lands declared forfeit by Paul. To avenge his father's killing he next attacked Olvir Rosta near Helmsdale 1139 burning his house. Olvir escaped but his mother, *Frakokk, died in the fire.

Went to Holdbodi's aid 1140 when Tiree was over-run by Welsh raiders and with him pursued them to the Isle of Man but the Welsh leader eluded them having first killed local chieftain whose widow Margaret m. Sweyn. Holdbodi then 1141 switched loyalties, sided with the Welshman and with him attacked Sweyn on his newly acquired Manx estates but was repelled. Sweyn returned to Gairsay 1142.

Holdbodi returned to Tiree c1143 and Sweyn sought revenge attacking him with 5 ships including one commanded by *Thorbjorn Klerk with whom he had patched up a brittle friendship after previous animosity. Holdbodi fled but they took much booty before returning to Caithness where disputes arose over allocation of the loot, Thorbjorn Klerk alleging that Sweyn had seized more than his fair share. He complained to Rognvald in Orkney while Sweyn and his Caithness henchman, Margad, raided throughout their own territory before retiring to sea-girt castle of Lambaborg where they were besieged by Thorbjorn and Rognvald without success. Sweyn slipped away and swam to safety taking refuge with Scottish King David who effected reconciliation between him and Rognvald.

During so-called 'War of the Three Earls' 1152-54 when *Erlend III and *Harald II Maddadsson vied for control of Earldom with *Rognvald II on his return from the Holy Land 1153 Sweyn supported Erlend until the other two killed him in his longship moored off Damsay 1154 while Sweyn, who had been acting as his adviser and protector, was absent. The 2 Earls pursued Sweyn through the islands but he won free and eventually all 3 made peace, a reconciliation extending even to Thorbjorn Klerk with whom he once again went a-viking and in a sea-fight off the west coast killed Somerledi, ancestor of the Macdonald Lords of the Isles.

In Spring 1171 he went on his penultimate viking raid known as the 'Broadcloth Cruise' from the booty won from merchant shipping. On his return Rognvald suggested he give up these raids on account of age. He agreed but wanted to make one last cruise that autumn. He did and it was his last. He captured Dublin but on going ashore to collect the ransom was ambushed and killed.   1,2,3,10,22,35(7),50.

Sweyn Breastrope - d.1135 Orphir. Member of Earl *Paul II's hird and at sea his forecastleman. At battle of Tankerness 1135 threw huge boulder which knocked leader of attacking force *Olvir Rosta unconscious so that his fleet broke off engagement and fled south. Described as 'unlucky-looking' (OS), was said to practise 'black arts'. Killed by namesake *Sweyn Asleifsson at Paul II's Yuletide feast in Orphir 1135.   1,3,35(7),50.

Sydserff, Bishop Thomas - b.1581 d.1663. s. of Edinburgh burgess. Educ. Edinburgh. Bishop of Galloway until deposed during Commonwealth; re-instated at Restoration and appointed Bishop of Orkney 1602 when aged over 80. Never visited Orkney but bequeathed 400 merks to St Magnus Cathedral.   21.

T

Tait, Professor John, MD DSc FRSE FRS Canada - b.1878 Kirkwall d.1944 Montreal. Physiologist. Educ. Kirkwall Burgh (Grammar) School, George Watson's College, Edinburgh, Universities of Edinburgh, Gottingen, Berlin.

Assistant in Physiology Department, Edinburgh University 1906 and after service in Royal Army Medical Corps in Italy and Macedonia during World War I appointed Professor of Physiology, McGill University, Montreal 1919. Director Experimental Medicine, McGill 1924 initiating and engaging in wide field of research. Retired due to ill-health 1938.

An accomplished linguist fluent in German, French, Italian and latterly Spanish, was also a classical scholar reading Latin and especially Greek literature throughout his life. His wide ranging interests also included detailed studies of birds, animals and plant-life. Involved in production of first 'Orkney Book' 1909 contributing section on zoology.   Orc 2/11/44.

Taylor, Alexander Burt CBE DLitt - b.1904 Earlston, Berwickshire d.1972 Edinburgh. Registrar General for Scotland, translator of Orkneyinga Saga; s. of Rev. A. B. Taylor, one-time Minister of Paterson (now East) Kirk, Kirkwall. Educ. Hamilton Academy, Kirkwall Grammar School, Edinburgh and Columbia Universities.

Teacher in Stirling and Falkirk before becoming Inspector of Schools 1933; Principal, Department of Health for Scotland 1939 being seconded for Civil Defence duties during World War II and Asst. Secretary after war dealing with specialist services, medical research, rehabilitation and mental health; Registrar General for Scotland 1959-65.

Continued Icelandic and Scandinavian studies throughout his life with special reference to Norse influence on early Scottish maps.

Publications include translation of 'Orkneyinga Saga' with detailed introduction and analytical notes 1939, Lindsay's 'Rutter of Northern Seas' and many papers to learned societies.   49, Orc March 72, OH 16/11/58.

Tennyson, Alfred Lord - b.1809 d.1892. Poet Laureate. Visited Kirkwall 1883 while on cruise with Prime Minister *William Gladstone when both were made Freemen of Kirkwall at ceremony in the Paterson (now East) Kirk. After visiting the Cathedral, Palaces and Tankerness House went out to Maeshowe and Ring of Brogar.

Orc Jan/Feb 1967 and Sept 1883, OH Sept 1883.

Thomas, Captain F. W. L., RN FSA Scot - d.1883 Edinburgh. Naval Officer, surveyor, antiquarian, anthropologist. Commanded HM Survey Ship *Woodlark* carrying out survey work in Orkney and Shetland waters and later in the Western Isles. An interest in archaeology resulted in his making detailed studies of the Ring of Brogar and other pre-historic monuments in Orkney and submitting innovative papers with detailed plans of them to the Scottish Society of Antiquaries. He did the same for Shetland and the Western Isles. He also pioneered research on Orkney rentals with his paper 'What is a Pennyland?' for the Society of Antiquaries

OH 4/11/1885, *Proceedings of Society of Antiquaries Scotland* 1885.

Thomas of Kyrknes - Kirkwall bailie 1481.   2.

Thoms, Sheriff George Hunter MacThomas - b.1831 Dundee d.1903 Edinburgh; father was Provost of Dundee. Educ. Dundee qualifying as advocate; called to Scottish Bar 1856; appointed Sheriff Principal Caithness, Orkney and Zetland 1870.

First became interested in church architecture in St Giles Cathedral, Edinburgh and after coming north as Sheriff, continued his interest in St Magnus Cathedral, leaving a substantial residue of his estate to be administered by Kirkwall Town Council, owners of the Cathedral, as the Thoms Trust Bequest for the restoration and upkeep of its fabric. Was Commissioner for Northern Lighthouses and Provincial Grand Master of Freemasons of Orkney and Shetland.   OH 4/11/1903.

Thomson, Albert John, BEM, FSA (Scot) - b.1914 Kirkwall d.1995 Kirkwall. Curator of St Magnus Cathedral 1946-78. Educ. Kirkwall Grammar School; cabinet-maker to trade but man of many parts. Always interested in Orkney history he was appointed Curator of the

Cathedral after demobilisation from the army 1946. Was steeped in its colourful story and carried out detailed research of the building especially into the mason marks by which the various periods of building can be identified and even where some of the master masons came from, published in 'Orkney Miscellany' Vol II 1954. He also established how the interior would have appeared in early times by minute observation of remnants of the colour patterns appearing in obscure corners especially in damp weather. He had intended to publish in more detail the results of his researches on retirement but for health reasons was unable to do so. His notes, however, are preserved in the Orkney Archive.　　　　　　　　　　　　　Orc 10/8/95.

Thora - dau. of *Somerledi Ospaksson; m. (1) *Erlend II (2) Sigurd of Paplay; mother of *St Magnus by Erlend; grd. mother of *St. Rognvald.
　　At Easter 1117, or 1116 she had prepared a feast in Paplay, Holm to welcome both her son Magnus and his cousin *Hakon back from their fateful meeting in Egilsay but Hakon came alone having agreed to the killing of Magnus. After the feast she pleaded with him and obtained his permission to bury her son in Christ Church, Birsay.　　1,3,35(7).

Thorbjorn Klerk - b.pre-1117 d.1158 Caithness. s. of Thorstein Clumsy-mouth and Gudrun Frakokk's dau.; grd. s. of *Frakokk; m. Ingigerd, sister of *Sweyn Asleifsson but divorced her during dispute with Sweyn over division of plunder.
　　Brought up by Frakokk along with *Olvir Rosta and others probably near Helmsdale. Fostered his second cousin *Harald II Maddadsson accompanying him to Orkney 1139 as counsellor when he became joint earl with *Rognvald II. Quarrelled with Sweyn Asleifsson after burning of Frakokk in her house near Helmsdale during Sweyn's revenge attack on Olvir Rosta who escaped. After reconciliation, arranged by Rognvald, together with Sweyn attacked and plundered *Holdbodi in Hebrides 1143 Thorbjorn commanding one of Sweyn's ships only to fall out with him again over share-out of plunder. Appealed to Rognvald and with him unsuccessfully besieged Sweyn in his Caithness stronghold, Lambaborg. Sweyn escaped to Scottish Court and once again Rognvald patched up the quarrel.
　　Counsellor to Harald II when Rognvald left him in charge of Earldom while away on his Crusade 1151-3 and also supported him in War of the Three Earls on Rognvald's return from the Holy Land resulting in resumption of joint rule by Harald and Rognvald. But when he killed one of Rognvald's followers, Thorarin Bag-nose 1155 during a long-running feud he was outlawed by the Earl and fled to the Scottish Court 1156 where he was well-received.
　　Back in Caithness 1158, however, he ambushed and killed

Rognvald who was across from Orkney on a hunting expedition with
Harald and was then himself killed by the Earl's men.
    Described as 'a wise man and man of mark, valiant but
overbearing'. (OS).   1,2,3,35(7).

Thorfinn Brusisson - Chieftain in Stronsay 1152; m. Ingigerd, sister of *Sweyn
    Asleifsson after she was divorced by *Thorbjorn Klerk 1143.   1,3.

Thorfinn I Einarsson Skullsplitter - Earl of Orkney c954-c976; s. of *Torf-
    Einar; m. *Grelod grd dau. of *Thorstein the Red; father of Earls
    *Arnfinn, *Havard Harvest-Happy, *Ljot, *Hlodver and *Skuli; became
    sole Earl of Orkney when his bros. *Arnkel and *Erlend I were killed
    supporting *King Erik Bloodaxe of Norway at battle of Stainmore 954.
    Orkneyinga Saga has little detail of his rule although his nick-name
    suggests it may well have been violent. Howe of Hoxa, South
    Ronaldsay is believed to be his burial mound. 'A mighty chief and
    warlike' (OS).   1,2,3,35(7),76,100.

Thorfinn Haraldsson - s. of Earl *Harald II Maddadsson. Mutilated by
    William the Lion of Scotland while hostage in place of his father after
    Harald's unsuccessful invasion of Moray territory c1197.   1,2,3.

Thorfinn II Sigurdsson The Mighty - b.c999 d.c1064 Orkney. Earl of
    Orkney 1014-c1064; youngest s. of Earl *Sigurd II by dau. of Malcolm
    II of Scotland; half bro. of *Hlodver (Hundi), who died as hostage in
    Norway and Earls *Sumerledi, *Einar II Wrymouth, *Brusi, all sons of
    Sigurd by his first and unidentified wife; father of Earls *Paul I and
    *Erlend II; grd. father of Earl *Hakon and St *Magnus.
    Brought up in Scottish Court of his grd. father, Malcolm II, who
    granted him Earldom of Caithness and Sutherland 1004 where he was
    fostered by *Thorkel Amundisson Fostri, while his surviving 3 half-
    bros. held Orkney Earldom jointly. It was maintained that as another
    son of Sigurd II, though by a different mother, he was equally entitled
    to a share of Orkney, a claim strenuously denied particularly by Einar
    II. In a protracted power struggle aided by Thorkel Fostri and pressing
    his claim with threat of force he acquired his third share on the death
    of Sumerledi 1018 taking over another third after the killing of Einar
    by Thorkel Fostri 1020. Brusi protested at this and for arbitration took
    his case to King Olaf of Norway who, claiming overlordship of the
    islands himself, divided Orkney into three parts granting one each to
    Brusi and Thorfinn on feudal terms while retaining one third for
    himself but passing it to Brusi also on feudal terms.
    A mild man, Brusi, unwilling or unable to protect his two-thirds
himself against the currently frequent incursions by viking-type
raiders handed this royal third to Thorfinn on condition that he defend

the entire Earldom against such attacks, an agreement which held until Brusi died c1033 after which Thorfinn assumed overall control of the Earldom without opposition until Earl *Rognvald I Brusisson returned from Russia and Norway 1037 to claim, with backing from the Norwegian Crown, his father's share.

In the meantime Thorfinn had embarked on campaign c1033-36 to extend his influence in the north and west of Scotland defeating a so-called Scots King *Karl Hundison, first in sea-battle off Deerness and then at Tarbatness in the Moray Firth. From there it is claimed he raided as far south as Fife and may have been in alliance with Macbeth after Duncan's death 1040.

On Rognvald's return to Orkney Thorfinn diplomatically agreed to share rule of the Earldom with him 1037-45 while apparently retaining the dominant role. For several years they raided together down the west coast of Scotland, the Hebrides and into north-west England and Ireland so that at one time it was claimed, with perhaps only a slight element of exaggeration, that he controlled 9 earldoms, including Orkney and Shetland, from his Palace in Birsay.

His already extravagant life-style now came under increasing strain with having to entertain and maintain *Kalf Arnesson, uncle of his wife Ingibjorg and his numerous followers, who had been expelled from Norway. His affairs further south having stabilised Thorfinn ended his agreement with Rognvald once again assuming overall control of the Earldom and its revenue. Rognvald immediately and successfully sought help in Norway to regain his share of the Earldom obtaining ships and fully armed men. With them he sailed at once to meet Thorfinn's fleet in the Pentland Firth 1046 probably off the Berry in Hoy. Rognvald was decisively defeated in a close-fought battle Thorfinn gaining victory through the last-minute intervention of Kalf Arnesson and his 6 ships.

Rognvald again sought help in Norway and with one lone ship made an immediate mid-winter surprise counter-attack catching Thorfinn off guard, burning his house over him. He escaped, however, and with his wife rowed across the Pentland Firth in an open boat to his estate in Caithness.

He retaliated right away with a night raid across the Firth to catch Rognvald unawares on Papa Stronsay where he had gone to collect malt for Yule ale and in turn burned his house over him. There was another spectacular escape with Rognvald leaping though the flames only to be betrayed by the barking of his pet dog when hiding among the rocks where he was killed by Thorkel Fostri.

Thorfinn, now secure in possession of his Earldoms, ruled them well and in peace for the next 20 years from Birsay coming to terms with both Scotland and Norway and making a pilgrimage to Rome 1049-50 to receive absolution from Pope Leo IX for his earlier sins. It seems likely that during his pilgrimage he discussed the provision of a bishop for Orkney with the Archbishop of Bremen-Hamburg and probably pressed the request while in Rome. A bishop was certainly appointed, *Thorolf, the first in Orkney, and once back home in Birsay Thorfinn established Christ Church and a palace for him next his own residence but whether this was on the Brough as originally thought or on the Mainland opposite is uncertain.   1,2,3,35(7),76,100.

Thorir Treskegg (Treebeard) - d.c894. Danish viking who, with *Kalf Scurvy, set themselves up as 'Lords of Orkney' after ignominious departure of Earl *Hallad from the islands. Killed by *Torf-Einar when he took over as Earl.   1,3.

Thorkel Flettir - Chieftain possibly connected with Tuquoy, Westray. Commanded a warship supporting Earl *Paul II at battle of Tankerness 1135. Granted lands in Stronsay originally held by *Valthjof, *Sweyn Asleifsson's bro. after his death by drowning and forfeited by Sweyn after he killed *Sweyn Breastrope at Paul's Yule feast in Orphir. He was burned in his Stronsay dwelling-house by Sweyn's followers.   1,3.

Thorkel Fostri Amundisson - s. of Deerness chieftain *Amundi. Driven out of Orkney c1018 by Earl *Einar II Wrymouth for having supported the smaller farmers by advocating reduction of the Earl's heavy demands on them to fund his raiding expeditions. In exile fostered *Thorfinn II when he was granted Earldom of Caithness and Sutherland at age of 5 and became his lifelong adviser and friend returning to Orkney with him when Thorfinn, through Thorkel's negotiating skills, acquired his third of the Earldom in spite of Einar's opposition.

Einar's resentment continued, however, so Thorkel went to Norwegian Court for advice and to enlist support of *King Olaf. It was agreed that on Thorkel's return to Orkney the 2 protagonists should each attend a banquet at the other's homestead. Thorkel was host to Einar at the first in Skaill, Deerness. They were both then to travel together to Einar's feast but justifiably suspecting treachery and discovering an ambush laid for him, Thorkel killed his guest in the drinking hall at Skaill and as a result Thorfinn acquired yet more of the Earldom.

He continued his staunch support of Thorfinn and was present at his winter attack on *Rognvald I in Papa Stronsay 1046 in order to regain the Earldom which Rognvald had seized and in fact killed Rognvald himself in the affray.   1,2,3,30,35(7),76.

Thorolf - First Bishop of Orkney c1050 with seat at Christ Church, Birsay during time of Earl *Thorfinn II who probably negotiated the appointment while on his pilgrimage to Rome c1048. Was certainly approved by Rome and consecrated Bremen-Hamburg.   21,77,100.

Thorstein the Red - s. of Olaf the White, King of Dublin by *Aud the Deepminded; grd. s. of *Ketil Flatnose; grd. father of *Grelod who m. Earl *Thorfinn I Skullsplitter. Controlled large part of northern Scotland and Hebrides during latter part of 9th century.

In alliance with Earl *Sigurd I raided as far south as Moray and Ross and was at battle against *Maelbrigte Tusk c892 when Sigurd met his death. Murdered by Scots in Caithness.   1,2,3,30,71,76.

Tomison, William - b.c1740 South Ronaldsay d.1829 South Ronaldsay. Joined Hudson's Bay Company in Canada 1760 rising to become factory Governor and 'Chief, Inland'. Retired to South Parish of his native island and having made his fortune in the Nor' Wast left a substantial sum of money to endow the South Parish school bearing his name, Tomison's Academy.   2,23.

Torfaeus, Thormodus, Latinised version of Thormodur Torfason - b.1636 probably Iceland d.1719 Norway. Historian; m. a Norwegian woman who owned farm near Kopervik on the island of Karmo between Stavanger and Bergen where he lived from 1682 until his death. Appointed historiographer to King of Norway he compiled series of histories in Latin including 'Orcades' which was translated by Rev. Alexander Pope, Minister of Reay in Caithness as 'Ancient History of Orkney, Caithness & the North' 1866. Described by Dr. Hugh Marwick as '. . . this father of Orcadian history'.   73.

Torf-Einar - see Einar I.

Traill, George William, b.1792 d.1847 London, of Rousay and Wyre - Indian Civil Administrator. Of Westness and Woodwick branch of Traill family.

Educ. Haileybury College of East India Company 1808; joined Bengal Civil Service in India 1810; Nepal 1815 and in charge of administration of 11,000 sq. mile Himalayan province of Kumaon from 1816 until retirement 1836. Described as a 'benevolent and active despot' he also became known as the 'uncrowned King of Kumaon'.

On retirement returned to Orkney, assumed guardianship of distant relative, the future General *Sir Frederick Burroughs, then a minor but eventually his heir, and using fortune made in the East began to build up estate in Rousay. Achieved ambition of bringing Westness back into Traill possession 1846 after which became notorious for initiating 'clearance' of Quandale in Rousay by eviction of crofters to make way for sheep - the only Orkney example of similar, but much more extensive, clearances taking place in the Highlands. This policy was actually planned and put into effect by his factor *Robert Scarth to be continued by Burroughs when he inherited the estate.   2,9,64.

Traill, George, of Quandale - Provost of Kirkwall 1690 and 1695-1698. Successful Kirkwall merchant. m. (1) Elizabeth Irving 1674 (2) Anna, dau. of James Baikie of Tankerness 1682 for whom he built his house on Bridge Street 1684.   4,64.

Traill, George. b.1696, of Holland, Papa Westray - m. (1) Jean Traill of Kirkness 1727 (2) Margaret Stewart of Brugh 1743.
    Played ambivalent role during the '45. Paid his feudal dues to pro-Hanoverian Earl of Morton but at the same time sympathetic towards the Jacobite North Isles lairds to whom he gave assistance when they were in hiding and indeed married the dau. of one of them, Stewart of Brugh. Admitted to Electoral Roll 1745.   11,64.

Traill, George, of Hobbister - Earldom Chamberlain; m. Isobel Louttit of Lyking 1712; father of Sibilla, later wife of *John Traill of Elsness. Replaced as Chamberlain for Earl of Morton and factor for Earldom by *Hay of Balbithan 1725.
    Member of committee of heritors investigating weights and measures 1743 and involved in Pundlar Process 1733-59 participating in funding of the anti-Morton lairds' legal costs.   1,11,64.

Traill, George, b.1787 d.1871, of Hobbister and Rattar - s. of *James Traill of Hobbister and Rattar. Advocate; MP for Orkney and Shetland 1830-1835, he was thus MP both before and after Reform Act 1832 narrowly defeating the favourite to win, *Samuel Laing, in 1833 poll, the first in which Shetland was given the franchise. The declaration of the result at the Mercat Cross, Kirkwall caused a riot on Broad Street during which, *John Traill Urquhart, one of his supporters was injured and subsequently died. Traill was in turn defeated 1835 but was later elected MP for Caithness holding that seat 1844-1869.   2,4,14,64.

Traill, James, b.1683 d.1733, 1st of Woodwick and North Ronaldsay - Edinburgh lawyer and merchant; s. of William Traill, 1st of Westness; m. Margaret, dau. of John Traill of Elsness, 1712 who bore him 9 children all of whom died in childhood.
    Bought Woodwick estate and North Ronaldsay and retired to Orkney from Edinburgh 1728. Provost of Kirkwall 1730-33. Estate inherited by his nephew, *John Traill of Westness.   64,73.

Traill, James, b.1758 d.1843, of Hobbister and Rattar - Sheriff of Caithness with lands in Sanday but made his fortune from freestone quarries in Caithness; m. Lady Janet Sinclair, dau. of William, Earl of Caithness 1784; father of *James Traill MP. Burgess of Kirkwall 1818.   4,64.

Traill, John, b.1657, 2nd of Elsness - Merchant laird, shipowner; s. of *Patrick Traill 1st of Elsness and Elspeth Pottinger; m. (1) Helen Stewart (2) Margaret Stewart of Brugh 1712.

Owned lands in both Sanday and Stronsay. Traded to Continent visiting Bergen himself 1713 and 1714 with cargoes of grain. His ship, *Elephant*, was captured by a French privateer off Shetland 1697 and ransomed.   64,73,77.

Traill, John, b.1718 d.1758, 3rd of Elsness - Grd. s. of *Patrick Traill of Elsness; m. Sibilla, dau. of *George Traill of Hobbister, Earldom Chamberlain.

One of the North Isles Jacobite lairds who took refuge in the Gentlemen's Ha' caves in Westray after Culloden and whose Sanday mansion-house, built by his grd father *Patrick, was burnt down by Hanoverian troops under *Benjamin Moodie of Melsetter during their unsuccessful search for the fugitives, an episode vividly described in fictional form by *Walter Traill Dennison in his 'Orcadian Sketch Book' entitled 'Why the Hoose o' Hellsness was Brunt'.   4,7,11,64.

Traill, John, d.1793, of Westness - s. of *George Traill of Westness and Margaret, sister of *William Bellenden of Stenness; m. Mary Balfour, dau. of *John Balfour of Trenaby 1745.

One of the North Isles Jacobite lairds who had to go into hiding after the '45. Owned Woodwick estate, Evie, North Ronaldsay and a town house in Kirkwall, all inherited from his uncle. *James Traill of Westness.   11,48,64.

Traill, Patrick, b.c1627 d.1690, 1st of Elsness - Merchant laird; s. of George Traill, Blebo, Fife and Isobel Craigie; m. Elspeth Pottinger c1654. Successful ship owner, skipper and merchant trading to the Continent. Bought Elsness in Sanday 1668 where he built his mansion-house and also owned town house in Kirkwall 1677. Elsness remained in family until c1817 when it passed to collateral branch, Traills of Rattar. He was still sea-going master of one of his 2 sloops 1676.   4,7,64.

Traill, Patrick. b.c1737 d.1795 Leith, of Sabay - General of Artillery; s. of James Traill of Sabay and Margaret Bellenden of Stenness. Freeman of Kirkwall 1794.

According to records in Royal Artillery Library which lists only one Traill he appears to have joined the Artillery as a cadet 1755 rising to Lieutenant Colonel 1782 and Major General 1795. Saw service in North

America and was CRA (Commander Royal Artillery) at siege of Charleston 1780. Transferred 1793 to Invalids (Reserve).   4,64.

Traill, Colonel Thomas (Germany Thomas), 1st of Holland - s. of George Traill, Blebo, Fife and Jean Kennedy; m. Marian Craigie c1632.

Joined army of Gustav Adolfus of Sweden as mercenary taking part in Thirty Years War (1618-48) in Germany. Is credited with having written poem on which, it is thought, Robert Burns, based his love-song 'My Love is like a red, red rose' which contains similar, almost identical, verses.   64.

Traill, Thomas - d. 1753. s. of *George Traill of Quandale. m. Sibilla Grant, dau. of South Ronaldsay Minister. Master Kirkwall Grammar School 1719-27 resigning to become Parish Minister, Orphir and then Minister of Lady Parish, Sanday 1733.   4,7,64.

Traill, Thomas, d.1779 Savill, Sanday, of Westove - s. of James Traill of Westove and Barbara Fea of Clestran; m. Marian Stewart of Brugh. Lived in and farmed Savill. One of the North Isles Jacobite lairds.   48,64.

Traill, Dr. Thomas Stewart, b.1781 d.1862, of Tirlot - Professor of Medical Jurisprudence, Edinburgh University; s. of Rev. Thomas Traill of Tirlot and Lucia Traill of Westray; m. Christian, dau, of Harry Robertson DD.

Superintended production of 8th edition of 'Encyclopaedia Britannica'. Successful physician Liverpool 1805-32; man of many talents, health reformer, educationalist, popular lecturer. Outside his medical career he was interested in mineralogy and built up a collection of fish fossils in Orkney which was the inspiration for *Hugh Miller's study of fossils from the Stromness area resulting in his classic work 'In the Footprints of the Creator'.   17,44,47,48,64.

Traill, Thomas William, M Inst CE - b.1829 Kirkwall d.1910. Naval officer and engineer; s. of Lieut. Gilbert Traill RN of Hatston.

Joined Royal Navy 1853 when it was changing over from sail to steam. Served in Baltic and at Sebastapol during Crimean War 1854-56 becoming Fleet Engineer. Retiring from Navy served on Board of Trade for 31 years as Engineer Surveyor-in-Chief and Inspector of Chain Cable and Anchor Proving Establishment.   35(3).

Traill, Rev. Walter, b.1768 d.1846, of Westove - s. of *Thomas Traill of Westove and Marian, dau. of *Alexander Stewart of Brugh; m. (1) Margaret MacBeath 1789 (2) Catherine Watt, Kirkwall 1825.

Minister, Burra, Shetland 1790; Lady Parish, Sanday 1791 though living at Savill in Burness. Resigned from Ministry 1810 on inheriting Westove estate from bro. James who died without issue. Re-admitted as Minister of Lady 1825 having suffered 'great losses' financially, being very, and frequently unwisely, liberal with his money. His reinstatement caused great resentment in Sanday being regarded as a mis-use of patronage. Author of 'Vindication of Orkney' 1823, answering some of the criticisms levelled at 'tyrannical Orkney lairds' by *Alexander Peterkin.   6,7,64.

Tredwell (Triduana), Saint - Mythical female saint who was believed to have plucked out her eyes to escape the amorous attentions of a Pictish king. Her chapel in Papa Westray (Papay) was a place of pilgrimage, especially for those with eye-sight problems and blindness, up until the Reformation.

This chapel dedication along with that of St Boniface, the island's name Papay, the *St Findan legend and extensive but largely uninvestigated archaeological remains suggest that Papay was an important pre-Norse Christian centre, possibly an episcopal seat.
                        84, *St Boniface Church* - Christopher Lowe.

Tudor, John R. - Feature writer for *The Field* magazine London who spent some months during summer 1880 collecting material for his monumental account of 'Orkney and Shetland' published 1883.

Tulloch, Bishop Thomas - c1418-c1460. Closely associated with Danish/Norwegian Court and acted on its behalf in administering Danish possessions in Orkney 1422 resulting in friction with *David Menzies of Weem who was given management of Earldom a year later and whose rule became so oppressive that the people of Orkney complained to Denmark. Bishop Tulloch took over the administration again 1427 at least until absentee *William Sinclair was confirmed as Earl 1434. The Bishop was present at coronation of Christian I in Copenhagen 1442.

Credited by *Jo Ben with building Noltland Castle in Westray as the country residence of Orkney Bishops but this is now regarded as inaccurate; he did, however, restore St Olaf's Church, Kirkwall. During restoration work in St Magnus Cathedral in the 19th century his reputedly magnificent tomb was destroyed and his bones were said to have been scattered over fields near the town.   2,4,20(6),21.

Tulloch, Bishop William - d.1482. Bishop of Orkney 1461-1478. Cousin of Bishop *Thomas Tulloch whom he succeeded in the diocese. Described in Craven's 'History of the Orkney Church' as 'A prelate of high accomplishments and great suavity of manners' who had the confidence of both King Christian I of Denmark and King James III of Scotland and whose standing in Orkney was equal to that of Earl *William Sinclair with whom he was at odds.

He was member of ambassadorial commission to Denmark charged with arranging marriage of Margaret, Christian's dau. to James III 1468 resulting in the consequent pawning of his lands and sovereign rights in Orkney by Christian for part of her dowry. Bishop Tulloch received the tack of Orkney and Shetland after the impignoration being entrusted with the management of the islands and although he later acquired a reputation of being rapacious and corrupt there is no evidence to support this charge. In actual fact he was an able administrator, trusted by both Scotland and Denmark, his good offices helping Orkney through a difficult period of transition.

He was member of Scottish Parliament 1471 and Keeper of the Privy Seal 1473 and was first suffragan Bishop of Orkney when the Scottish Church formally annexed the diocese from Norway and it came under the newly erected See of St Andrews 1471.   2,21.

Tyrie, Rev. James - b.1708 d.1778; s. of Sir David Tyrie of Aberdeenshire, related to Royal House of Scotland; m. Helen Traill of Elsness. Educ. Scots College, Rome for priesthood and on return to Scotland acted as missionary and 'secular priest' before converting to Protestantism 1734 and working as itinerant preacher and missionary for Presbyterian Church. He was then recommended for a charge in the Fort William area but as he had no Gaelic was sent to Orkney instead 1744 and presented to the charge of Cross and Burness in Sanday 1745. That congregation, however, wanted Rev. George Traill of Hobbister (later Minister of Dunnet, Caithness) as their Minister and at Tyrie's inaugural service 1746 they walked out on him.

The following year he was translated to the joint charge of Sandwick and Stromness where he was admitted in face of 'great opposition' by some members of that congregation using force to prevent others, who did want to attend the service, from entering the church. Grounds for their opposition appeared to be his Roman Catholic background, alleged irregularities in his domestic life but particularly their dislike of having a Minister thrust upon them through the patronage system - in both instances he had been 'presented' by the Earl of Morton. After some of the unruly elements, mainly women, had been disciplined by the Presbytery, however, the hostility subsided and he remained their Minister until his death 1778.   6,7,11,14(4).

U

Ufi - Follower of Earl *Erlend III who tried to save the Earl when his ship, moored off Damsay, was attacked by Earls *Rognvald II and *Harald II ending 'War of the Three Earls' 1154. Taking the drunken Earl in his arms he jumped overboard with him in a vain attempt to escape. Erlend was killed. 1,3.

Urquhart, John - b.1756 d.1794; s. of Sanday merchant James Urquhart and Marion Drever; m. 1786 Helen, dau. of *John Traill 3rd of Elsness. Clerk to *Thomas Balfour of Huip from 1774. Merchant in Kirkwall. 14(3).

Urquhart, John Traill - b.1789 d.1833. Advocate; s. of *John Urquhart and Helen Traill of Elsness through whom he inherited the Elsness estate. Built new Elsness dwelling-house 1812 and also mansion house of Geramount both in Sanday and owned town house in Kirkwall High Street. Owned Houseby in Stronsay and was agricultural improver. Referred to as Convener of Commissioners of Supply (forerunner of County Council) 1823 and Commissioner for Kirkwall at General Assembly of the Church of Scotland 1825-32. Fond of field sports especially shooting.

Died 1833 as result of injuries received during riot on Broad Street following announcement of 1833 parliamentary election won by his friend *George Traill whom he had supported. 4,7.

Urquhart, Thomas - hanged 1797 Edinburgh. Kirkwall Postmaster operating from his house in what is now Victoria Street. Elected Kirkwall Town Council 1794 and re-elected 1795. Stood trial in Edinburgh, along with his 16-year-old son, David, on 8 charges including theft from Post Office, falsehood and forgery and on conviction was hanged, his son being set free on account of his youth although he admitted some of the charges. 4.

V

Valthjof Olafsson - d. 1135; s. of Olaf Hrolfsson of Gairsay; elder bro. of
*Sweyn Asleifsson. Drowned while on way from estate in Stronsay to
attend Earl *Paul II's Yuletide feast in Orphir at which his bro. Sweyn
killed his namesake *Sweyn Breastrope, one of the Earl's favourites. As
a consequence, instead of allowing Sweyn to succeed to his bro's lands
in Stronsay, Paul declared them forfeit in favour of *Thorkel Flettir but
Sweyn eventually managed to acquire them for himself.   1,3,35(7),50.

Vedder, David - b.1790 Deerness d.1854. Poet, journalist. Went to sea for
a time, later becoming Customs officer before entering on journalistic
and literary career. On staff of *Blackwood's Magazine* and associated
with *Edinburgh Literary Gazette*. His work was published as 'Poems,
Lyrics and Sketches' with an essay on his life and writings by Rev.
George Gilfillan, Kirkwall 1878. Perhaps best remembered locally for
his poem 'To Orkney' with its opening line, 'Land of the whirlpool -
torrent - foam'.   5.

W

Wallace, Rev. James - d.1688. Historian and last Minister of St Magnus
Cathedral before abolition of Episcopacy in Scotland. Educ. King's
College, Aberdeen. Schoolmaster, Fortrose before becoming Minister
of 'Marie Kirk', Sanday 1668 and subsequent translation to 1st charge
in St Magnus Cathedral 1672.

Described by Craven as Orkney's first historian, he supplied Sir
Robert Sibbald, Geographer Royal for Scotland, with material on
Orkney for his surveys. Five years after his death his own 'Description
of the Isles of Orkney' using much of the same material was published
1693 by his son Dr. James Wallace. A 2nd edition with additional
chapters appeared 1700 again published by son James who this time
produced it under his own name.

Bequeathed his library to be added to what became the Kirkwall
Bibliotheck, Scotland's first public library developing into the Orkney
Library of today.   6,7,21,69.

Wallace, Professor Robert Charles, CBE MA BSc PhD FGS LLD - b.1881 Deerness d.1955 Ontario, Canada. Geologist, petrologist, mineralogist; s. of James Wallace, Sanday and Mary Swannay, North Ronaldsay; m. Elizabeth Harcus MA Kirkwall 1912.

Educ. Deerness Public School (under *Magnus Spence), Kirkwall Burgh (Grammar) School, Edinburgh University, Research Scholar in Crystallography, St Andrews University 1910.

Lecturer in Geology and Mineralogy, Manitoba University, Winnipeg 1910-12 becoming Professor of these subjects in the same University 1912-28 and President Alberta University 1928-36 when he was appointed Principal, Queen's University, Ontario.

Commissioner for Northern Manitoba 1912-21; Commissioner Mines and Natural Resources, Manitoba 1926-28; President Royal Society of Canada 1940-41 and Executive Director of Arctic Institute of North America.

Specialised in physical chemistry of rock magmas, petrology and crystallography. Orc 10/2/55, 49(1951-60).

Wason, John Cathcart - b.1848 Ayrshire d.1921 London. MP for Orkney and Shetland 1900-21; s. of Rigby Wason, MP for Ipswich. Educ. Laleham, Rugby. Member of New Zealand Parliament while farming there for several years but returned UK becoming barrister-at-law Middle Temple. Successfully fought Orkney and Shetland Parliamentary election 1900 as Unionist defeating sitting Liberal member *Sir Leonard Lyell but two years later resigned his seat on disagreeing with Unionist Government and became Independent Liberal. In subsequent by-election was re-elected as a Liberal and surviving 2 further elections served in that capacity for next 19 years dying in office 1921.

A fitting memorial to his popularity is the buoy marking a skerry about a mile off Scapa Pier which had troubled mariners, including the Navy, for many years. He fought unsuccessfully for a long time to get it marked by some sort of warning beacon and in the end providing the necessary funds to do so himself. It naturally became known locally as 'Wason's Buoy'. 49, OH 27/4/21. Orc 28/4/21.

Watson, Governor Hew - Cromwell's representative in Orkney c1650 during Commonwealth, occupying Cathedral manse, Watergate rented from the Minister, Rev. James Douglas.

Took possession of 16-gun frigate, a present from Queen of Sweden to the Marquis of Montrose, still lying in Kirkwall Roads after Montrose had left Orkney for battle of Carbisdale 1650. Crew mutinied and handed ship over to Commonwealth. 4,35(4).

Watson, James - b.1770 Dumfries d.1808 Crantit, St Ola. Factor of Earldom

estate for Lord Dundas 1799-1808. Incurred local hostility when he
enforced Lord Dundas's rights as Vice Admiral of Orkney with
jurisdiction over wrecks. He strove to prevent 'nefarious collusions
often formed between masters of . . . vessels and persons residing in
the county'. A printed circular against him in the Orkney Archive
describes him as 'a broken down pedlar of Dumfries'. Said to be
'motivated by blundering self-interest'.   2.

Watt, Alexander - b.1738 Kirkwall d.1814. Kirkwall merchant and farmer;
s. of *William Watt snr; bro. of *William Watt jnr from whom he rented
farm of Corse near Kirkwall; m. Isobel Stewart 1769, dau. of
*Archibald Stewart of Brugh.
       Co-founder and minority shareholder in family firm, William Watt
jnr & Company, Merchants, Kirkwall 1766. Postmaster, Kirkwall
1800.   4,14(2),74.

Watt, Captain Alexander Gibson - b.1766 Kirkwall d.1811 Skaill,
Sandwick. Army officer. Oldest surviving s. of *William Watt jnr by 1st
wife, Jean Mowat. Educ. privately Kirkwall, Caithness and Marischal
College, Aberdeen.
       Spent several years in the family merchant firm, William Watt jnr &
Company, but joined Army 1795 being commissioned as Ensign in
Scotch Brigade through influence of *Honyman of Graemsay (Lord
Armadale). Transferred as Lieutenant to 88th Regiment of Foot
(Connaught Rangers) in which saw active service in West Indies,
English invasion coasts threatened by Napoleon, Channel Islands,
India, Egypt and after promotion to Captain in 75th Foot (Gordon
Highlanders) took part in pre-emptive strike 1807 to deny Napoleon
the Danish fleet lying off Copenhagen. On transfer to Veterans Reserve
was posted to Orkney where he died only a few months after his
father.   74.

Watt, James - b.1742 Kirkwall, d.1817. Shipmaster and ship owner,
Whitby; s. of *William Watt snr; bro. of *William jnr, *James and
*Alexander; m. Eliza Newton, grd niece of Sir Isaac Newton of gravity
fame. Became partner in family firm 1777 acting as its agent in
Whitby.   14(2).

Watt, John/Jon - b.1660 probably in Keith where father, William Watt was
merchant, possibly with Kirkwall interests, d.pre-1738; m. Margaret
Kirkness 1690.
       After university educ. came to Orkney from Edinburgh as Master,
Kirkwall Grammar School 1688; treasurer to Kirk Session and Session
Clerk. Later qualified as physician Edinburgh and returned Kirkwall
to practise.   4,69.

Watt, John Gibson - b.1735 Kirkwall d.1832 London. Physician; s. of *William Watt snr; bro of *William jnr, *Alexander and *James Watt.

Started out as barber and wig-maker before going to sea where he was pressed into the Navy becoming surgeon's mate on board man o' war 1759. Coming ashore was apprentice chemist in London 1762 and successful apothecary there by 1766 when he became co-founder and minority shareholder in family firm with his father and brothers *William jnr and *Alexander but was in dispute with them after several years presumably resigning from the firm and by 1807 had established his own company, John Watt & Sons, surgeons, in London where he founded and endowed what became known as Watt's Hospital.   4.

Watt, William, snr - b.1700 Kirkwall d.1777 Kirkwall. Merchant. Grd s. of *John Watt; m. Katherine Gibson, dau. of Rev. John Gibson, Evie 1729; father of *William Watt jnr.

A staunch Jacobite he was captured 1746 by *Benjamin Moodie's Hanoverian troops in Burray along with his friend and business associate, Orkney's leading Jacobite laird *Sir James Steuart. They were held overnight in Kirkwall Tolbooth before being marched to Stromness to board the Government sloop *Shark* taking them to await trial in London where Sir James died in jail. Watt, however, was released and returned to Orkney 1747 with the Act of Redemption reinstating to their forfeited estates those North Isles lairds who had themselves escaped arrest for their Jacobite sympathies.

Resumed his interrupted business activities and in 1766 became a partner in the merchant company established by his son *William Watt jnr.   4,74.

Watt, William, jnr - b.1730 Kirkwall d.1810 Skaill, Sandwick, 6th of Skaill - Merchant. Eldest s. of *William Watt snr and Katherine Gibson; m. (1) Jean Mowat, dau. of Rev. Hugh Mowat, Evie (2) Margaret Graham, dau. of Robert Graham 6th of Breckness (3) Margaret Gilchrist, widow of Thomas Baikie of Burness; father by (1) of 5 daughters and 2 sons including *Capt. Alexander, by (2) of 1 dau. and 2 sons including *William Graham Watt, who succeeded him.

Successful and thrusting businessman, amassed considerable fortune to help realise his social ambition of becoming one of the landed gentry as well as a merchant laird, an ambition achieved 1787 with the acquisition of the Breckness and Skaill estate from his former bro-in-law, Robert Graham. Along with his father, *William Watt snr, and bros. *Alexander of Corse, *John in London and later, *James in Whitby, founded trading firm of William Watt Jnr & Company, Merchants, Kirkwall being principal (59%) shareholder. For 2 decades or more it was Orkney's premier business enterprise trading to ports in Britain, the Low Countries, Germany and especially Scandinavia, exporting kelp, hides, meal and butter, importing luxuries such as tea, coffee, tobacco, wines and spirits, often smuggled, as well as necessities like timber, slates and coal, while in Orkney itself operating banking and insurance services, buying and selling of property as well as dealing in groceries, clothing, stationary, footwear and much else besides.

On becoming laird of Skaill interested himself in agricultural improvements on his estate, which by further acquisitions, planking and enclosures became one of the largest in Orkney. Took an increasing interest in public affairs now being on the county voting panel where he supported Balfour against Dundas in the 1790 Parliamentary election but switched to Honyman's candidature in 1796.   4,67,74.

Watt, William Graham, b.1776 Kirkwall d.1866 Skaill, Sandwick, 7th of Breckness and Skaill - Eldest s. of *William Watt jnr by 2nd wife Margaret Graham inheriting estate although his father's oldest s. *Alexander by his first wife, 10 years his senior was still alive; m. Ann, dau. of *Thomas Traill of Frotoft, Provost of Kirkwall.

Educ. Edinburgh High School. Managed and improved the estate, now comprising about a third of Sandwick, enclosing and reclaiming waste land, and also entered into trading partnership with father-in-law. Appointed Kirkwall Burgess 1812, Commissioner of Supply 1817-1818, JP, chairman of Parish Council and School Board. Described as 'a liberal Tory, well educated and moderately well-read', interested in local history and archaeology he supervised first excavation 1850 of Stone Age village of Skara Brae situated close to Skaill House.   67,74,79.

Watt, William George Thomas, b. 1849 Tasmania d.1909 Skaill, 8th of Breckness and Skaill - Inherited estate from uncle *William Graham Watt; m. Mary Barry, grd dau. of *Rev. Dr. George Barry.

Active in public life and management of estate. Convener of County Council, chairman of Parochial and School Boards. Continued his uncle's interest in antiquarian research and with the artefacts from the Skara Brae excavations he set up and maintained his own museum at Skaill.   35(2),67.

Webster, Professor Thomas - b.1773 Orkney d.1848 London. Geologist, artist, architect. Grd s. of Rev. Thomas Baikie of Burness and Elizabeth Traill; father was a Londoner who died young; Webster brought up by Stewarts of Brugh at Cleat in Westray and educated privately with their children whose tutor was Rev. Dr. *George Barry, the historian. Showed early interest in drawing and painting. At Aberdeen University and Royal Academy studied art, architecture, draughtsmanship and agriculture but became increasingly interested in geology and in 1841 was appointed London University College's first Professor of Geology. He also designed the building for the Royal Institute in Albemarle Street, London.

Author of numerous research papers mainly on geology of south coast of England and his name is associated with a rare British mineral called Websterite.   Orc 15/7/71, 44.

William I The Old - c1102-1168. First resident Bishop of Orkney. 'Paris Clerk' (scholar). Described as 'a warrior-prelate and an able statesman' (Clouston) he was reputedly related to *Kolbein Hruga and other members of Norse nobility so probably consecrated in Scandinavia, certainly not supported by papacy in Rome who regarded him as an 'intruder' preferring their own nominee *Ralph II Novell of York. In effect when William began his episcopate Orkney had not only 2 Earls, *Hakon and *Magnus, but 2 Bishops as well, William leaning towards Hakon and Ralph, who may never have set foot in Orkney, being the choice of the Magnus faction.

Took up residence in Egilsay where he later welcomed *Sweyn Asleifsson 1135 after his killing of *Sweyn Breastrope during Earl *Paul II's Yuletide feast in Orphir and thanked him for 'cleansing the land' of an evil man. He may also have been present when Magnus was martyred on Egilsay but for the next 20 years or so opposed the growing 'sanctity of Magnus' cult supporting Hakon and subsequently his son Earl *Paul II. After visiting Norway c1134 where *Rognvald II, preparing the expedition to claim his share of the Orkney Earldom, vowed to build and dedicate 'a stone minster the finest in the north' to his martyred uncle, Magnus and to endow the bishopric, Bishop William switched allegiance, recognised Magnus's sanctity and agreed to the translation of his relics from Christ Church, Birsay to St. Olaf's Church, Kirkwall pending final enshrinement in the Cathedral when it was ready to receive them. A more consistent political objective was his promotion of Earl *Harald II Maddadsson and thereby of Scottish interests. It was Bishop William who 'managed' Sweyn Asleifsson, negotiated with Scotland so that Rognvald II's rights in Caithness were recognised and he also negotiated Rognvald's acceptance of Harald II Maddadsson as co-earl.

Accompanied Rognvald on his Crusade to the Holy Land 1151, commanding one of the ships and, sometimes acting as much in a military or diplomatic capacity as a spiritual one.

He survived Rognvald by 10 years and was buried near him in the Cathedral they had striven to establish. His tomb was destroyed during restoration work in 1848 and his bones, like those of a later Bishop, *Thomas Tulloch, were said to have been scattered in fields near the town.   4,21,100.

William III, Bishop of Orkney - Consecrated Norway 1310 but appears to have had pro-Scots affiliations. Was temporarily suspended by Bergen Provincial Council 1321 after being accused, among other misdeeds, of 'hawking and boisterous hunting', embezzlement, and carelessness in spiritual matters in that he was too tolerant of heresy and witchcraft. He appears to have been re-instated by 1324.   2,21.

William IV, Bishop of Orkney - Succeeded Bishop William III at date unknown but is recorded in the Annals of Iceland as being 'slain in the Orkneys' 1385. Although probably a Scandinavian appointment he was pro-Scots and aligned himself with Earl Henry I Sinclair and the Earl of Ross and was opposed at times to Norwegian Crown.   2,21.

Wilson, Major Alan - b.1856 probably Moray d.1893 S. Africa. Soldier, trader, gold prospector; s. of Robert Wilson, contractor, engaged to build main roads and bridges in Orkney early 1860s.

   Educ. Kirkwall Grammar School walking both ways from home at Rossmyre, Firth every day. After 11 years in Orkney family moved back to Moray and he was apprenticed to a bank. But banking did not suit him so he emigrated to South Africa 1874 and in the Cape Mounted Rifles fought in Zulu War 1889 and first Boer War 1891. After a spell of trading and gold prospecting became Chief Inspector, Bechuanaland Mining and Exploration Company.

   During Matabele Rising 1893 raised, trained and commanded an irregular force, the Victoria Rangers, and on patrol to the Shangani River led 17 of these mounted troops in an attempt to capture the Matabele King Lobengula. Misled as to the numbers of tribesmen opposing them they found themselves surrounded by hundreds of Matabele warriors and fighting to the last round of ammunition all were killed in what became known as 'Wilson's Last Stand'.   Orc 11/9/69.

Wilson, Edward Adrian - Chief of the scientific staff on Scott's second expedition to the Antarctic and one of those who died with him. He visited Orkney and Shetland in his youth and his diary contains a reference to his paying respects at the tomb of John Rae in St Magnus Cathedral - this is unusual in being an example of a member of the exploring 'establishment' paying tribute to a man they usually tended to hold in suspicion. The episode is noted in George Seaver, 'Edward Wilson of the Antarctic'.

Y

Young, Andrew, d.1679, of Castleyards - Keeper of Earldom Girnel, s. of *William Young; m. Marion Meason; father of William Young II who pre-deceased him. 4,69.

Young, Andrew d.1734, of Castleyards - 2nd s. of Bailie William Young and Barbara Moncreiff from whom he inherited Castleyards estate; grd s. of Andrew I of Castleyards; m. (1) Jean Moncreiff 1687 (2) Margaret MacKenzie, grd dau. of Bishop *Murdoch MacKenzie.

Receiver of Earldom rents 1693; Clerk and Collector of Cess for Commissioners of Supply 1703; Dean of Guild becoming Provost of Kirkwall 1710-12. Involved in early stages of Pundlar Process in Mortonian interest. Bought lands at Weyland 1708. 4.

Young, Andrew, of Castleyards - eldest s. of Andrew II by his 2nd wife Margaret MacKenzie; m. Barbara Baikie of Tankerness, widow of David Traill of Sebay 1725, the marriage, however, was considered irregular, the service having been conducted by an Episcopalian clergyman and Young found himself in trouble with the Presbyterian Synod and Kirk Session of the day and was fined. Their son, also Andrew, an officer in the 16th Foot (Bedfordshire Regiment) was killed in action 1762 at Belle Isle in France.

Surveyor of Customs 1747 the same year in which he organised the first reasonably regular postal service between Orkney and the south; he was appointed official Deputy Postmaster for Orkney 1774. 4.

Young, William, d.1675, of Castleyards - Came to Orkney c1647 as Girnel Keeper for Earl of Morton from whose factor, *Douglas of Spynie, he bought and extended property at foot of Strynd in Kirkwall then known as King's Yards and later Castleyards. He also acquired lands at Seatter, Holland and Weyland all near Kirkwall founding estate and 'Castleyards dynasty' which played an important part in administration of Orkney and particularly Kirkwall for over a century. 4,69.

Young, William - eldest s. of Andrew I but pre-deceased him; m. Barbara Moncreiff 1660. Successful businessman; Bailie and Burgh Treasurer, Kirkwall Town Council. Bought Orquil, St Ola 1674. 4,69.

Yule, Rev. John - d.1792 Kirkwall. Minister St Magnus Cathedral 1757; m. (1) Christina Baikie 1748, dau. of a previous Minister of the Cathedral (2) Barbara Traill, dau. of *Rev. Thomas Traill of Hobbister, Minister of

Lady Kirk in Sanday 1756. His own dau. Sibilla, m. *Rev. George Barry, the historian.

Educ. Marischal College, Aberdeen. Schoolmaster Rhynie; missionary Portsoy before coming to Kirkwall.

Praised on a visit to Orkney by Principal Gordon of the Scots College, Paris for keeping the Cathedral in a good state of repair. 4,6.

Z

Zeno, Nicolo and Antonio - 14th century Venetian travellers and navigators. Although they actually existed, much doubtful speculation has grown up about their presence in northern waters as a result of the 'Zeno narrative' published in Venice two centuries after their deaths and purporting to be the story of a voyage to Faroe c1390. According to this, Nicolo was shipwrecked there c.1390. Rescued by someone called 'Zichmni' who claimed to be ruler of a neighbouring group of islands. It has been suggested that 'Zichmni' may have been an Italian mispronunciation of 'Sinclair' and that his rescuer was possibly *Henry I Sinclair, Earl of Orkney. Nicolo is said to have entered 'Zichmni's' service taking part in an attack on Shetland where Henry certainly had interests and may have built a fortress there putting Nicolo in charge of it.

Having apparently become bored with garrison duties, however, Nicolo set off on a voyage of exploration getting as far as Greenland where there was a Norse settlement. Dubious legend has it that hearing of his exploits Henry was inspired to accompany him on a second expedition and may even have reached North America. So runs the story which does in certain aspects coincide with Henry's known career but should be regarded with extreme caution.   2,35(4).

Appendix I

Members of Parliament - U.K. Parliament

Sir Alexander Douglas of Egilsay	1707-13
Col. George Douglas of St Ola (became Earl of Morton, 1730)	1713-15
James Moodie, Younger of Melsetter	1715-22
Col. George Douglas of St Ola	1722-30
Col. Robert Douglas of St Ola#	1730-46
James Haliburton of Firth# (brother-in-law of the Earl)	1747-54
Capt. James Douglas of St Ola	1754-61
Commodore Sir James Douglas of St Ola (re-elected)	1761-68
Thomas Dundas of Fingask (brother of Sir Lawrence)	1768-71
Capt. Thomas Dundas, Younger of Fingask#	1771-80
Robert Baikie of Tankerness (unseated on petition)	1780
Charles Dundas of Fingask (on petition)	1780-84
Col. Thomas Dundas	1784-90
John Balfour of Trenaby	1790-96
Capt. Honyman R.N. (later Admiral)	1796-06
Col. Robert Honyman	1806-07
Malcolm Laing of Strenzie	1807-12
Richard Bempte Johnstone Honyman (Younger) of Armadale and Graemsay	1812-18
Capt. the Hon. G. H. L. Dundas, R.N. (later Admiral)	1818-20
John Balfour of Trenaby	1820-26
Hon. G. H. L. Dundas	1826-30
George Traill of Hobbister	1830-35
Thomas Balfour, Younger of Elwick	1835-37
Frederick Dundas	1837-52
Arthur Anderson	1852-57
Frederick Dundas	1857-72
Samual Laing of Crook	1873-85
Sir Leonard Lyell of Kinnordy	1885-00
John Cathcart Wason (Conservative)	1900-02
" " (Liberal)	1902-21
Sir Malcolm Smith	1921-22
Sir Robert Hamilton	1922-35
Sir Basil H. H. Niven-Spence	1935-50
Joseph Grimond	1950-83
James Wallace	1983-

#By-election

Appendix II

Members of Parliament - Scottish Parliament

James Stewart of Graemsay (declared ineligible) 1607
Edward Sinclair of Essenquoy
Robert Henderson of Holland
Hugh Craigie of Gairsay 1652
Hugh Craigie of Gairsay 1661-63
Patrick Blair of Little Blair 1663
Arthur Buchanan of Sound 1667
William Douglas of Egilsay
Patrick Blair 1669-72
Andrew Dick 1678
Sir William Craigie of Gairsay 1861-62
Charles Murray of Haldane 1685-86
Harie Graham of Breckness . . . .
Sir William Craigie of Gairsay 1689-02
Charles Mitchel (election not sustained) .1700
Sir Archibald Stewart of Burray 1702-07
Sir Alexander Douglas of Egilsay 1702-07

Appendix III

Members of Parliament for Kirkwall

James Moncrieff, Merchant, Burgess 1669-74
David Craigie of Oversanday 1681-82
David Craigie of Oversanday 1685-88
George Traill of Quendale 1689-98
Sir Alexander Home 1698-02
Robert Douglas (who Voted for the Union) 1702-07

Appendix IV

Members of Parliament - Northern Burghs
(Kirkwall, Wick, Dornoch, Tain, Dingwall, Cromarty)

John Haddon 1707
Lord Strathnaver 1708
Col. (afterwards Sir) Robert Munro 1710-41
Robert Craigie of Glendoig 1742-47
Sir Harry Munro 1747-61
Maj. Gen. John Scott 1761-68
Hon. Alexander Mackay 1768-73
Gen. James Grant of Ballindalloch 1773-80
Col. Charles Ross of Marangie 1780-84
Rt. Hon. Charles James Fox (sat for Westminster, for which
         he had also been elected) 1784
George Ross 1785
Capt. C. Ross 1786
Sir Charles Ross of Balnagowan 1786-96
William Dundas 1796-02
Rt. Hon. John Charles Villiers 1802-05
James MacDonald of Langdale 1805-06
Sir R. Mackenzie 1806
Brig. Gen. J. R. Mackenzie 1806-08
Rt. Hon. Sir W. H. Freemantle 1808-12
Sir Hugh Innes 1812-30
James Loch 1830-52
Samuel Laing the Younger 1852-57
Lord John Hay 1857-59
Samuel Laing the Younger 1859-60
Viscount Bury 1860-65
Samuel Laing the Younger 1866-68
George Loch 1868-72
Sir John Pender 1872-85
J. Macdonald Cameron 1886-92
Sir John Pender 1892-96
T. C. H. Herrerwick 1896-00
Arthur Bignold 1900-10

Appendix V

Lord Lieutenant of Orkney

John, Earl of Morton 1715

Lord Lieutenants of Orkney and Zetland

John, Earl of Sutherland 1717
George, Earl of Morton 1730
James, Earl of Morton 1738
Sir Thomas Dundas 1794
Lord Dundas 1831, 1837
John Charles Dundas 1839
Frederick Dundas of Papdale 1866
John Charles Dundas 1872
Capt., Malcolm Alfred Laing, Yr., of Crook, Rendall 1892
Sir William Watson Cheyne, K.C.M.G. 1919
Alfred Baikie of Tankerness 1930

Lord Lieutenants of Orkney

Patrick Neale Sutherland Graeme, C.B.E., B.A. 1948
Lt. Col. Robert Scarth of Binscarth, O.B.E. 1959
Col. Henry William Scarth of Breckness 1966
Col. Sir Robert Andrew Alexander Scarth Macrae, K.C.V.O., M.B.E. 1972
Brig. Malcolm Gray Dennison 1990
Mr George Robert Marwick, J.P. 1997

Appendix VI

Coveners of Orkney

John Riddoch, Provost of Kirkwall 1780
Robert Baikie of Tankerness 1781-1786
    No Minutes 1786-1791
Robert Baikie of Tankerness 1792
    No Minutes 1793-1815
William Graham Watt of Breckness 1816-1818
Rev. Walter Traill of Westove 1818
William Traill, Younger of Frotoft 1819-1821
John Traill Urquhart of Elsness 1821-1823
James Baikie of Tankerness 1823-1825
Samuel Laing of Papdale 1825-1831
James Baikie of Tankerness 1831-1833
Samuel Laing of Papdale 1833
James Baikie of Tankerness 1834
    No Minutes 1835
Capt. William Balfour of Elwick 1836-1838
Capt. William Balfour of Elwick and James Baikie of
    Tankerness (joint) 1838
James Baikie of Tankerness 1839-1852
John G. Heddle of Melsetter 1852-1855
John G. Heddle of Melsetter and William Balfour of
    Gairsay (joint) 1855-1856
David Balfour of Balfour and Trenabie 1856-1886
Lieut.-Col. James William Balfour of Berstane 1886-1907
William George Thomas Watt of Breckness 1907-1909
Alfred Baikie of Tankerness 1909-1917
James Johnston of Coubister 1917-1926
William MacLennan, OBE, Grainbank 1926-1930
J. Storer Clouston of Smoogro 1930-1944
Alexander Calder, Sebay 1944-1959
Henry W. Scarth of Breckness 1959-1970
J. Donald Brown, Stromness 1970-1975
George R. Marwick, Swannay House, Birsay 1975-1978
Edwin R. Eunson, Kirkwall 1978-1990
John A. Tait, Campston, Toab 1990-1994
Hugh Halcro-Johnston, Orphir House 1994-

Appendix VII

Provosts of Kirkwall

Harry Sinclair	1549-	James Baikie	1737-64
Patrick Bellenden	1565-	John Riddoch	1764-84
Earl Robert Stewart	1567-	William Lindsay	1784-88
David Scollay	1586-	Robert Laing	1788-92
Earl Robert Stewart	1590-	Thomas Traill	1792-12
Earl Patrick Stewart	1591-12	Thomas Jameson	1812-14
Harie Stewart	1619-	John Riddoch	1814-18
Capt. Thomas Knightsone	1619-21	Thomas Pollexfen	1818-20
Edward Sinclair	1621-35	Samuel Laing	1820-34
Thomas Buchanan	1635-47	Capt. William Balfour	1834-36
George Drummond	1647-50	James Baikie	1836-50
James Keith	1650-	James Spence	1850-62
Patrick Blair	1654-58	Alexander Bain	1862-72
Patrick Craigie	1658-70	Col. David Balfour	1872-76
James Baikie	1670-74	Samuel Reid	1876-87
Arthur Baikie	1674-79	Thomas Peace	1887-92
David Craigie	1679-88	Nicol Spence	1892-04
George Traill	1688-91	John Sclater	1904-07
Hugh Craigie	1691-94	James Slater	1907-13
Thomas Louttit	1694-95	William B. Baikie	1913-19
George Traill	1695-98	John White	1919-25
David Traill	1698-10	John M. Slater	1925-40
Andrew Young	1710-12	Peter C. Flett	1940-47
David Traill	1712-18	Robert Slater	1947-54
John Covingtrie	1718-30	James Flett	1954-57
James Traill	1730-33	James Scott	1957-69
George Traill	1733-37	Georgina W. Leitch	1969-75

Appendix VIII

Provosts of Stromness

J. A. Brown	1893-	James G. Marwick	1931-46
Andrew Stewart	1893-96	George S. Robertson	1946-53
John Rosey	1897-99	Thomas N. F. Hourston	1953-59
Andrew Wylie	1900-18	Rosetta C. B. Groundwater	1959-65
Capt. G. G. Baillie	1918-19	James R. T. Robertson	1965-68
Robert W. Clouston	1919-25	William E. Knight	1968-71
James Corrigall	1925-31	James R. T. Robertson	1971-75

Appendix IX

Genealogy of the Earls of Orkney

(Late 9th Century to 1206)

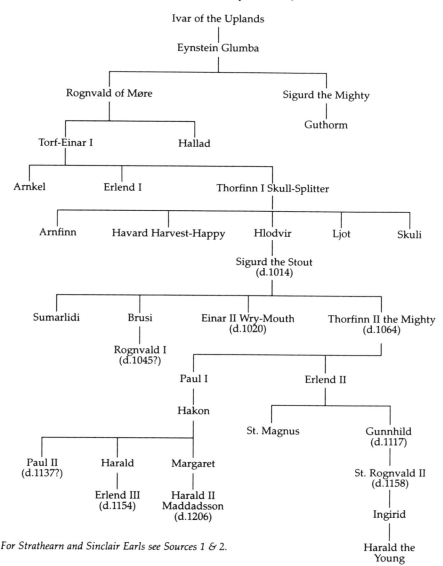

For Strathearn and Sinclair Earls see Sources 1 & 2.